DESIGNING & PLANNING

ENVIRON MENTAL GRAPHICS

EDITED BY
WAYNE HUNT

DESIGNED BY
GERRY ROSENTSWIEG

TEXT EDITED BY
ERIC LaBRECQUE

PUBLISHED BY
MADISON SQUARE PRESS

DESIGNING & PLANNING

ENVIRON MENTAL GRAPHICS

ISBN 0-942604-35-0
        Library of Congress Catalog Card Number 93-079606

Distributors to the trade in the United States and Canada:
        Van Nostrand Reinhold 115 Fifth Avenue, NY 10003

Distributed throughout the rest of the world by:
        Hearst Books International 1350 Avenue of the Americas
        New York, NY 10019

Published by:
        Madison Square Press 10 East 23rd Street, New York, 10010

DESIGNING AND PLANNING ENVIRONMENTAL GRAPHICS
        Edited by: Wayne Hunt / Gerry Rosentswieg
        Designed by: Gerry Rosentswieg/The Graphics Studio
        Text edited by: Eric LaBrecque

PRINTED IN HONG KONG

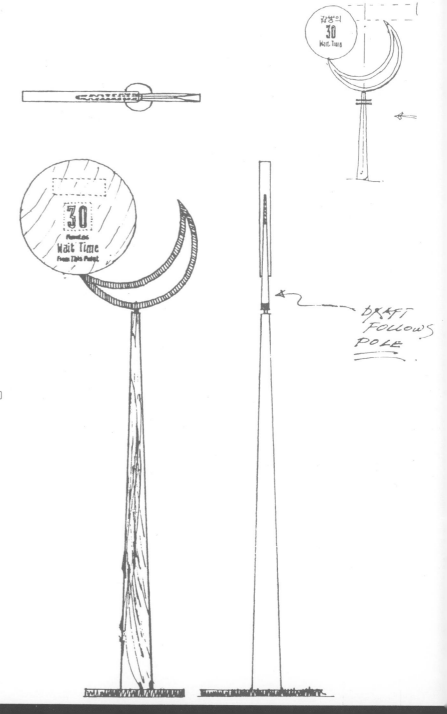

TABLE of CONTENTS

Environmental graphics designed by Gerry Rosentswieg, The Graphics Studio.

PREFACE

I remember how excited I was whenever, as a young designer, I succeeded in getting my hands on a studio's internal forms. To share the information on a bid sheet or proposal was an instant high, a lesson in how my profession worked. This basic information, impossible to get then, is still hard to come by — especially if you're just starting out.

And the need for it never goes away. For advice on a bid or a fabricator referral or any of a hundred other matters, designers routinely turn to their peers. That's what we have done here. The practical information assembled in this book comes from some of the best environmental graphic designers working today.

With new technology and an ever-widening range of resources at our disposal, environmental graphic design has never been more exciting. With regulations imposing new areas of control, it has never been more difficult. And with more firms in the business than ever before, it has never been more competitive.

In short, to succeed you need more than aesthetic judgment and the skills of a designer versed in the printed page. You must familiarize yourself with a specialized body of knowledge. The projects we have chosen demonstrate what's possible when that knowledge has been applied with mastery, imagination and insight.

Gerry Rosentswieg

*Environmental graphics
designed by
Wayne Hunt Design.*

INTRODUCTION

Environmental graphics is a relatively new design discipline. Consisting of unequal parts architecture, industrial design, lighting and, of course, graphic design, environmental graphic design — or EGD — is growing at an unprecedented rate. Graphic designers trained in two-dimensional work are trying their hands at three-dimensional expression; architects practiced as spatial designers are adding graphics to their roster of services.

Known for years as Architectural Signing, EGD now has a broader definition and acceptance. It isn't limited to signs on buildings; it often comprises the entire environment. EGD commands new respect among building developers, retailers, city planners, architects and facility managers. Major building projects, from corporate towers to sports facilities, now list graphics alongside the more familiar disciplines of landscape and lighting design. EGD has arrived!

Schools of art and design are following suit with EGD classes, and even majors. Architecture schools are also beginning to accept EGD as an important part of the building arts. In addition, the field has its own thriving professional organization, the Society for Environmental Graphic Design, which fosters professionalism, uniform standards, and camaraderie.

What's lacking in this exciting, emerging field is a substantial body of literature and documentation. Textbooks don't exist. Neither, for the most part, do authoritative essays, papers and case histories. Hence this book.

While not literally a "how to," this book documents many interesting and important projects, and peeks behind the scenes at the design and production process. We have tried to make environmental graphics more visible, more understandable, and fun. We hope you enjoy the book.

Wayne Hunt

Business Environments

Joining landscape and lighting design, environmental graphics have become an integral part of the corporate workplace.

Richard Poulin Design Group
THE MERCHANDISE MART

A comprehensive graphics program
for a Chicago landmark Built in the 1930's, Chicago's famed Merchandise Mart is the world's largest wholesale building and design center. As part of a comprehensive renovation and restoration of the four million square foot complex of showrooms, retail and office space, designers developed a comprehensive graphics program that includes logotypes for The Mart as well as a new retail complex and food service area, and retail tenant design manuals that outline graphic design criteria for storefronts, awnings and banners.

1.

2.

4.

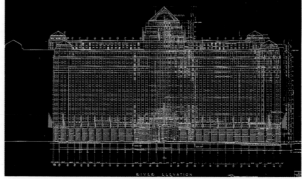

3.

1. Street entrance.

2. Building logo in terrazzo floor.

3. Presentation board showing exterior metal banner program.

4. Exterior view of building at dusk.

5. Presentation board for a tenant construction barricade.

6. Lobby map directory - a daunting task - for one of the largest buildings in the world.

7. Examples of retail tenant signs in common areas.

8. - 9. Studies for metal banner program.

5.

6.

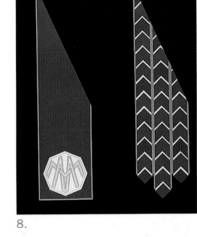

8.

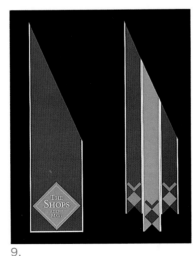

9.

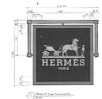

7.

Project Facts

The two-year project for Merchandise Mart Properties involved two designers. Implementation budget was $300,000.

Technical Information

The program makes use of Muntz metal, etched and sandblasted glass, terrazzo, marble, and ceramic frit glass. Graphic identities for The Merchandise Mart, The Shops at the Mart, and The Mart Food Court were incorporated into the terrazzo floor patterning, glass handrails, and sidelights. Signs were fabricated using a variety of materials and processes, including rear-illuminated lightboxes, metal etching and paint-fill, waterjet-cut bronze letters, and metal-inlay terrazzo. Sizes of typical sign elements range from 3 ft x 3 ft. x 7 ft. 6 in. high for a directional/wayfinding kiosk to 6 x 6 in. room identification panels. Internal fluorescent tubing illuminates all directional/wayfinding kiosks and elevator bank identification flag signs.

Design Details

Designers worked to incorporate the Art Deco flavor of the building's detailing into every graphic element. The use of a consistent typeface, Bembo, as well as a subdued color palette echoes the original architect's intent for graphic and typographic elements.

Credits

Design Firm: Richard Poulin Design Group, Inc.
Design Team: Richard Poulin
Design Director: Mieko Oda
Architect: Beyer Blinder Belle, P.C., Chicago, IL
Fabricator: Cornelius Architectural Products, Pittsburgh, PA

Spagnola & Associates
MERCK & CO., INC. WORLD
HEADQUARTERS SIGNAGE PROGRAM

Signage for a new corporate headquarters

Chemical and pharmaceutical giant Merck & Co.'s new head-quarters occupies 1.8 million square feet on a 460-acre site in Whitehouse Station, New Jersey. Some 1,900 employees work there. To make sure a new signage program functioned properly, designers spent many hours programming vehicular and pedestrian flow. Interior signs also needed to meet guidelines set down in the Americans with Disabilities Act (ADA). At the same time, the assignment called for an elegant system that would reflect the company's quality. The facility's main ID exmplifies this quality; its glass sign panel's transparency changes with the angle of the sun.

1.

2.

3.

1. - 3. Monument signs of tempered, patterned glass, are designed to change in varying light conditions.

Project Facts

With an overall project budget of $335,000, a team of four designers worked on the assignment for Merck & Co., Inc. over a two-and-a-half year period. The scope of work included programming, designing and supervising the installation of all signs in the program.

Technical Information

Exterior main identification sign is a tempered glass panel, 10 ft. x 4 ft. 6 in. x 3/4 in., with a ceramic frit pattern baked onto the back surface. Cut-out letters and logo have a baked enamel finish and are mounted flush onto the glass panel. Sign base footings are poured concrete and steel, with two-piece aluminum mounting brackets installed flush with grade. Granite base stone is installed around the sign base, with a weed brake installed under the stone setting bed. Ground lights flush with grade illuminate the sign at night. Other exterior signs feature fabricated aluminum sign panels with reflective vinyl typography. Photopolymer laminated onto 3/8 inch acrylic was specified for most interior signs. In some cases, raised and foil-stamped typography is used; in others, letters are vinyl die cuts to allow for future changes.

Design Details

Designers integrated the program into the environment and architecture, with colors and materials that complement the buildings. Their objectives were clear communication and elegant design.

Credits

Design Firm: Spagnola & Associates, New York, NY
Design Team: Tony Spagnola and James Dustin,
Design Directors: Robert Callahan, Haesoon Chang
Architect: Kevin Roche, John Dinkeloo, Hamden, CT
Fabricators: Architectural Graphics, Inc., Norfolk, VA;
Adelphia Graphic Systems, Exton, PA

1.

Lorenc Design
MCI BUSINESS SERVICES HEADQUARTERS

Expressing a communications company's maverick style

MCI's divisional headquarters occupies ten floors — 400,000 square feet — of a highrise tower in Atlanta, GA. Designers collaborated with architects and interior designers to develop an integral signage and exhibit program, requiring them to comprehend complex interior layouts and materials palettes to insure an orchestrated fit. Fortunately, a progressive client allowed great freedom within the given architectural aesthetic, including an extensive use of metals in their "raw" state.

2.

3.

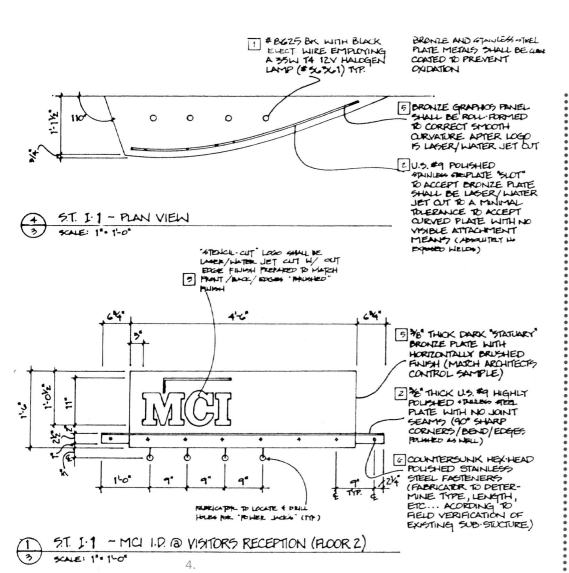

① #8625 B/K WITH BLACK
ELECT. WIRE EMPLOYING
A 35W T4 12V HALOGEN
LAMP (#56961) TYP.

BRONZE AND STAINLESS STEEL
PLATE METALS SHALL BE CLEAR
COATED TO PREVENT
OXIDATION

⑤ BRONZE GRAPHICS PANEL
SHALL BE ROLL-FORMED
TO CORRECT SMOOTH
CURVATURE AFTER LOGO
IS LASER/WATER JET CUT

② U.S. #9 POLISHED
STAINLESS STEELPLATE "SLOT"
TO ACCEPT BRONZE PLATE
SHALL BE LASER/WATER
JET CUT TO A MINIMAL
TOLERANCE TO ACCEPT
CURVED PLATE WITH NO
VISIBLE ATTACHMENT
MEANS (ABSOLUTELY NO
EXPOSED WELDS)

④/③ S.T. I-1 ~ PLAN VIEW
SCALE: 1" = 1'-0"

"STENCIL-CUT" LOGO SHALL BE
LASER/WATER JET CUT W/ CUT
EDGE FINISH PREPARED TO MATCH
③ FRONT/BACK/EDGES "BRUSHED"
FINISH

⑤ 3/8" THICK DARK "STATUARY"
BRONZE PLATE WITH
HORIZONTALLY BRUSHED
FINISH (MATCH ARCHITECTS
CONTROL SAMPLE)

② 3/8" THICK U.S. #9 HIGHLY
POLISHED STAINLESS STEEL
PLATE WITH NO JOINT
SEAMS (90° SHARP
CORNERS/BEND/EDGES
POLISHED AS WELL)

⑥ COUNTERSUNK HEX-HEAD
POLISHED STAINLESS
STEEL FASTENERS
(FABRICATOR TO DETER-
MINE TYPE, LENGTH,
ETC... ACORDING TO
FIELD VERIFICATION OF
EXISTING SUB-STRUCTURE.)

FABRICATOR TO LOCATE & DRILL
HOLES FOR "POWER JACKS" (TYP)

①/③ S.T. I-1 ~ MCI I.D. @ VISITORS RECEPTION (FLOOR 2)
SCALE: 1" = 1'-0"

4.

1. Building exterior.
2. - 3. Display in
elevator lobby.
4. - 5. Working drawing
and finished sign for
visitors reception area.

5.

Project Facts

Three designers spent approximately 1,000 hours over a two-year period on the assignment for the Business Services Division of MCI Telecommunications Corporation. Overall project budget was $100,000, of which $60,000 was design and $40,000 was implementation.

Technical Information

Bronze, copper, aluminum, stainless steel, black oxidized steel, fabric-wrapped cord and fiber optics were specified. Materials were etched and welded, and installed with mechanical fasteners. The project demanded tight coordination between site conditions and as-built elements for final integration. Main reception signs were laser cut using stencils. Cut-out letters were illuminated by light cast against a background wall. All metal surfaces were illuminated by accent lights on the ceiling to highlight metal patterns and add richness.

Design Details

A primary design goal was to provide cohesiveness from main spaces to base core spaces. In doing so, designers referred to the idea of motion and the dynamics of telecommunication — giving static components a kinetic yet sophisticated presence. Sign curves suggest the dispersal of signals into space. Colors of natural materials integrated with the overall interiors palette.

Credits

Design Firm: Lorenc Design, Atlanta, GA
Design Team: Jan Lorenc, Design Director; Chung Youl Yoo, Lee Jones
Building Architect: Kevin Roche, John Dinkeloo & Associates, Hampden, CT
Interior Architect: Heery International, Atlanta, GA
Reception Area: Design South Signage Division, Atlanta, GA
Lighting: Ramon Noya, Ramon Luminance Design
Other Collaborators: Arlin Buyert, Project Manager, MCI Telecommunications; Robert Voyules, Mary Hill, Hines Interests Limited Partnership
Photo Credit: Jan Lorenc

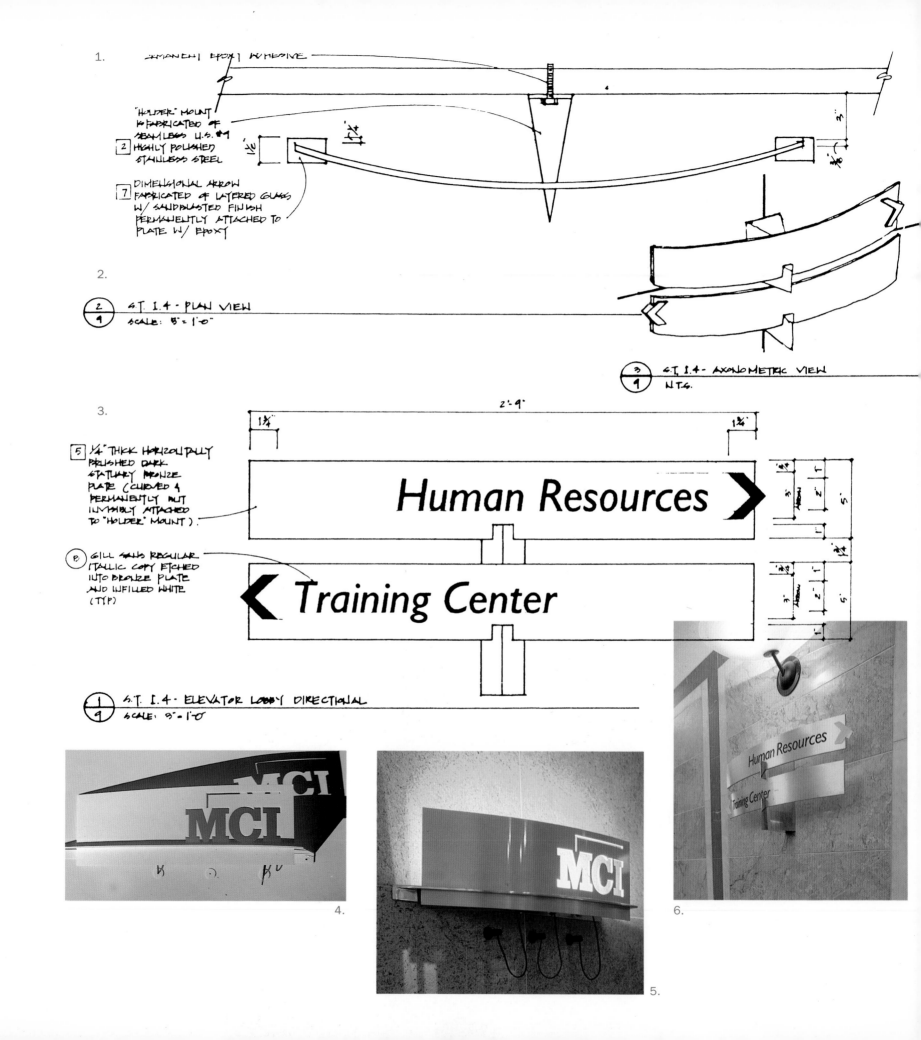

1.

PERMANENT EPOXY ADHESIVE

"HOLDER" MOUNT
TO FABRICATED OF
SEAMLESS U.S. #4
[2] HIGHLY POLISHED
STAINLESS STEEL

[7] DIMENSIONAL ARROW
FABRICATED OF LAYERED GLASS
W/ SANDBLASTED FINISH
PERMANENTLY ATTACHED TO
PLATE W/ EPOXY

3"

2.

(2/9) S.T. I.4 · PLAN VIEW
SCALE: 3" = 1'-0"

(3/9) S.T. I.4 · AXONOMETRIC VIEW
N.T.S.

3.

2'-9"

1¾"   1¾"

[5] ¼" THICK HORIZONTALLY
BRUSHED DARK
STATUARY BRONZE
PLATE (CURVED &
PERMANENTLY BUT
INVISIBLY ATTACHED
TO "HOLDER" MOUNT).

Human Resources ❯

[8] GILL SANS REGULAR
ITALIC COPY ETCHED
INTO BRONZE PLATE
AND INFILLED WHITE
(TYP)

❮ Training Center

(1/9) S.T. I.4 · ELEVATOR LOBBY DIRECTIONAL
SCALE: 3" = 1'-0"

4.

5.

6.

9.

7.

10.

1. Working drawing for directional signs.

2. Axonometric view of sign helps explain design concept.

3. Working drawing - front view.

4. Full sized paper study model shows dramatic shadow play.

5. Installed sign featuring exposed power jacks.

6. Finished directional sign.

7. - 8. Directory features articulated granite base.

9. Room identity plaque of folded metal.

10. Curved metal surfaces enliven static signs.

11. Project monument sign.

8.

11.

Stuart Karten Design
SONY MUSIC CAMPUS

Weaving an element of fun into a
low-key environment

Sony's new three-building campus in Santa Monica, CA, receives relatively few visitors, and most are guided to their destinations by a person. As a result, designers developed a wayfinding system that "functions without jumping out at you." At the same time, in keeping with the music industry's lively nature and supported by an open-minded, design-oriented client, they attempted to take advantage of opportunities to introduce elements of fun as well. The fuzziness of ADA guidelines, newly implemented at the time, posed the greatest challenge in signing the 100,000 square foot project. Stuart Karten Design hired a special consultant to help ensure the guidelines were met.

5.

6.

1.

7.

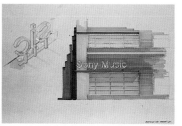

2.

3.

4.

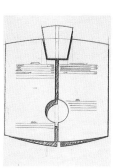

9.

10.

8.

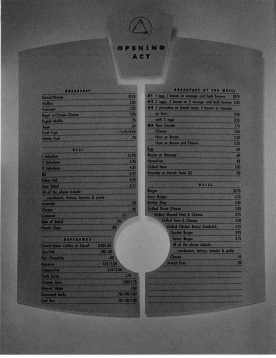

OPENING ACT

11.

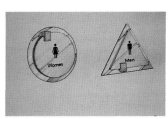

12.

13.

14.

1. Main identity sign.
2. Design presentation board.
3. - 4. Backlit signs identify music divisions.
5. Reception area sign integrates with office interior.
6. Atrium lobby.
7. Secondary exterior identity of polished stainless steel.
8. Interior and graphic designers worked together to create a consistent program.
9. - 10. Design study and full sized mock-up of menu board.
11. Actual cafeteria menu board.
12. - 14. Study and completed restroom signs.

Project Facts

A five-designer team spent approximately 800 hours over an eight-month period on the project for Lowe Enterprises and Sony Music Entertainment. Overall project budget was $160,000, of which $100,000 was implementation and $60,000 was design. Scope of work included directional, code, and informational signage for the entire campus, including parking, building identification and cafeteria menu signage.

Technical Information

Stainless steel, stained ash, acrylic, and vinyl die-cut letters were specified. Signs were fabricated using conventional techniques and illuminated with fluorescent, neon and quartz halogen lighting. Typical interior signs measure 12 x 12 inches.

Design Details

Designers strived for integration in their design approach, achieving it by using materials consistent with elements of the architecture, colors that blended with building interiors and exteriors, and typestyles based on the Sony Music corporate identity. Signage matched the individual color palettes of each of the three buildings. Inside, a sconce with accompanying nameplate was specified for every office door. Initially, the interior designer was selecting sconces without relation to the signage. Once designers saw the opportunity to introduce an ensemble, they created a custom sconce and matching nameplate. Their forms derive from the buildings' architecture viewed in plan.

Credits

Design Firm: Stuart Karten Design, Marina Del Rey, CA
Design Team: Stuart Karten and Josh Freeman, Design Directors; Vickie Sawyer-Karten, Bob Loza, Dennis Schroeder, John Protti, Jennifer Bass, Steve Reinisch, Designers.
Architect: Steven Ehrlich Architects, Santa Monica, CA
Interiors: Pizzulli & Associates, Santa Monica, CA
Fabricators: Karman Ltd., Canoga Park, CA; Ampersand Signs & Sphere, Los Angeles, CA
Code Review Consultant: Bonnie Blacklidge, Venice, CA

Debra Nichols Design
SEARS TOWER RENOVATION

Complete interior and exterior graphics for the world's tallest building

With 4.4 million square feet and 109 floors, not to mention 96 elevators and four sky lobby transfer floors, Chicago's Sears Tower poses complex and challenging circulation problems. Besides developing programs to meet these, designers also developed a highly-specific materials palette that would extend the building's character. Stainless steel was the obvious choice, in keeping with the architect's desire to express the building's structural steel in interior finishes, but a variety of sign finishes enabled designers to maintain interest. The steel serves as a backdrop for clean, modern graphics that reflect the influence of signage for early "skyscraper" style architecture.

1.

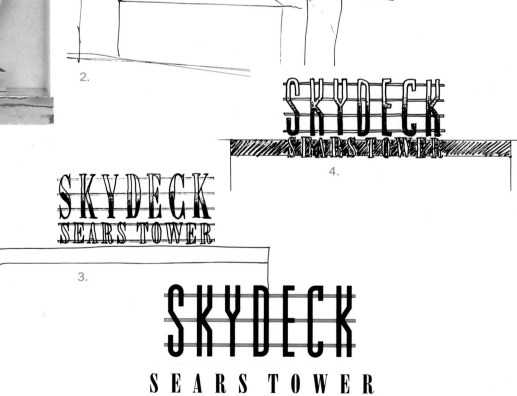

1. Materials board supplements the designer presentation.

2. - 5. Concept sketches show alternative designer directions.

6. - 7. Working drawings and installed elevator bank signs.

8. Ceiling mounted directional sign echoes transparent quality of smaller elements.

6.

TYP. FOR ALL DETAILS THIS SHEET.
- COPY TO BE CENTERED ON BARS.
RS: STAINLESS STEEL #8 FINISH, CLADDING ON ALUM. TUBE. BARS TO
TIGHT AGAINST WALL OR GLASS, FLUSH FASTENERS ON TOP ONLY.
D SHOULD BE CAPPED W/ NO VISIBLE JOINT LINES.
TTERS: FABRICATE FROM 6 GAUGE STAINLESS STL #6, VERT. GRAIN.
TACH LETTERS TO BARS W/ STUD & SPOT WELD TOP & BOTTOM
ANUFACTURER RESPONSIBLE FOR BRAILLE TEXT.

7.

8.

Project Facts

The two-year assignment for The John Buck Company involved two designers and included a complete interior directional wayfinding program; retail and restaurant signage; multi-tenant and code signage; exterior plaza signage; and Skydeck identity and signage. Implementation budget was $300,000.

Technical Information

Stainless steel was a primary material. Designers specified polished #8, brushed #6, and a custom swirl pattern. Tempered glass and acrylic were also specified. Bars and letters were fabricated steel. Fabrication called for eight-foot spans, hanging stainless steel bars and three-foot deep cantilevered bars mounted to columns. Since fabricated letters would be visible front and back, all edges needed to be finished. Supports for cantilevered flag signs were mounted to columns by structural steel installers from the fabrication pattern. Column cladding fit over these supports; signs were added last. Major directional letters are 12 inches high.

Design Details

The web and flange of structural steel beams and columns inspired the building's interior architectural column cladding. Directly inspired by the cladding in turn, signage appears to grow out of the columns. A limited palette of stainless steel caused designers to focus on a solution that relied on style, scale, and technique; influenced by the clean lines of skyscraper graphics, they developed signage that is simple, elegant and refined. They chose a Futura sans serif typestyle for its clarity and clean geometry as well as its historic association with skyscraper graphics.

Credits

Design Firm: Debra Nichols Design, San Francisco, CA
Design Team: Debra Nichols, Design Director; Kelan Smith
Architect: De Stefano + Partners, Chicago, IL
Fabricators: Martinelli Environmental Graphics, San Francisco, CA

1.

Calori & Vanden-Eynden
ROYAL EXECUTIVE OFFICE PARK

Using graphics to increase marketability

An upscale but otherwise unremarkable six-building office campus on an 80 acre site in the Town of Rye, New York became more visible and appealing with a simple yet colorful exterior graphic system. A minimal budget imposed tight restrictions on materials use and fabrication techniques. Nonetheless, designers found a way to create impact with sculptural numerals of sheet aluminum to identify buildings and sheet aluminum banners to reinforce the park's name and add color to the site. Designers also found a way to save materials and eliminate waste: The original site ID sign was reused as the base for the new site sign. Twice the size of the original, the new sign makes the entry compatible with the rest of the project.

CURB
W/ PLANTED
INFIL

5'-0"

PLAN

2.

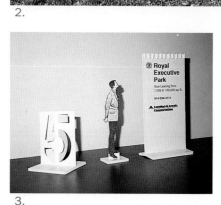

3.

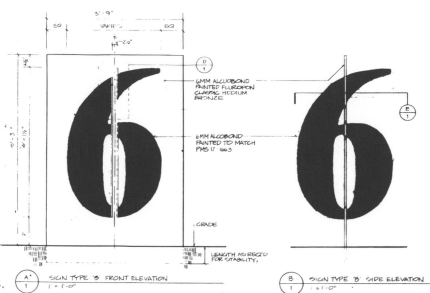

4.

6.

1. Installation of sheet aluminum banner.
2. Plan and installed building identity numeral of handcut sheet aluminum.
3. Study models.
4. Working drawing indicates the sculptural qualities - front and side views.
5. Concept sketches show "folded" design motif.
6. Actual installed banner.

Project Facts

One principal and one staff designer worked approximately 225 hours over a four-month period on the London & Leeds Corporation project. Scope of work included temporary leasing signs and leasing office directional signs, building ID numbers, decorative banners and a site ID sign. Overall budget was $40,000, of which fabrication was $28,000 and design fees were $12,000.

Technical Information

Numerals and banners were created with the simple yet effective use of hand-cut, sabre-sawed aluminum sheet. Aluminum plate, aluminum angle, acrylic polyurethane, plywood and concrete were also specified. Banners and numerals were stencil cut, the counters rotated 90 degrees and reattached using aluminum angle and rivets. Wind load was calculated for banners attached to existing light standards. Banners are 1 ft. 3 in. x 4 ft. Numerals are 4 x 6 ft. above grade.

Design Details

Responding to the owner's desire to use graphics and color to increase the appeal of suburban office space in a declining market, designers chose colors for their brightness and regal richness. Heraldic shields were a logical theme for decorative graphics, given the site's name and the owner's London location. The typeface was chosen because it was classic, easy to obtain and reproduce.

Credits

Design Firm: Calori & Vanden-Eynden, New York, NY
Design Team: David Vanden-Eynden, Design Director; Julie Vogel
Fabricator: Signs & Decal Corporation, Brooklyn, NY
Lighting Consultant: LSI (Lighting Systems Inc.), Cincinnati, OH
Photo Credit: James R. Morse, New York, NY

Calori & Vanden-Eynden
CORNING GLASS CENTER

Improving circulation and defining
spaces in a popular museum

The Corning Glass Center attracts some 250,000 visitors a year. To develop a unique and workable sign program that would direct them through a maze-like three-building complex, designers removed more than ten years' worth of accumulated signage and replaced it with one-third the amount of new signs. As the program was installed in an existing, extensively renovated facility, the team had to work with little or no information regarding visible architectural elements, much less hidden dimensions and conditions.

1.

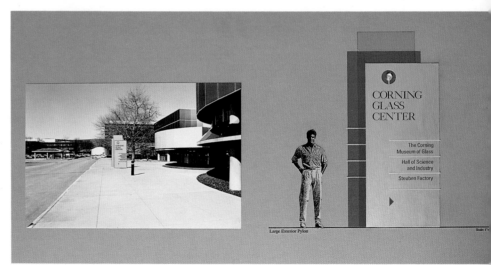

2.

3.

4.

5.

6.

7.

1. Paper study model for monument sign.

2. Presentation board shows proposed design in site context.

3. Sign prototype and fabricator color samples prepared for designer approval.

4. Actual monument sign demonstrates changes in design from study model.

5. Plaza directional sign with pole-mounted dimensional logo.

6. Corridor of exhibit signs make an architectural statement.

7. Sign panels are mounted on aluminum bar stock that spans the corridor.

Project Facts

A design principal, senior designer, and junior designer spent approximately 1,000 hours developing the signing and wayfinding system for the Corning Glass Center. Project duration was 14 months. The scope covered front-of-the-house items from concept development through punch list. Of a $170,000 total budget, $100,000 was for fabrication and $70,000 for design.

Technical Information

Aluminum sheet, aluminum angle, acrylic sheet, polycarbonate sheet, automotive paints, vinyl sheet, steel plate, aluminum bar stock, and plywood were specified. Fabrication processes included brake forming, drilling, routing, acid etching, silkscreening, and cutting. Letter forms were cut with a water jet.

Building conditions demanded precise field measurements. Interviews with security guards and Corning personnel provided valuable insight into common visitor navigational problems.

Design Details

Glass and the "look" of glass drove the theme and aesthetic. Asymmetrical sign forms and graphics were used to impose a unique order in a chaotic environment. Colors were selected to resemble glass doors; the type style (Univers) was chosen for its availability and legibility; design details evoke layers of glass.

The designers defined and emphasized transition points and spatial separations using sign forms and placement. The Steuben factory hallway was transformed into an exhibit space using signs and sign forms to unify varying ceiling heights, hallway widths, and handrails.

Credits

Design Firm: Calori & Vanden-Eynden, New York, NY
Design Team: David Vanden-Eynden, Design Director; Robert Henry, Douglas Morris, Designers
Fabricator: Cornelius Architectural Products, Pittsburgh, PA
Engineer: Geiger Engineers, Westchester, NY
Lighting Consultant: Howard Branston Lighting Design, New York, NY
Photo Credit: James D'Addio, New York, NY

The Gnu Group
OAKLAND FEDERAL BUILDING

A contemporary government office
building with a high level of finish.

The elegant character of a pair of 20-story office towers over a
five floor atrium finds its counterpart in a comprehensive sign system's traditional use of rich materials and finishes. Besides its
aesthetic appeal, the system also complies with Uniform Federal
Accessbility Standards. A six-year project timespan for the one
million square foot building made staff continuity a challenge.

10 Location Plan

0 2 4 6 8

1.

2.

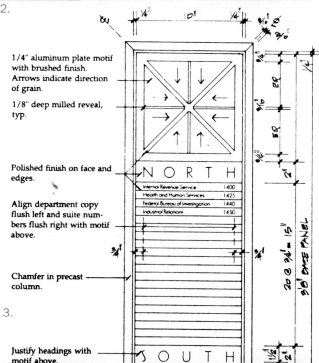

1/4" aluminum plate motif
with brushed finish.
Arrows indicate direction
of grain.

1/8" deep milled reveal,
typ.

Polished finish on face and
edges.

Align department copy
flush left and suite num-
bers flush right with motif
above.

Chamfer in precast
column.

3.

Justify headings with
motif above.

N O R T H

Internal Revenue Service	1400
Health and Human Services	1425
Federal Bureau of Investigation	1440
Industrial Relations	1450

S O U T H

1. Directory is centered
between architectural
columns, which it recalls.
2. Signage complements
grand scale of entry.
3. Detail of directory,
working drawing.
4. - 5. Uplit glass signs
identify elevator banks.
6. Typical floor directory.
7. Building standard tenant
identification sign.

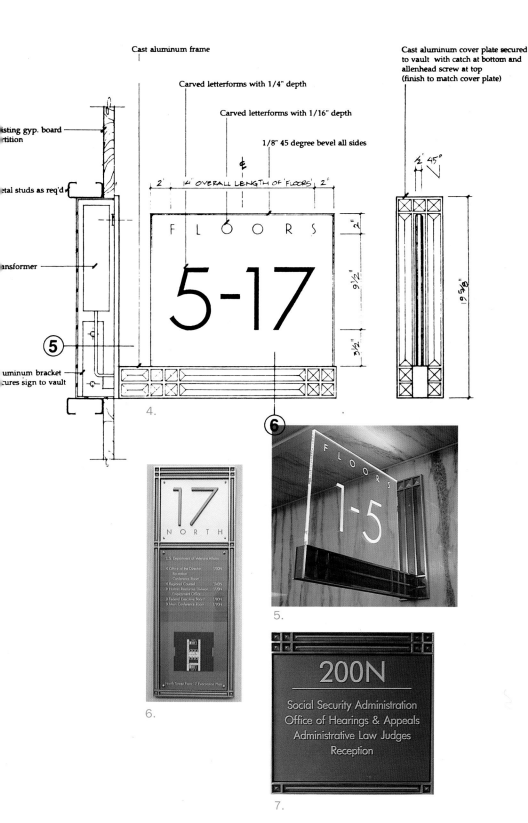

Cast aluminum frame

Carved letterforms with 1/4" depth

Carved letterforms with 1/16" depth

1/8" 45 degree bevel all sides

Cast aluminum cover plate secured to vault with catch at bottom and allenhead screw at top (finish to match cover plate)

isting gyp. board rtition

etal studs as req'd

ansformer

⑤

uminum bracket cures sign to vault

F L O O R S

5-17

4.

⑥

5.

6.

7.

Project Facts

Three designers worked with Kaplan McLaughlin Diaz Architects and the U.S. General Services Administration during the project's six-year duration.

Technical Information

Designers specified fabricated and cast aluminum, carved stone, edge-lit glass, acrylic, and etched polymer that was selected to meet UFAS compliance. Challenges for the fabricator included providing a durable but natural-looking finish on cast aluminum to prevent tarnishing and creating deep, "V" carved letterforms in limestone at small scale. Exterior signs are non-illuminated; edge-lit glass illuminates some interior signs. The interior system includes a backlit directory.

Design Details

With the primary intent of creating elegant and richly textured signage that was compatible with the building but did not compete or distract, designers worked with a color palette taken directly from the architecture and a typeface chosen to reflect the geometric architectural detailing. Cast aluminum decorative framing proved a cost-effective way to produce a complex profile for multiple units.

Credits

Design Firm: The GNU Group, Sausalito, CA
Fabricator: Karman Limited, Canoga Park, CA
Architect: Kaplan McLaughlin Diaz, San Francisco, CA
Design Consultant: The Office of Michael Manwaring, Oakland, CA

Geoffrey Scott Design Associates/GSDA
SOUND HOUND RECORDING STUDIOS

A recording studio with three-dimensional
graphic furniture, architecture

By treating architecture and furniture as three dimensional graphic elements, designers were able to contrast a 2,700 square foot Manhattan recording studio with an existing Fifties-vintage office environment — and meet an extremely tight budget. Inventive use of materials combines with the eclectic introduction of recycled auto seats and framed "Hollywood Hound" images, including Toto, Lassie and Rin Tin Tin, to give the studio an image

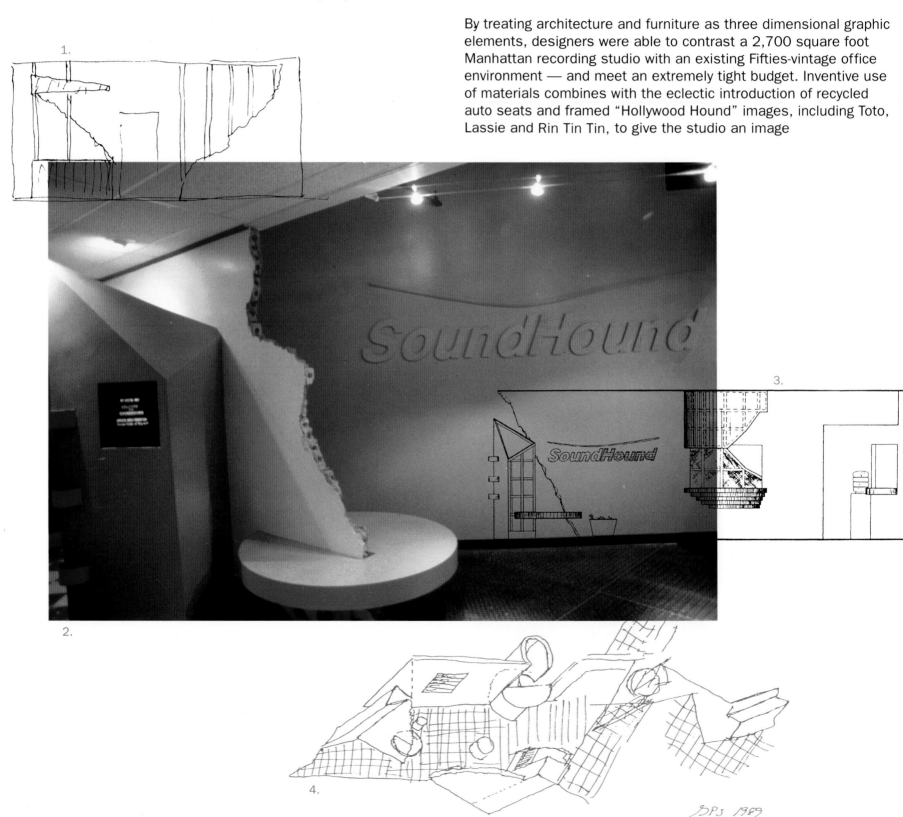

1.

2.

3.

4.

30

5.

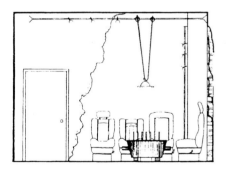

6.

1. *Early concept drawing.*
2. *Details of "cutaway" wall and entry signage.*
3. *Illustrated elevation explains unusual design concept.*
4. *Axonometric sketch demonstrates irregular space.*
5. *Dramatic view of entry.*
6. *Detail and sketch of glass topped dog-toy filled table.*

Project Facts

The six-month project for studio owner Jeff Berman involved a team of two designers, who spent 15 hours per week each (720 total). Overall project budget was $72,500, of which design was $7,500 and implementation was $68,000.

Technical Information

Materials include diamond steel plate (floor) exposed metal lath (walls); sheet rock (sculptural video directory); recycled scrap metals, 3-D furniture elements; painted video kiosk, plastic laminate details, trim and furniture; and clear polyurethane-finished letters and furniture tops. Lettering was cut from particle board. Metal lath was left exposed as a translucent wall finish. Recycled auto seats were used in the VIP lounge. The "Dog Toy Table" features a clear acrylic tabletop with an oversized, exposed nut-and-bolt fastener.

Fabrication included carpentry, painting, and welding. The installation of cantilevered forms required careful bracing. Elements are illuminated with individual halogen spotlights on horizontally- and vertically-suspended cables.

Design Details

To contrast fully with the monotone colors and orthogonal geometry of adjacent existing conditions, designers introduced contrasting shapes, a diagonal organization of space, and different circulation methods. Their overall philosophy was to challenge the user and stimulate interest in the environment. Colors distinguish forms and establish a hierarchy within the space; type plays off the existing company logo and typestyle with a new italicized interpretation expressed in clear-coat particle board letters on the wall.

Credits

Design Firm: Geoffrey Scott Design Associates/GSDA Venice, CA
Design Team: Geoffrey Scott, AIA, Design Director; Peter Schwob, Ellen Goldman
Architect: Geoffrey Scott, AIA
Fabricator: National Millwork, Sattler, TX

1.

Sussman/Prejza & Company
GAS COMPANY TOWER

Identifying a new corporate headquarters

Southern California Gas Company is the largest natural gas distributor in the country. For its new 54-story headquarters and seven-story parking garage in downtown Los Angeles, Sussman/Prejza's assignment was to develop an image of The Gas Company as a major tenant in an architectural as well as graphic way. At the same time, the design team was also responsible for developing a comprehensive sign program for the building itself. Working closely with the client as well as the architect, designers met criteria for the two assignments in tandem, developing a shared design vocabulary expressed through typography, materials and finishes. The program proved so successful that it served as the impetus for a comprehensive corporate image program for The Gas Company.

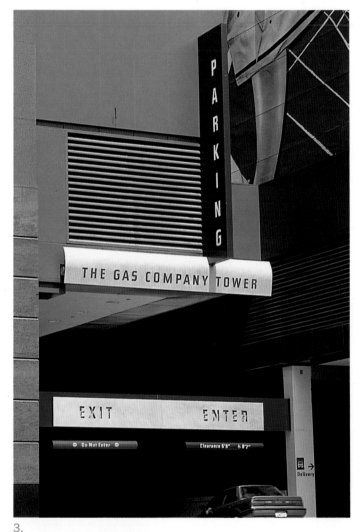

3.

2.

4.

5.

6.

1. Building exterior in
Los Angeles cityscape.
2. Building identification sign
with blue accent signature.
3. High image sign extends to
parking entrance.
4. Typical multi-tenant floor
identification.
5. Emergency exit plan is
integrated with elevator call button.
6. Street level view of
building signage.
7. Strictly decorative sculpture
goes beyond signing to a retro-view
of building ornamentation.

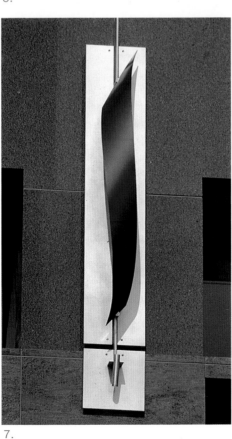

7.

Project Facts

Design budget for base building signage and graphics for Maguire Thomas Partners (Los Angeles, CA) was approximately $300,000. An additional $300,000 design budget was allocated for The Gas Company's sconces, chandeliers, and exterior signs. A core team of four designers worked on the building graphics assignment over a two-year period.

Technical Information

Signs generally are aluminum panels with stainless steel hardware; chandeliers are aluminum (due to weight restrictions). Except for minor garage signs, all signing is made of fabricated pieces with exposed hardware attachments. Scaled to fit the building, sconces were approximately 10 ft. high overall, with 6 foot flames. In the Olive Street lobby, a 10 foot chandelier consists of three paired flame pieces in a linear formation. As part of a second chandelier in the building's rotunda, three flame pieces rotate around a central axis.

Design Details

Initially, designers studied a wide range of rudimentary designs. They eventually developed a design based on The Gas Company's traditional flame logo and the bowed shape of the building itself. Materials and fabrication techniques such as the use of exposed fasteners instead of welded joints recall the building's architectural detail. A Steel Futura typeface also reflects the building's character as well as that of The Gas Company. Designers used a simple palette of silver (aluminum, stainless steel, and paint), black, white and blue. The blue relates to The Gas Company's traditional use of blue to represent a clean-burning flame. With modification, the building identity became the new logotype of The Gas Company.

Credits

Design Firm: Sussman/Prejza & Co., Inc., Culver City, CA
Design Team: Deborah Sussman, Principal; Scott Cuyler, Associate; Trent Fleming, Project Manager; Holly Hampton, Senior Designer
Architect: Skidmore, Owings & Merrill, Los Angeles, CA

Lorenc Design
HOLIDAY INN HEADQUARTERS

An integrated environment communicates
a worldwide image As the result of restructuring, Holiday Inn moved its worldwide headquarters from Memphis to Atlanta, and in doing so brought together staff who had formerly worked at disparate locations into a single highrise building. The designers' task was to reunite the company's divisions visually, allowing employees and visitors to grasp its worldwide image. This required interviewing all key executives as well as evaluating the overall interior architecture. Each division has a dedicated floor; the reception area on each of ten floors has a central map of the world rendered in a different medium. (Personnel: a collage of faces from around the world. Legal: colored square glass chips. Franchise: a series of globes illustrating hotel locations. Information Technology: PC boards. Company-Managed Hotels: a map of the Western Hemisphere, which is also a sconce light.) Thus the company expresses both its unity and diversity.

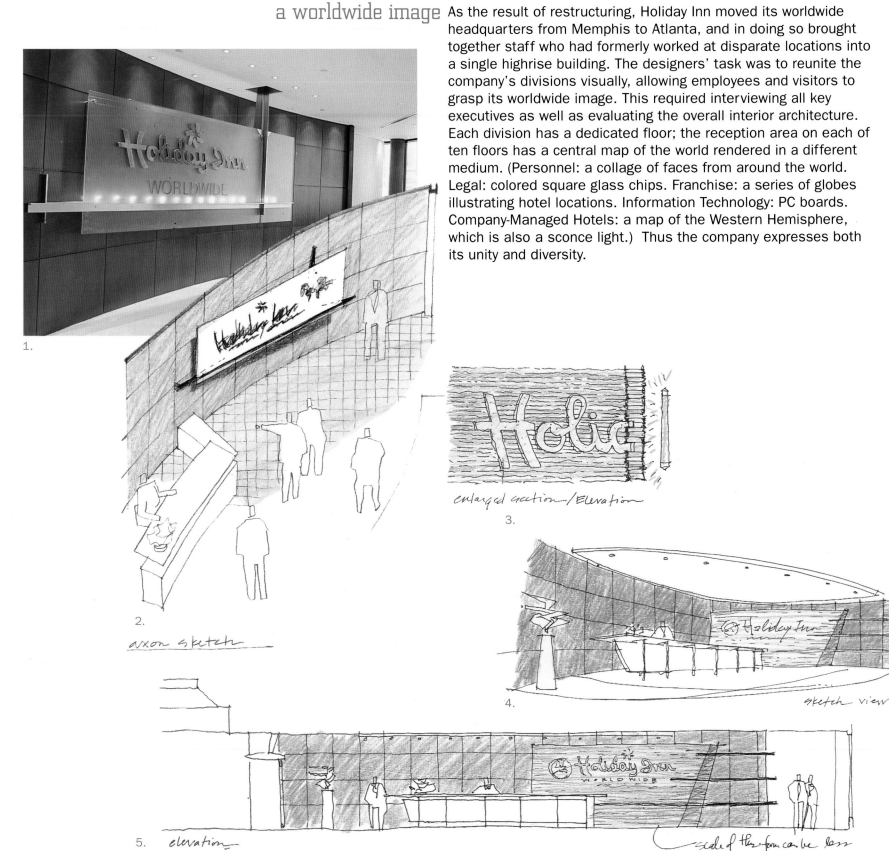

1.

2.
axon sketch

3.
enlarged section/Elevation

4.
sketch view

5. elevation
scale of this form can be less

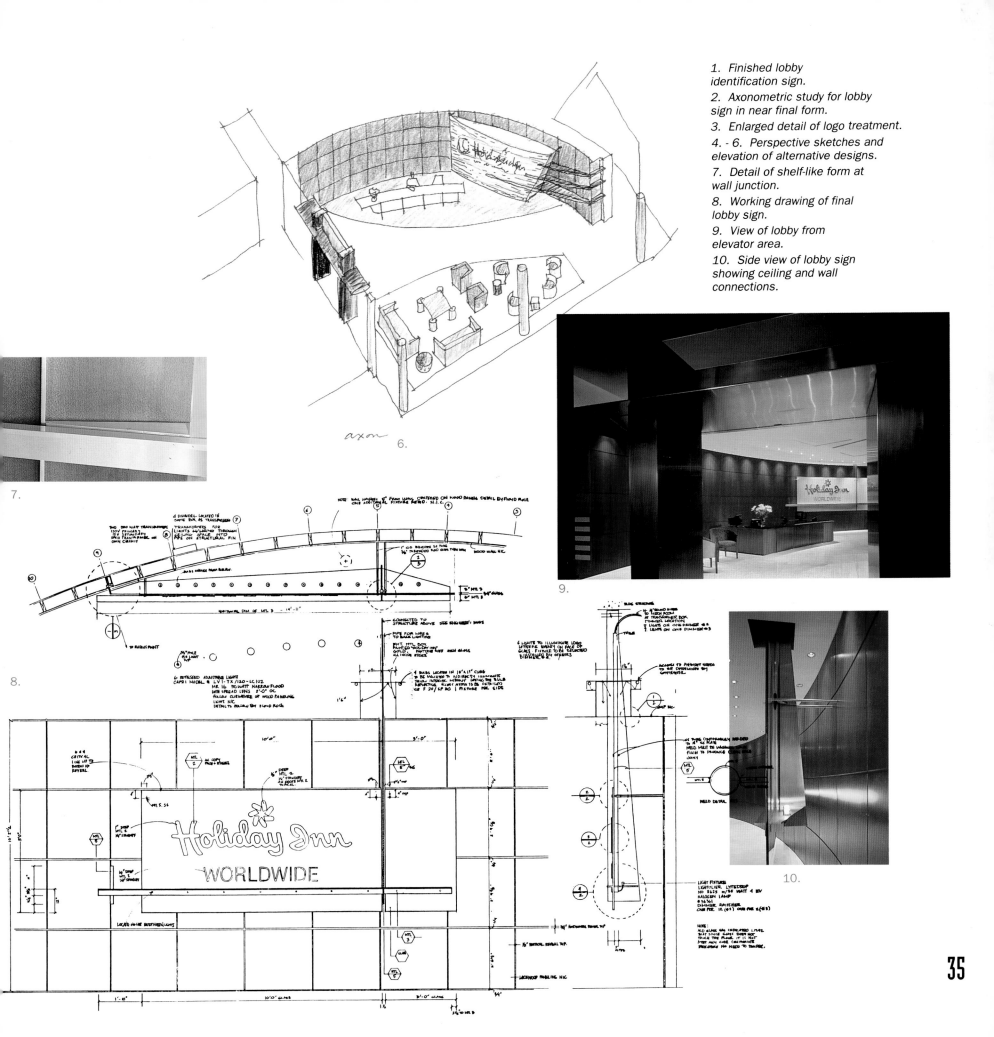

1. Finished lobby identification sign.
2. Axonometric study for lobby sign in near final form.
3. Enlarged detail of logo treatment.
4. - 6. Perspective sketches and elevation of alternative designs.
7. Detail of shelf-like form at wall junction.
8. Working drawing of final lobby sign.
9. View of lobby from elevator area.
10. Side view of lobby sign showing ceiling and wall connections.

6.

7.

8.

9.

10.

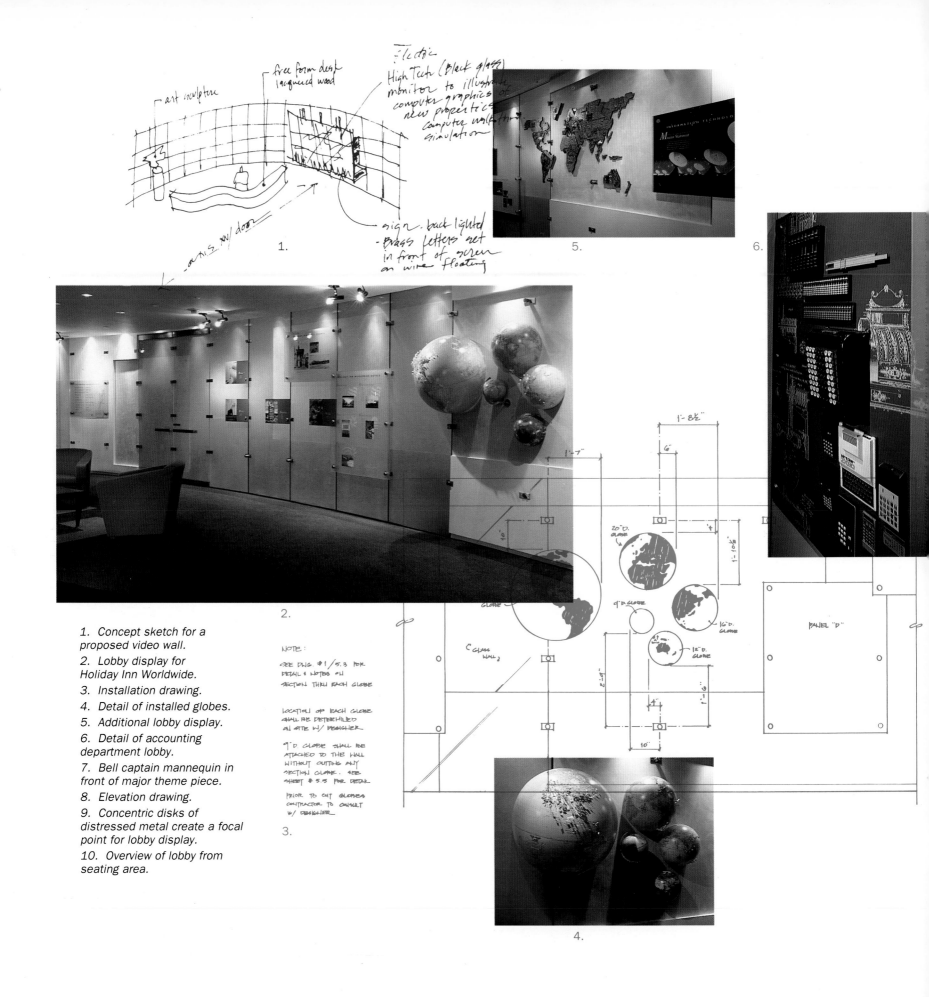

1.

2.

3.

5.

6.

4.

1. Concept sketch for a
proposed video wall.

2. Lobby display for
Holiday Inn Worldwide.

3. Installation drawing.

4. Detail of installed globes.

5. Additional lobby display.

6. Detail of accounting
department lobby.

7. Bell captain mannequin in
front of major theme piece.

8. Elevation drawing.

9. Concentric disks of
distressed metal create a focal
point for lobby display.

10. Overview of lobby from
seating area.

7.

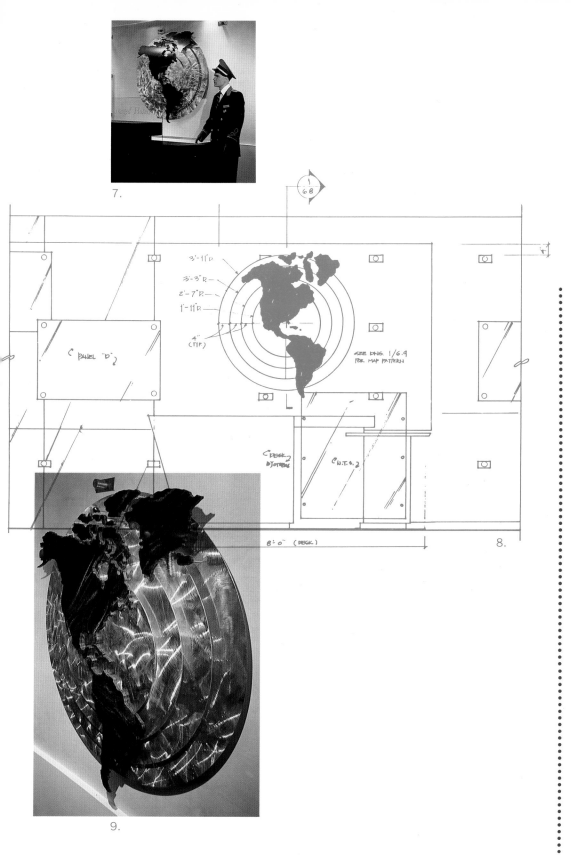

10.

8.

9.

Project Facts

Four designers spent 2,000 hours on the year-long project for Holiday Inn Worldwide. Overall project budget was $200,000, of which $75,000 was design and $125,000 was implementation.

Technical Information

Bronze, glue chipped glass, and stainless steel were the primary materials specified. Glass was sandblasted to yield an icy, textured appearance. Fabricators needed to be careful to keep expensive connectors clean. The lobby sign contains a string of exposed fixtures on its rear metal fin. The sign punctures the ceiling, revealing a glowing, internally illuminated square of Holiday Inn yellow. Additional fixtures highlight the face of the sign and exhibits.

Design Details

Signs and graphics needed to respond to the modern vocabulary of the interiors, using understatement to communicate a new Holiday Inn. They also needed to express hospitality. While structurally attached at two points, the main lobby sign appears to be floating in space. Exhibit elements are attached by bronze connectors. Garamond Old Style Italic type was selected as a foil to the more contemporary Futura.

Credits

Design Firm: Lorenc Design, Atlanta, GA
Design Team: Jan Lorenc, Design Director; Chung Youl Yoo, Steve McCall, Patricia Kennedy.
Architect: Heery International, Atlanta, GA
Fabricators: Design South Signage Division, Atlanta, GA (lobby sign); Designers Workshop, Atlanta, GA (exhibit construction) Maridee Pohlmann,

Donovan and Green
CORNING CORPORATE
HEADQUARTERS ENTRY

Light as a company's metaphor

In the 1850's, Corning Glass Works moved to Corning, New York to manufacture red and green glass lenses for railroad signal lights. A century and a half later, the altered transmission of light is a major part of Corning's business. Fiber optics, the next century's communications medium, is a product Corning helped invent and will continue to develop in the future. Designers were asked to develop an entry to Corning's new international corporate head-quarters in New York City. After extensive research, they proposed that the essence of light has always been a consistent element in the company's business. This discovery became the basis for a visceral entry experience that tells a story about the client.

1.

2.

3.

4.

1. Detail of light source for spectacular light show.
2. Lobby entry showing sign integrated into light display.
3. - 5. Details of ever changing light animation.

5.

Project Facts

Two designers worked on the project over a three-and-a-half-month period. The process involved extensive client interviews, close coordination with the architect and general contractor, and extensive testing of light relative to interior lighting and carpet samples. These affected a $100,000+ implementation fee, which also included development of a prototype.

Technical Information

Using dichroic filters, prisms, and optical mirrors combined with a pure white source, lighting was focused on 50 feet of wall, with a changing pattern of spectral light. Dichroic filters separate light into the various colors of the visible spectrum. By carefully selecting dichroic filters and aiming them through mirrors and prisms, the color palette became an ever-changing array. Light sources were programmed by computer so the presentation would change over the course of the day.

Design Details

The use of basic optical principles of science and advanced technology was the designers' solution for explaining Corning's technological advances. The presentation communicates the essential aspects of Corning's corporate values wrapped in a memorable visual experience.

Credits

Design Firm: Donovan and Green, New York, NY
Design Team: Michael Donovan, Design Director; Allen Wilpon
Lighting Designer: Jerry Kugler Associates, Inc., NY
Fabricator: Maltbie Associates, Mt. Laurel, NJ
Engineer: Cosentini Associates, New York, NY

Maestri
PACIFIC FIRST CENTRE

Creating a "Center of Attention"

1.

Long before the groundbreaking for this now-significant downtown Seattle property, designer Paula Rees was developing a two-year marketing strategy to position the high-risk development as a highly desirable mixed-use location. In addition, she oversaw all events, promotion and advertising for the Centre. As part of the comprehensive graphics program she and her team subsequently went on to develop, three dozen works of glass art commissioned from the internationally known Pilchuk Glass studio serve not only as a public art collection but as a system of portable wayfinding elements to create a continually changing experience of the space. Today, the *Seattle Times* calls the widely visited and successful Pacific First Centre the "Center of Attention"

2.

1. View of building.

2. Entry canopy to office tower.

3. Secondary entrance to retail areas with glass and neon sculpture.

4. An original typeface was designed for the project.

5. Detail of sculpted elevator numerals.

6. Two piece evacuation sign allows background granite wall to show through.

7. Colorful graphics in escalator landings reinforce level numbers.

8. 15 foot "sun-ring" is suspended and dominates interior space at entrance.

9. Design study for decorative emblem.

3.

4.

40

6.

5.

7.

8.

9.

Project Facts

A team varying in size from three to five developed the environmental graphics portion of the project for Prescott (Seattle, WA) over a span of two-and-a-half years. Completion of the graphics program culminated a seven year involvement for design director Paula Rees. EGD scope includes logotype/identity, graphic themes, construction banners, temporary site signs, building signs, code signs, color, pattern, texture, displays for the Pilchuk glass art collection, focal points, and retail lighting. Ultimately, more than 100 different artists and designers were brought into the project.

Technical Information

Diverse materials include glass, historic restoration of cast stone, metals, plastics, cast and etched bronze, porcelain and 20-color porcelain enamel tiles used in floor patterns (where, contrary to the designer's recommendations, the use of mechanical floor polishing equipment has begun to abrade them). Historic cast stone arches belonging to a theater that once occupied the site were reused as portals to the escalators. On the second floor, a glass portal by artist Norie Sato is illuminated by TV monitors in its base. Torchier stanchion lamps uplight to draw attention to retail signs, which hang from custom-blown sconces.

Design Details

The creative concept was defined by the phrase light travels. The retail component of the enclosed, mixed-use project suffers without light; therefore, the designers decided to give it its own sense of light. Placed in portable cases, the works of glass art they commissioned serve as "signs without words," helping to attract and move people through a series of rotundas. Celestial ideas provided further visual inspiration; the myth of Helios is a conceit for the transition from the East Rotunda's "sun ring" design to the West Rotunda's "celestial vessel." North-pointing cast silver stars are set into the ceiling. Elsewhere, a custom alphabet in cast bronze reinforces the building's Postmodern feeling.

Credits

Design Firm: Maestri, Inc., Seattle, WA
Design Team: Paula Rees, Design Director;
Fabricators: Signtech, Seattle, WA; Meyer Sign, Seattle, WA; Pioneer Porcelain, Seattle, WA
Architect: Callison Partnership, Seattle, WA
Special Consultants: Bruce Hale, Seattle, WA (typography and design); Marjorie Aronson, Seattle, WA (art); Craig Graham, Seattle, WA (art installation); John Koval (writer and researcher)
Photo Credits: Frederick Housel, Seattle, WA; David Emery, Seattle, WA; Chris Eden, Seattle, WA

Pentagram
SONY BARRIER WALL

Alerting New York to a landmark
change of owner For a construction bridge concealing the conversion of Philip Johnson's eccentric AT&T Buidling for Sony Corporation, designers created a concept for a city block-long mural that would announce the conversion of what is now the Sony Building. The project was never implemented: After the design was developed, the client decided to take the assignment in-house.

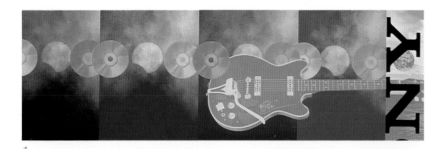

1.

4.

2.

5.

3.

6.

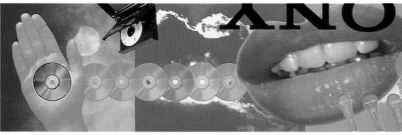

7.

8.

9.

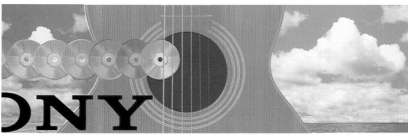

10.

*1. - 10. Conceptual
presentation boards.*

Project Facts

Two designers spent 50 hours on the Sony project over a two-month period. Design budget was $20,000.

Technical Information

Canvas and vinyl were both considered as the material for the wall, with vinyl ultimately selected because the edges of the material could be easily heat-sealed together. Computer generated imagery was produced with a laser scanner.

Design Details

Imagery from Sony's film, electronics and recording companies (Columbia Pictures, Sony Electronics, Sony Music, Columbia Records and Epic Records) was used to create a striking impression of the corporation as an entertainment and technology giant. The mural was designed to create visual excitement in the streetscape on many levels.

Credits

Design Firm: Pentagram, New York, NY
Design Team: Paula Scher, Design Director; Ron Louie, Daphna Bavli
Fabrication: Rathe Productions, New York, NY

Lorenc Design
MCI CUSTOMER SERVICE
WALL OF FAME

A dynamic display honors a
company's top performers

A 1,000 square foot elevator lobby in the Atlanta headquarters of
MCI's Southern Division offers an unusual opportunity to express
the motion, energy, and devotion of MCI consumer service personnel. Designers mounted award plaques against sculptural metal
panels that project into the space at a progressively skewed
angle. The lobby's "funneling" towards the entry door accentuates
a warped, kinetic perspective, and the panels' bottom edge lifts
off the floor to create a void underneath. With a black wall, ceiling
and carpet — and the use of specialty track lighting to highlight
the "raw" metal — the exhibit appears to hover or float with an
energy all its own.

2.

1.

3.

4.

5.

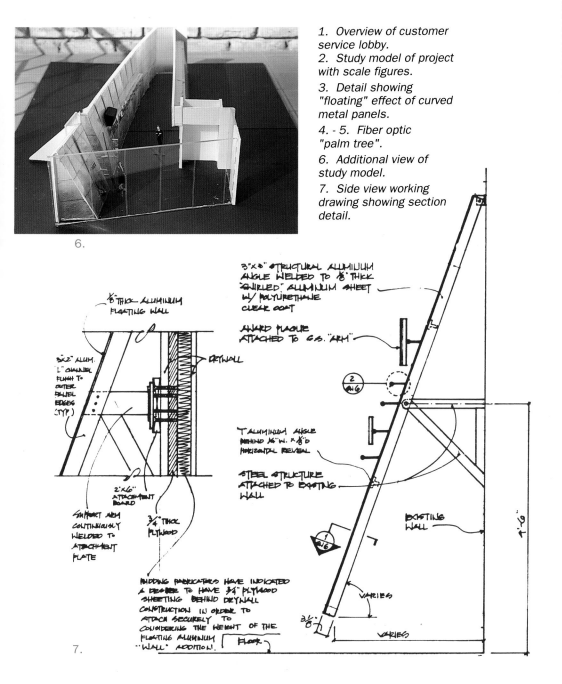

6.

1. Overview of customer service lobby.
2. Study model of project with scale figures.
3. Detail showing "floating" effect of curved metal panels.
4. - 5. Fiber optic "palm tree".
6. Additional view of study model.
7. Side view working drawing showing section detail.

7.

Project Facts

Working for the MCI Telecommunications Corporation's Southern Division Headquarters, three designers tallied an estimated 700 to 1,000 hours on the year-long project. Of an $85,000 overall budget, $50,000 was implementation and $35,000 was design.

Technical Information

Materials included ground aluminum, polished stainless steel, bronze, copper and fiber optic strands that illuminate two "heroic" lanterns flanking the entry portal. Patterns made by grinding the aluminum heighten the display's sense of energy. Stainless steel rods needed to run level across the warping backdrop. The wall is fabricated from flat, standard-sized aluminum panels (4 ft. x 8 ft. by 3 1/8 in.) on a structural aluminum framework. Award plaques are 1/2 in. thick curved bronze panels mounted on 5/8 in. diameter solid stainless steel rods. Changeable, easy-to-maintain plaques are updated by MCI using a master-designed desktop publishing progam. The MCI logo is cut one foot deep into the wall; mysteriously glowing "MCI Corporate Orange" comes from a concealed neon source.

Design Details

The exhibit needed to convey MCI Business Services' high-energy spirit and the corporation's forward-looking personality. Various sizes of fish scale-shaped commemorative plaques represent different categories of awards. Designers chose Gill Sans Italic type for its subtle yet dynamic connotation.

Credits

Design Firm: Lorenc Design, Atlanta, GA
Design Team: Jan Lorenc, Design Director; Lee Jones, Chung Youl Yoo
Fabrication: Designers Workshop, Chamblee, GA
Interior Architect: Heery International, Atlanta, GA
Lighting Design: Ramon Noya, Ramon Luminance Design, Atlanta, GA
Other Collaborators: Arlin Buyert, Project Manager, MCI Telecommunications Corporation, Southern Division Headquarters

Clifford Selbert Design
EDITEL

A bold graphic identity for
a video production company

1.

Editel's Boston facility didn't always stand out. Two modest signs identified its nondescript brick building — when they weren't ripped off by vandals. The company ultimately decided to make a more forceful statement, and turned to the designers who had recently completed its new graphic identity to create it. Editel initially wanted a canopy to extend from the building to the street, but when the city would not approve it, designers convinced the client to create an identity with light instead. Adapting the new graphic identity to signage, Clifford Selbert Design created a bold identity for both day and night.

2.

1. - 3. Views of installation showing light pipe, an alternative to neon, and illuminated spheres.

Project Facts

The project involved one designer. Overall project budget was $23,000, of which $8,000 was design and $15,000 was implementation.

Technical Information

Light pipe — tubing illuminated by the refracted light from a bulb at one end — was chosen as the illumination source. A new product at the time (1989), it provided an interesting alternative to neon. To mount the lighting elements, installers drilled through the facade of the four-story building. 10 and 17 foot lengths of light pipe were used together with 8 inch internally illuminated custom spheres.

Design Details

The non-traditional identity was adapted from the firm's logo. The brightly-illuminated building graphic is appropriate to the bright, active neighborhood in which the facility is located.

Credits

Design Firm: Clifford Selbert Design, Boston, MA
Design Team: Clifford Selbert,
Design Director: Linda Kondo
Fabricator: Design Communications, Boston, MA

Richard Foy is a principal and co-founder of Communication Arts in Boulder, Colorado. He has served as Chairman of the Downtown Boulder Mall Commission and served on the board of the Downtown Boulder Association for seven years. In addition, he has been a member of the boards of the Society for Environmental Graphic Design, Downtown Steering Committee, and Colorado Music Festival. In 1980, Communication Arts won the National Honor Award from the Department of Housing and Urban Development for design of the Downtown Boulder Mall.

RICHARD FOY

Total Design Environments

There are signs and there are buildings. But when one comes close to being the other, we suddenly get a totally designed environment: a seamless unfolding of events, information, and experience. When we find ourselves immersed in a place that surprises, delights, comforts, or appeals to us more than the usual, we are probably in one of these spaces.

A totally designed environment is deliberately orchestrated to bring us to an intended level of feeling, understanding, or purpose. These spaces effectively communicate with their occupants by making us feel acknowledged, connected, and pleased to be there.

Sitting on poles, signs often appear disconnected from their environments. Others, attached to buildings, often appear as afterthoughts. Sometimes the graphics are made thicker in a gesture to help them exist in three-dimensional space. Most buildings are sound and functional but stop short of creating a truly integrated environment of information and experience. Imagine a building made as a sign, where every decision is based on its ability to communicate. Or imagine a sign big enough to hold people. Gateways, facades, spaces, and amenities would all be parts of the message. Now we are talking about a total design experience.

This is hardly a new idea. A cathedral, a castle, an Amish house, a Greene and Greene house, the classic movie theatre of the Thirties, the passenger train or ship, a teepee, a factory, and the Golden Gate Bridge are but a few types of these environments. They are linked by a level of execution or purpose that delivers a complete set of thoughts along a theme. Many are said to be works of art, beautiful and enjoyable. They become attractions by themselves.

Many cultures have needed to imbue their buildings with totally integrated messages, in words, pictures, bas-relief, and sculpture. Even their buildings' forms were shaped by the messages to be communicated. Ancient Inca, Aztec, Egyptian, East Indian, Roman, Greek, Thai, Chinese, Japanese, Nordic, and Russian architecture are covered with blatant symbolism, imagery, or narrative. As recently as the late 1800's in all Western countries, messages were inscribed across great buildings, monuments, and places. However, the world (including its architects and designers) got carried away by the age of machines and technology. Designers moved on to modernist, post-modernist, and deconstructivist pursuits, movements that have more emphasis on expression rather than communication. As a consequence, we have temporarily lost much of the interest and skill to make buildings and places that really talk to us. We inherit a great many bland and mute places and a norm that builds little else.

Meanwhile, a hyper-competitive climate for customers and an all-time high level of consumer sophistication has emerged. The times are suddenly ripe for buildings that talk again. People and businesses want places of distinction to help attract and retain customers. Resort, hospitality,

recreation, superstore, retail, entertainment, and restaurants are but a few types of industries looking for more expressive environments. Also, others wishing to create more specialized or further-considered environments are turning to comprehensive design solutions. Museums, courthouses, corporate parks, hospitals, convention and sports facilities, residential enclaves, town centers, cultural centers, and theaters exemplify this category. There are virtually no boundaries to where a totally designed environment can occur, because there is no limit to what may be enhanced by a broader range of human expression. When successful, the advantages and rewards of this design approach are vast.

A total design approach encompasses a spectrum of disciplines, abilities, and resources. Not all projects are suited for this type of effort. A likely candidate is a place that requires a high volume of patronage; many people and frequent return visits. A richer environment sustains a longer period of discovery, interest, and appreciation. Another condition of probability is a client looking for the next step, something extra that a competing project doesn't already own.

The total design process is further assisted by the following:
- Designers and architects who approach an assignment with an open mind and let the solutions arise out of the project's context rather than with preconceived styles and dispositions.
- Aiming for the highest common denominator. This intrigues the broadest audience while providing something for everyone.
- A shared willingness by client and designers to risk a little more to achieve a greater return by involving sign design at the project start and adequately budgeting for it.
- A higher level of project management to control and coordinate the efforts of many team members.
- A shared vision by client and designer. Both must care about the experience of their customers because they themselves appreciate encountering the same surprising level of experience.

A growing number of architects are realizing the excitement and potential of these seamless environments. They assemble cross-disciplinary teams of interior, graphic and environmental designers in pursuit of large projects. Some interior designers and graphic designers have been able to leap off the page and into the full-blown three-dimensional world of environmental communication. Their numbers are rapidly growing to fill the increasing need. The Society for Environmental Graphic Design (SEGD), based in Cambridge, Massachusetts, attracts architects and interior, industrial, landscape and graphic designers, and craft and trade people. It is ardently moving to build awareness and provide assistance to environments in need of better-integrated communications. There are many highly-skilled technological craft and trade people eager for new challenges and opportunities.

We are moving from an age of information to an age of experience, from stimuli to sensation. The screen media's appeal is so seductive that increasingly effective spaces and places are needed to recreate the community experience, to reinterpret our physical world for today. Some of today's more innovative environments are blending in electronic media to inform and entertain large numbers of people. The social need to mix, feel, and interact is basic. Spaces that consider human needs, provide comfort, and give pleasure are rare. It is these positive interactions within the built environment, among fellow human beings, where civilization takes small steps forward.

Designers who create these environments are setting the stages of real-life dramas. Spaces can be given personalities. They can be friendly, gracious, helpful, and considerate. They can surprise, delight, and give a sense of well-being. The payoff for designers is connecting with people and being able to give them pleasure. The only architectural and environmental power is in the creation of spaces that people love. This is the goal of a seamlessly designed environment.

Retail Spaces

Signage and graphics enhance the shopper's experience of the marketplace.

Communication Arts
ALFALFA'S MARKET

Showcasing a cornucopia of natural foods

A pair of natural foods markets in Littleton and Cherry Creek, CO express a refreshing departure from conventional food store environments while allowing products to retain their prominence. Both goals are achieved through careful planning of product adjacencies, lighting, coordinated graphics and a minimum of interior structural elements. Kiosks for food demonstrations and a display of specialty food items serve as focal points.

Casework, graphics and floor colors harmonize to link the various departments, yet each is also designed to accommodate individual management operations and display needs. Enameled refrigerator cases are standard white porcelain; black rubber bullnoses replace the usual wood grain vinyl trim to create a custom look and provide protection from shopping carts. The same clean white finish and bullnose detail also provide continuity for specialty island kiosks.

1.

1. Supermarket signage, conceptually mainstream - but treated with special flair.

2. Dimensional signs identify market check-out counters.

3. Overview shows importance and clarity of signage concept.

4. - 5. Details of department signs.

2.

3.

4.

5.

Project Facts

Three designers worked on the Alfalfa's Market project over a six-month period. Scope of work for the 8,800 square foot space included colors, finishes and materials for store interiors as well as all identity and display graphics.

Technical Information

Cut, bent and folded sheet metal and sign foam letters were specified. Translating complex paper sculptures into large sheet metal sculptures required close collaboration between the design team, paper sculptor, and sheet metal fabricator. Typical sculptures are approximately 30 x 72 inches. They are illuminated by incandescent wall washers.

Design Details

Practical as well as aesthetic considerations drove Communication Arts' solution: First, space was limited; elements had to be eye-catching and quickly readable. By working with local fabricators, designers could watch and make corrections instantly. Second, colors and materials were used to express the idea of fresh, natural, wholesome products.

Credits

Design Firm: Communication Arts Inc.
Design Team: Richard Foy, Design Director; Gary Kushner, Paula Mosely, Designers
Fabricators: Rainbow Signs, Boulder, CO (assembly, painting, and installation)
21st Century Metalworks, Longmont, CO (cutting and fabrication of sheet metal sculptures)
Illustration and Paper Sculpture: Chris Butler, Boulder, CO
Photo Credit: R. Greg Hursley, Little Rock, AR

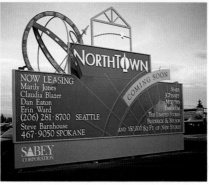

1.

Maestri
NORTHTOWN MALL

Giving visitors compass points in
a major regional mall

A 1.5 million square foot regional mall in Spokane, Washington serves five states and two Canadian provinces. Given this vast territory, it's no surprise to learn the mall is a serious shopping destination: People caravan long distances to get there, the average shopping stay is eight hours, and purchases commonly range as high as $1,500. Northtown Mall wasn't always so immense, however, and when another one and a half levels were added to the original single-level structure, increased size and exceptionally tall ceiling height created a need to enhance visibility, increase up and down traffic wherever possible, and provide visitor orientation in a confusing figure-eight plan.

In addition to satisfying these needs, designers created an identity for the mall, named the public spaces, developed the environmental graphics, assisted the client in marketing ideas and strategies, and produced leasing materials.

2.

1. Pre-opening leasing sign.
2. Signature marquee at night.
3. Monumental tenant directory
with dramatic lighting.
4. Detail of directory lighting.
5. Mall logo is repeated in
transparent, small-scale
hanging signs.
6. Streetside monument sign.
7. Night detail.
8. Detail of area
identification sign.

3.

4.

5.

6.

7.

8.

Project Facts

A team of six designers spent a total of 1,400 hours on the year-and-a-half assignment for Seattle-based Saby Corporation. Overall project budget was $120 million. EGD budget and scope of work were drastically reduced due to financial constraints, although deleted elements may be added (three years after conclusion of the original assignment). Design fee (after reduced scope) was $115,000. Implementation budget was scaled back from $850,000 to $400,000. Time constraints were also tight; elements were being built during the design process.

Technical Information

Materials specified included painted aluminum, neon low voltage lighting, hand blown glass light fixtures, brass, wrought iron, and custom tiles. A series of ten directories function as oversize way-finding pieces in themselves: Their etched glass tops and dimensional compass points help them to be seen floor to floor at major intersections. To keep the 12 foot tall by 4 foot wide directories from becoming their own footprinted objects in the space, designers worked the colors and materials of the railing into them.

Design Details

Playing off the Northtown name, designers used north-pointing arrows as compass points throughout the project to help give people a subliminal sense of direction. While a series of immense two-and-a-half-story directional beacons, visible on any level from all directions, were dropped from the project, oversized directories serve a similar purpose. Throughout the mall, 30 additional colors extended the architect's basic palette of dark green, black, and cream. Graphics based on animal motifs, enhanced lighting, and a distinct name and identity make Discovery Park, the mall's food court, a focal point for shoppers waiting for a second wind.

Credits

Design Firm: Maestri, Seattle, WA
Design Team: Jeff Thompson and Paula Rees, Design Directors; David Hoffman, Phil Jones, Linda Sokup.
Architect: Kober Sclater
Fabricators: Signtech, Seattle, WA; Kendar Tile, Seattle, WA
Lighting Consultant: Candela, Seattle, WA

1.

Wayne Hunt Design
WELLER COURT

Economical graphics system completes
"California style" remodeling

Renovating and updating dining and shopping malls often relies heavily on new signage to make a difference. A three-level open air mall in the Little Tokyo district of downtown Los Angeles is no exception. With a majority of restaurants as tenants, Weller Court caters mainly to an Asian community. While successful, the original architecture and public space were stark and uninviting by today's standards. Designers addressed the need to make the center more appealing with tenant graphics, public space and owner signage

2.

3.

4.

5.

6.

YOKOHAMA Okadaya

7.

· ELK ·

Akasaka Hanten

Family Funland

8.

9.

1. Directional sign from adjoining hotel directs customers to project.

2. Three-sided tenant directory is major design element in plaza.

3. - 4. Early design concepts of directory.

5. Tenant signs at balcony edges identify upper level restaurants.

6. System of sign shapes and mesh backgrounds allows for display of varying tenant logo styles.

7. - 8. Metal mesh backs unify arcade tenant signs.

9. Three examples of wall mounted alternative shapes.

10. - 11. Front and back details of typical tenant signs.

10.

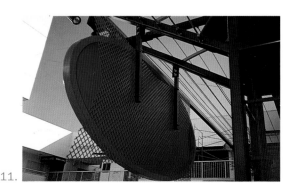

11.

Project Facts

Towards the end of the development of the major remodeling concepts, the architect brought the graphics team on board. Three consultant staff did the bulk of the work, including concept design, working drawings, and supervision. From start to opening day, the graphics project took nine months at a cost of approximately $120,000.

Technical Information

Virtually the entire project is aluminum sign technology with polyurethane paint finishes. Steel was used in the map directory tower for strength. Metal mesh pieces "intersect" with sign cans and act as backgrounds for tenant signs. Illumination of wall-mounted signs was challenging; a standard outdoor swivel fixture was specified.

Design Details

The mall owner, East West Development, requested a "California" look. The graphics team interpreted this to mean bright, airy, accessible and with a liberal use of color. A more functional objective was to improve upper floor tenant visibility by bringing signage to the deck railings; and since the restaurants' logos needed display, a modular system of shapes and colors was developed to entertain any combination of sign shape, color, and logo.

Credits

Design Firm: Wayne Hunt Design, Pasadena, CA
Design Team: Wayne Hunt, Principal; John Temple, Senior Designer; Christina Allen, Dinnis Lee
Architect: Kajima International, Los Angeles, CA
Fabricators: AHR Ampersand, Los Angeles, CA
Photo Credit: Jim Simmons/Annette Del Zoppo, Culver City,

The Gnu Group
EL CAMINO SHOPPING CENTER

An environmental graphics facelift
for a small shopping center

Besides enhancing and updating the look of a 130,000 square
foot shopping center in Woodland Hills, CA, graphics increase
visibility from the freeway and invite pedestrian traffic away from
the center's anchors. Because of the way anchors were
positioned, small arcade strips of stores ended at blank brick
walls. To make them inviting, designers augmented the walls with
primitive-inspired graphics and Mission style tile elements.

1.

4.

5.

2.

6.

1. Applied graphic shapes
and colorful tiles decorated
exterior walls.

2. - 3. Model and concept sketch
for directory.

4. - 5. Photographs of existing
project with paper cutouts of
proposed designs.

6. Study model of windchime.

7. Actual windchime and tile
pattern on tower fascia.

8. Perspective sketch and detail
of windchime.

9. Detail of wall graphics.

10. Hanging blade signs
in collonade.

11. Diagramatic detail of
repeating freeze pattern.

3.

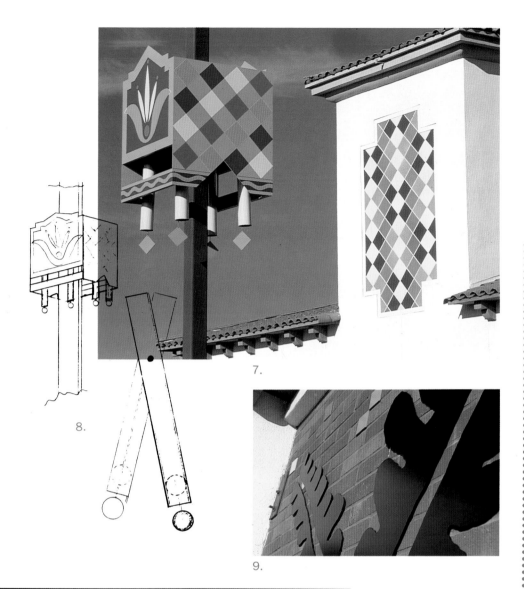

7.

8.

9.

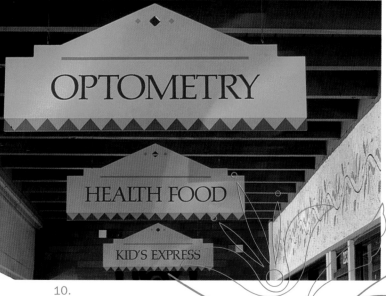

OPTOMETRY

HEALTH FOOD

KID'S EXPRESS

10.

11.

Project Facts

Three designers worked some 400 hours on the eight-month project for BRE Properties of San Francisco, CA. Overall project budget was $181,000, of which design was $44,000 (1990) and implementation was $137,000.

Technical Information

Twelve inch building tiles are porcelain enamel, aluminum and painted MDO (medium density overlay plywood). Frieze graphics were painted by hand. Fabricators were challenged to engineer 36 x 36 inch windchimes to clang pleasantly, not clunk. A bench was designed into the back of the freestanding project directory.

Design Details

The project had recently undergone a renovation in the Spanish Mission style; design research began with this. Its arena is inspired by the region's original missions, churches, and tile patterns; its friezes by Mexican primitive art, doorways, and other folk influences. The color palette is interpreted differently in the floral frieze, tile patterning and signing.

Credits

Design Firm: 2D+3D Graphic Design
(merged with the GNU Group in 1992)
Design Team: Nancy Daniels, Design Director; Maria Giannopoulou, Janna Solberg Hollis, Designers.
Fabricators: Pischoff Signs, Oakland, CA; Gene Siegrist Studios, Marina Del Rey, CA

1.

Sussman/Prejza & Co.
THE CITADEL

Exploring the post industrial possibilities
of a freeway landmark

The 1929 vintage "Hollywood Assyrian" facade that fronts a long defunct tire factory is one of Southern California's most recognized freeway landmarks. Behind it stretches a 35 acre site where the factory's industrial skeleton would become part of an adaptive reuse program consisting of a 157,000 square foot factory outlet retail center, 400,000 square feet of new office space, a 200 room hotel and an existing ziggurat-shaped six story office building. In addition to architectural design of the retail component, Sussman/Prejza developed graphic identity, signing and architectural color for the total project. In designing an entry monument for the 180 foot breach in the 1,700 foot wall, designers needed to be sensitive to any impact their work would have on the existing Assyrian motif facade. After all, it was incorporated into the logo of the City of Commerce, in which the project is located. Their solution draws upon its mythological figures, as well as on the tire factory's vocabulary of exposed steel trusses.

2.

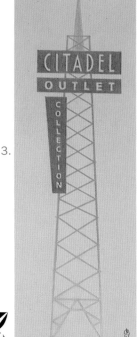

3.

5.

7.

4.

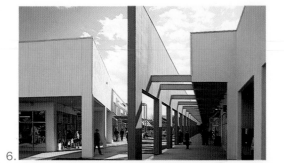

6.

9.

10.

12.

1. Building elevation from the freeway.
2. Study model of canopy detail.
3. Presentation sketch of tower marquee.
4. Evolution of project logo.
5. Entry monument sign demonstrating transparency and boldness.
6. Actual pedestrian canopy.
7. Formal pedestrian entry shows project color palette.
8.- 9. Presentation board and finished directory.
10. Rotating tire directory reflects building's past use.
11. - 12. Presentation board and actual directory sign.

Project Facts

The 18-month project involved a team of three graphic designers, four architects, and two color designers, who worked a total of approximately 1,800 hours. Overall budget on the Trammell Crow Company project was $118 million. Signing design budget was $150,000; signing implementation was $600,000.

Technical Information

Most signage is fabricated aluminum and steel. Designers used real tires on the retail directory in reference to the original factory. The moving tires give the illusion of spinning around each other. The 128 foot tower was fabricated in sections, assembled at the site, and then lifted into place.

Design Details

Designers were guided by the eclectic inspiration of the existing landmark building and by the nature of the adaptive reuse project. They also responded to a need for a strong freeway identity. The resulting aesthetic juxtaposes old and new, contrasting the "Hollywood mythical" vocabulary of the old facade and the industrial vocabulary of the original plant with new identity elements resulting from graphic and architectural intervention.

Credits

Design Firm: Sussman/Prejza & Co., Inc.,Culver City, Design Team: Deborah Sussman, Principal-in-Charge; Scott Cuyler, Design Director, Graphics; Fernando Vazquez, Design Director, Retail Architecture; Holly Hampton, Charles Milhaupt, Ena Dubnoff, Design Team Members.
Architect: Sussman/Prejza & Co., Inc. (Retail Design) The Nadel Partnership, Los Angeles, CA
Fabricators: Ad-Art Signs; Heath Sign Company; Kris Byk, (sculptural archers); Adelphia Graphic Systems, Exton, PA
Other Collaborators: Peridian, (Landscape Architect); Schwartz, Smith, Meyer, (Grand Allee Design); Grenald Associates (Lighting); Martin Weil, AIA (Restoration)

The Graphics Studio
HORIZON

A furniture store sheds its prosaic past

Horizon, an upscale furniture store in Los Angeles, has occupied the same location since the 1940's. The owners wanted to do something dramatic about its sadly out-of-date Fifties look on a very modest budget. A color-only assignment expanded to signage and identity when he decided to change the store's name from the prosaic-sounding Southern California Furniture Company and the designer suggested an element that might focus attention on the new name. An existing 15-foot high rooftop sign was modified to flash it intermittently with the existing "Furniture" message, and a striking new letter box sign identity was extended across a purple and aqua facade.

1.

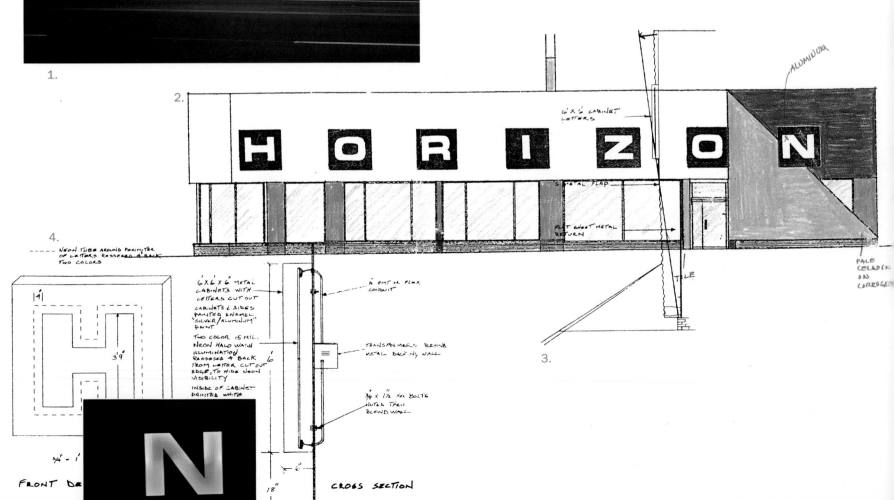

5.

6.

7.

1. Building elevation.
2. Color presentation study.
3. Section drawing of corrugated metal shape showing angle.
4. Working drawing and detail of light box.
5. Front detail showing angled wall and bi-colored illumination technique.
6. Side wall showing painted graphics.
7. Study and actual marquee showing neon with flashing painted sign.

Project Facts

The designer spent 40 to 50 hours on the Horizon Furniture Company assignment, which lasted 12 to 14 weeks. Scope of work included exterior signage, architectural color and project image. Design budget was $7,000; implementation budget, $28,000.

Technical Information

Letters are cut out from 60 inch square aluminum boxes. Blue and yellow neon tubes inside the boxes create a gradient effect. The corrugated steel triangle is 25 feet high and canted from the facade at a seven degree angle. Additional metal sheathing was pre-existing. A lacquer paint was used on the metal.

Design Details

The designer sought maximum street presence on a minimum budget. He wanted a solution that was a touch whimisical yet also offered the prospect of holding up well over time. A modified Copperplate typeface with serifs removed gives a subtle "retro modern" suggestion. The existing rooftop sign was enhanced by the addition of sheathing around its stanchions and a ball and pennant finial on top.

Credits

Design Firm: The Graphics Studio, Los Angeles, CA
Designers: Gerry Rosentswieg, Don Behrstock
Fabricator: Merit Sign Company, Sun Valley, CA
Photo Credit: Ferguson Kirchner, Newport Beach, CA

Bass Yager & Associates
SOHIO/BP SERVICE STATION

Graphics and architecture create
a standout service station

Sohio, one of the original Standard Oil companies that marketed primarily in Ohio, initially contacted Bass/Yager to modernize the look of its existing stations. Architectural features included rounded canopy fascia and the integration of pumps into the station columns for a streamlined, uncluttered look. After the design was developed and implemented as a Sohio station, it was extended to Sohio's Gulf chain, and finally to BP stations when British Petroleum acquired a majority interest in Sohio. Throughout these brand changes, the station's architectural expression remained the same.

1.

2.

3.

4.

1. Original gas station showing Sohio markings.
2. View from under the canopy.
3. - 4. Subsequent identity changes.

Project Facts

A team varying in size from eight to ten designers worked on the Standard Oil of Ohio project for a three-year period. The scope included development of all architectural and graphic elements of the station, including the use of new finish materials to express the rounded contours of the columns and canopy fascia.

Technical Information

An aluminum composite material (ACM) — basically an aluminum-plastic sandwich material — was specified for all finished surfaces, the first major use of this type of product for a retail facility. Initially too costly for widespread use, the material became substantially less costly when the program's rollout enabled quantity production. Ultimately, ACM's cost was comparable to more traditional products.

Design Details

The station was designed for high retail visibility through the use of color and shape. The introduction of the rounded front (bullnose) canopy fascia gives the station a visual quality that distinguishes it from competitors' traditional flat canopies. The curvilinear theme was carried through all of the station components including columns, the convenience store building, and car wash structure. Typography was selected to have a strong, contemporary appearance replacing many older typefaces used for the Sohio brandmark.

Credits

Design Firm: Bass Yager & Associates, Los Angeles, CA
Design Team: Saul Bass, Design Director; David Riedford (project manager),
Richard Huppertz (project account manager), Fulton Van Hagen (graphic design), Howard York (graphic design), Kraig Kessel (architectural design)

1.

Drenttel Doyle Projects
NEW YORK TRANSIT AUTHORITY GIFT SHOP AND INFORMATION CENTER

A temporary travel information center
for Grand Central Station

At Grand Central Terminal in New York City, designers created a temporary installation with a 1,000 square foot retail area using only surplus materials from Transit Authority yards. Built by Transit Authority craftspeople, the information center and transit museum gift shop is designed to be reassembled in a new location in a year's time. A large mural commissioned by artist Brian Cronin enhances the store's appearance.

2.

3.

4.

1. View showing Grand Central Station location.
2. Dramatic mural can be viewed through storefront.
3. Cubby hole display of merchandise forms a backdrop for curved counter.
4. Detail of counter, showing galvanized sheet metal.
5. Product display includes transit information.

5.

Project Facts

Three designers spent 180 hours over three months on the New York Transit Authority Project. Overall project budget was $60,000, of which $10,000 was for design.

Technical Information

Surplus Transit Authority materials included steel grates, industrial grade plywood, galvanized sheet metal, rivets, terrazzo tiles, and subway lighting fixtures. New finishes altered the appearance of these conventional materials.

Design Details

Economy of materials and the role of mass transit in an urban environment informed design for the space, formerly a bank, in Grand Central Station's main terminal. A bright, well-lighted mural offsets the shop's neutral wood and metal colors. Side-cut subway rails serve as "hooks" for displaying merchandise.

Credits

Design Firm: Drenttel Doyle Projects, New York, NY
Design Team: Miguel Oks, Design Director; Stephen Doyle, Mats Itakansson
Fabricators: Transit Authority Infrastructure Department; Bergen Shop, Brooklyn, New York
Lighting: Jerry Kugler Associates, New York, NY
Photo Credit: Scott Francis, New York, NY

Crate and Barrel
CRATE AND BARREL CONSTRUCTION BARRICADE

A retailer's icon inspires new store
construction barricades

Crate and Barrel's ubiquitous gift boxes and tags inspired construction barricade graphics for two new 8,000 square foot stores in the Chicago area. At a Michigan Avenue location in downtown Chicago, design not only needed to fit in an upscale shopping district, but materials and execution needed to last a full year and withstand a harsh winter. Panels could not warp or split, and needed to be secured for high winds. At a nearby Oak Brook location, the barricade needed to be viewable from greatly varying distances in four directions. While each barricade responds to different conditions, both reinforce Crate and Barrel's existing identity.

1.

2.

3.

4.

5.

1. Overall view showing prime Michigan Avenue location.

2. Flat MDO panels being installed over wood super structure.

3. - 5. Painted barricade gives the illusion of dimension.

Project Facts

One designer spent approximately 50 hours on the barricade, which will remain in place one year. Overall project budget was $40,000; implementation was $25,000.

Technical Information

Barricades are constructed of MDO, a medium-density fiber board, hand-painted and airbrushed for external use. The fabricator was challenged to make flat panels look three-dimensional both from up close and far away. Barricades run 300 feet and are 8 - 10 feet high. They are illuminated by ambient light.

Design Details

The designer sought simplicity and clarity of imagery, considered the context of store locations, and reinforced the existing graphic image of the company.

Credits

Design Firm: Crate and Barrel
(in-house department), Northbrook, IL
Designer: Alessandro Franchini
Fabricator: American Scene, Chicago, IL; Alex Broude
Photography: Francois Robert
Photo Credit: Alan Shortall

Morla Design
LEVI'S JEAN SHOP AND FIXTURE DESIGN

A new way to shop for jeans

In creating a new generation of Levi's shop environments, designers appealed to trend-conscious 16 to 28 year old shoppers without resorting to trendiness. A highly functional system of modular components allows the integration of graphics, image, product, light and sound in endless configurations for widely varying floor plans and high-volume inventory capacities.

1.

2.

3.

1. - 2. Gondola design with and without merchandise.
3. The entire system features casters to enable reconfiguration.
4. Detail of portable free standing shelving walls.

4.

Project Facts

Three designers worked approximately 600 hours on the nine-month assignment for San Francisco-based Levi Strauss & Company. The new environment has been introduced in one hundred 2,000 square foot shops nationwide.

Technical Information

Galvanized steel, mahogany and maple laminates, powder-coated metals and glass were specified, with galvanized steel as the primary surfacing material. All components were custom fabricated. Elements include seven foot tower fixtures and five foot wide floor fixtures. Recessed soffit lighting, wand-mounted halogen spots and ceiling track halogens provide illumination.

Design Details

Designers wanted to create an environment that would be functional, street-wise and fun, "cool" without being trendy, and would reflect a new, sophisticated image direction for the product. Fixtures incorporate an integrated sound, video and graphics display system. All components roll.

Credits

Design Firm: Morla Design, San Francisco, CA
Design Team: Jennifer Morla, Design Director; Scott Drummond, Senior Designer
Fabricators: Mobius, Eugene, OR; Store Fixtures Inc., Fort Worth, TX

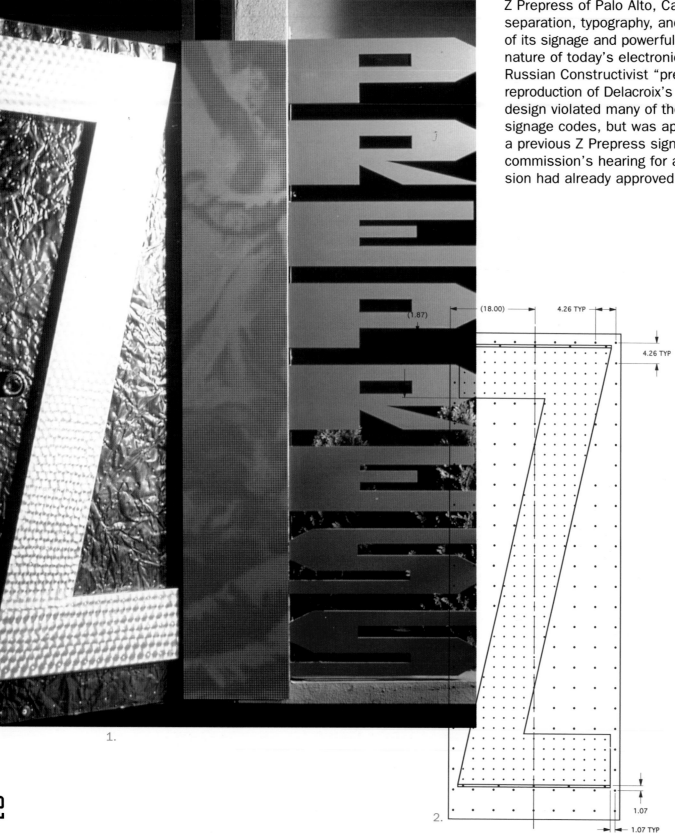

Mauk Design
Z PREPRESS ENTRANCE DOOR
Doorway to a service bureau's complete identity

Z Prepress of Palo Alto, California, is a leading electronic color separation, typography, and film assembly firm. Design elements of its signage and powerful entry door represent "the revolutionary nature of today's electronic prepress": a Bauhaus Futura "Z" and Russian Constructivist "prepress" typography, and a silkscreened reproduction of Delacroix's *Liberty Leading the People*. The door's design violated many of the City of Palo Alto's restrictive street signage codes, but was approved based on the positive impact of a previous Z Prepress sign. Designers arrived late to the signage commission's hearing for a variance only to discover the commission had already approved it.

1. Doorway to printing service bureau.

2. Diagram of Bauhaus Futura "Z", sheet steel and aluminum door.

3. Detail showing sculptural doorknob and richness of materials.

4. Detail of copper leaf letters.

5. Detail of screened image represents the revolutionary nature of today's electronic prepress.

3.

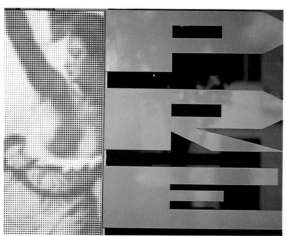
4.

5.

Project Facts

Two designers worked approximately 500 hours on the three month assignment. Implementation budget was $7,500. Door and signs are part of a complete identity program that extends to design of messengers' uniforms and bicycles.

Technical Information

Entry elements are made of steel, engine-turned aluminum, wrinkled copper with black oxide coating, copper rivets, and a hard to find four inch bolt. Sheet steel was folded; steel and aluminum were laser-cut. The grid for fiber optic holes and rivets was laid out using a computer-aided design program; fiber optic holes were drilled with a laser. Engine-turned aluminum evokes engine block detailing from a 1930's Duesenberg automobile. The bolt serves as a door handle. Prepress type is 30 inches wide on the 3 by 8 foot door. The giant "Z" contains 200 fiber-optic lines. A 75-watt light source is mounted on the wall inside the door.

Design Details

Designers were challenged to add visual excitement to an otherwise quiet suburban street-scape governed by some of the most restrictive sign ordinances in the country. Bold, constructivist-style type was chosen for its raw energy.

Credits

Design Firm: Mauk Design, San Francisco, CA
Design Team: Mitchell Mauk, Design Director; Tim Mautz, Designer
Fabricators: Curry Graphics, Hayward, CA (silkscreen); Schaeffer Sheet Metal, San Carlos, CA (Z letterform); Lazarus Lighting, Palo Alto, CA (fiber optics); Z Prepress, Palo Alto, CA (artwork production)
Photo Credit: Don Fogg

Paul Stuart Design Department
PAUL STUART WINDOW DISPLAYS

A specialty store expresses itself
in window displays Paul Stuart is a traditional men's specialty store in Manhattan where the tradition of retail window displays is also upheld — with engaging, theatrical environments that are fresh in spirit and passionately designed. Windows reflect the store's own image, simple and uncluttered by a variety of vendor images. According to Tom Beebe, the store's director of visual merchandising, the displays' objective is to communicate a sense of magic and drama to sales asssociates and customers alike.

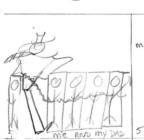

All: Informal, thinking sketches,
for approval and manufacture
and completed windows from
each series, New Years (tuxedo),
Me and My Dad" (Fathers Day),
and "Flying Carpet" (Summer).

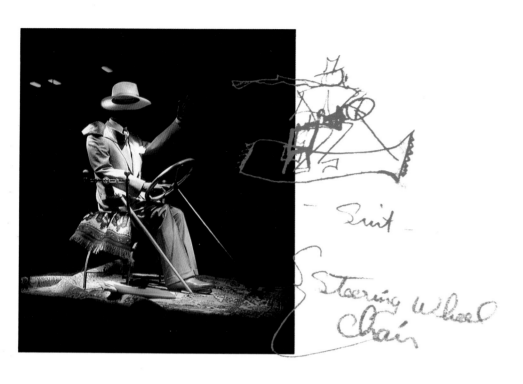

Project Facts

A team of three designers creates each display for a total of 14 windows, from development of the theme and scenario to execution. Planning displays for major events such as Christmas begins up to six months before execution.

Technical Information

Besides clothing, Beebe's displays use all manner of props as well as the traditional materials of display craft: colored filter, wires, thread, spray paint, nails and the ubiquitous straight pin. Designers are often challenged to attend to thousands of details for the complex scenarios.

Design Details

Displays often have the appearance of "magic," including clothing that appears to be inhabited by invisible figures or objects suspended in space, underscored by dramatic lighting. Whatever their theme or execution, they are intended to create customer excitement and reinforce the store's destination status.

Credits

Design Firm: Paul Stuart (in-house), New York, New York
Design Team: Tom Beebe, Director of Visual Merchandising; Gennaro Fredella, Michael Verbert.

PHILIP MURPHY

Forging a Winning Relationship with Environmental Graphics Fabricators

HOW IT ALL GOT STARTED

What began in 1973 as an impromptu meeting in Detroit to exchange information about how signs were created and produced became the genesis for the sophisticated industry of Environmental Graphic Design and Fabrication. From this auspicious gathering that included John Berry of Smith, Hinchman & Grylls, Richard Burns of the GNU Group, Jim Glass of Kelvin Group and Phil Meathe of Smith, Hinchman & Grylls, came a press release that read: "In the summer of 1973, several graphic designers met, almost accidentally, to discuss the general state of a new and elusive art which really has no name. The meeting was prompted by dissatisfaction with both the semantics and molasses-like flow of technological information in a neophyte field. Promotion of this specialty was determined to be desirable because its practitioners are entering a relatively unexplored territory, and because there is growing awareness of its importance by astute professionals in architecture."

In 1974, the group met for a second time in Houston, Texas to explore the potential for developing a national organization to serve this burgeoning industry. The term *environmental graphics* was coined from the following list: graphics engineering, graphics/signage, environmental signage, visual communications, architectural graphics, three-dimensional graphics, signage graphics, and directional graphics. The ensuing press release read: "The two most important accomplishments of the meeting were to select a name and to appoint an ad hoc steering committee to establish goals and by-laws. The name of the organization is the Society of Environmental Graphics Designers."

The Society of Environmental Graphics Designers (SEGD) was incorporated as a professional society in 1976. SEGD's primary goals were to define the qualifications of a professional environmental graphic designer and to recommend a curriculum which would help produce qualified graduates in this new field. In 1993, the organization elected to change its name to the Society for Environmental Graphic Design to better reflect the full range of activities in the profession. From the outset, SEGD membership included both professional designers and industry fabricators.

An early industry member, Hanley Bloom, summed up the initial problems that existed between designers and fabricators: "The environmental graphic designer and the fabricator didn't understand one another's needs. The fabricator felt put upon by the designers when samples, color matches, feasibility studies and budget estimates were requested without compensation. Designers had trouble understanding the fabricator's point of view — after all, the fabricator was going to make money off the opportunity he was being given. In addition, many designers were not completely familiar with "3D design," and their solutions were often unbuildable. We've come a long way in recognizing and respecting each other's needs and our joint contribution to the environmental graphics process."

THE PRESENT

Today SEGD promotes its members and initiates educational programs for the public. Information on designers and on the capabilities of fabricators is made available and continually updated. SEGD also provides a toll-free technical hotline to all of its professional membership. Fabricators answer a broad range of technical questions related to the fabrication process and how to specify projects efficiently. A technical sourcebook aids designers in specifying and preparing sign systems and bid documents. A "Tech Talk Bulletin" that reviews designer/fabricator trends, new materials, and fabrication techniques is also an important part of the SEGD quarterly newsletter, *Messages*. This sharing of information has been a boon to both the environmental graphic design professional and to the fabricators in sealing and confirming their interactive relationship.

HOW IT HAS PROGRESSED

As the organization enters its twenty-first year, SEGD has not only established a strong base for closer relationships between designers and fabricators but for the recipients of their services as well. In the realm of education, SEGD and its member designers are quick to explain that their custom designs require special fabricators who are expert and specialized in the processes, equipment and technology of environmental graphics.

New systems and technology have been created to allow for this specialization, and old systems have sometimes been eclipsed. Once considered standard for the environmental graphics world, the traditional bid process, for example, is not practiced as much as it once was. Fragmentation within the fabrication industry, improved quality control, and highly intricate custom designs have rendered the process less effective. Traditional bidding still has its place in the marketplace, but it frequently fails unless the fabricator selection process is painstakingly controlled and the designer manages the successful bidder on a time-and-materials contract.

Construction management services are now being offered by leading fabricators to aid designers. This team approach is implemented early in the project's design process and allows the fabricator to bring technology and budget problems to the team's attention. As design decisions are made, fabrication issues can be addressed and researched immediately. Simple material or fabrication changes can save the client money with little or no impact on design appearance or function. This approach relies on trust and good communications between all team members.

Many designers also help clients who purchase substantial amounts of environmental graphics or sign systems (i.e., medical facilities, institutions, corporate headquarters, asset managers, etc.) by recommending *strategic partnerships* with fabricators. The concept of designer-vendor-client partnering is relatively new in the United States. Clients who have created such partnerships report improved quality in product, delivery, and scheduling as well as lower costs and better communication between all parties. The GNU Group is currently negotiating strategic partnerships for the largest health care provider in the United States, a corporate headquarters campus, and a university campus.

Construction intent is a form of bid process similar to that used in the construction industry. It allows the designer to use design development drawings as a bidding tool. The drawings are annotated with measurements and text that explain construction intent without telling the fabricator how to build the finished product. Drawings are forwarded to two or three prequalified fabricators who are asked to prepare pricing, establish value engineering ideas with related savings, and to create a timeline for fabrication and installation.

Next, the designer and client meet with each fabrication team to ask specific questions about fabrication processes, project management, pricing, value engineering ideas and related savings, and durability and maintenance expectations. The interview process gleans a very clear picture for the client as to which fabricator understands the specific requirements that will provide the best value and the most appropriate working relationship for the project. The client, designer, and selected fabricator then meet to negotiate price, terms, and working strategy. Quite often, an exit interview with fabricators who were *not* selected also provides useful information for future opportunities.

WHERE IT'S GOING

With the foundation laid for closer and more interactive relationships, the environmental graphic designer and fabricator are positioned for new challenges ahead — projects with special needs, budgets with unique constraints, and a new breed of real estate owner with greater expectations than ever. With education, communication and a willingness to change, the profession will continue to flourish.

Philip Murphy is Vice President and Principal in Charge of Environmental Graphics at the GNU Group in Sausalito, California. He is a boardmember of SEGD and speaks nationally on the practice of environmental graphic design, fabricator relations, and strategic partnerships for environmental graphics users.

Institutional Environments

Well-executed signage is one way public and private institutions compete with their commercial counterparts.

1.

Richard Poulin Design Group
INDIANAPOLIS MUSEUM OF ART

A comprehensive graphic program
for a fine art institution Located on a 152-acre park-like site in the City of Indianapolis, the Indianapolis Museum of Art is comprised of the Eli Lilly Botanical Garden, four art pavilions including the newly constructed Mary Fendrich Hulman Pavilion designed by Edward Larrabee Barnes/ John M.Y. Lee & Associates of New York, a lecture hall, theater, concert terraces, restaurants and shops. A comprehensive design program coinciding with expansion of the museum's facilities provided the design team an opportunity not only to develop a new graphic identity but to establish graphic and sign standards for the entire complex.

1. Typical room number sign.
2. Working drawing for ground mounted monument sign.
3. Unique stairway installation.
4. Typical detail showing extruded aluminum bracket which "captures" the display panels.
5. Sign system for grounds features slim panels set into half-round concrete bases.
6. Good example of moveable interior sign.
7. - 8. Monument sign and detail of working drawing.

2.

3.

4.

5.

6.

7.

8.

Project Facts

The project involved three designers over a two-year period and included all architectural graphics and sign elements, exterior banners and site signs, stationery, brochures, a monthly magazine, promotional print materials, shopping bags and interpretive graphics for the museum's major collections. Implementation budget was $250,000.

Technical Information

Signs were fabricated out of a variety of materials and processes, including dimensional stainless steel letters, etched and gold leaf tempered glass panels, sub-surface silkscreened Plexiglas panels, baked aluminum panels with reflective vinyl die-cut letters, silkscreened brushed aluminum panels, and gold leaf on glass. Sign elements range in size from 2 ft. 1 in. wide by 6 ft. 2 in. high (free-standing kiosk) to 6 3/4 in. wide by 1 ft. 1 1/2 in. high (wall-mounted panel).

Design Details

A sans serif Univers typeface is used for all non-fine art related information (i.e., public information, directional, procedural) and a serif Bodoni Antiqua is used for all fine art information (i.e., art/caption labels, gallery identification). This allows a clear and concise distinction between the two major groups of information. Burgundy, turquoise and ochre are used as identifiers within the program. Each color symbolizes one of three pavilions; the colors are also used as key wayfinding symbols throughout the museum. The predominant component within the sign program is a panel sign produced in a system of proportionate sizes and materials and used throughout all areas of the project. A common panel system unifies elements within the program and strengthens the design approach.

Credits

Design Firm: Richard Poulin Design Group, Inc., New York, NY
Design Team: Richard Poulin, Design Director; Kirsten Steinorth, Debra Drodvillo
Architect: Edward L. Barnes/John Lee & Partners, New York, NY
Fabricators: Cornelius Architectural Products, Pittsbrugh, PA (sign program); Band-Art Banners, Indianapolis, IN (banners); Hamilton Displays, Indianapolis, IN (interpretive exhibit graphics)

The Design Offices
of Robert Bailey
OREGON MUSEUM OF SCIENCE
AND INDUSTRY

Museum graphics that entertain
as well as inform

The new, privately-funded Oregon Museum of Science and Industry in Portland is considered one of the best science museums in the country. The 18.5 acre site includes six exhibition halls totaling over 200,000 square feet, a 330 seat Omnimax theater, and a 210 seat planetarium. Since the project must compete for entertainment dollars, graphics needed to be lively as well as informative. Bright colors, massive forms and dramatic lighting add to their entertainment value.

1.

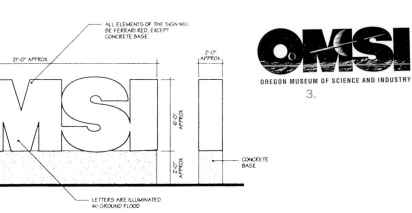

ALL ELEMENTS OF THE SIGN WILL BE FERRARI RED, EXCEPT CONCRETE BASE.

21'-0" APPROX.

2'-0" APPROX

6'-0" APPROX

2'-0" APPROX

CONCRETE BASE

FABRICATED 1/8" ALUMINUM DIMENSIONAL LETTERS ON CONTOURED CONCRETE BASE

LETTERS ARE ILLUMINATED W/ GROUND FLOOD

ELEVATION - SIGN TYPE E-C (Illuminated Letters Ground Mounted Entry Sign)
A3   Scale 1/4" = 1'-0"

2.

OREGON MUSEUM OF SCIENCE AND INDUSTRY
3.

1. Computer generated presentation of proposed monument sign.

2. Simple working drawing of monument sign.

3. Illustrative variation of logo designed for project.

4. Illuminated wall sign dominates streetscape.

5. Early conceptual sketch.

6. Poster cabinet features bottom lit layers of cut-out letter.

7. Detail of layered letter.

8. - 10. Conceptual presentation sketch, working drawing and actual directional pylon.

11. Neon tubing over stainless steel letter makes a powerful interior marquee.

4.

5.

11.

6.

7.

LOGO WILL BE DIMENSIONAL
TO THE FULL DEPTH OF THE SIGN.
INTERNAL ILLUMINATION
AT TOP OF THE SIGN WILL
ILLUMINATE BASE OF LOGO

WHITE REFLECTIVE VINYL
GLYPHS WILL APPEAR ON
PURPLE VINYL CIRCULAR FIELD.

REFLECTIVE WHITE TEXT
AND ARROWS CENTERED
IN SIGN WIDTH

FERRARI RED

STAINLESS STEEL
BASE CLADDING

8.

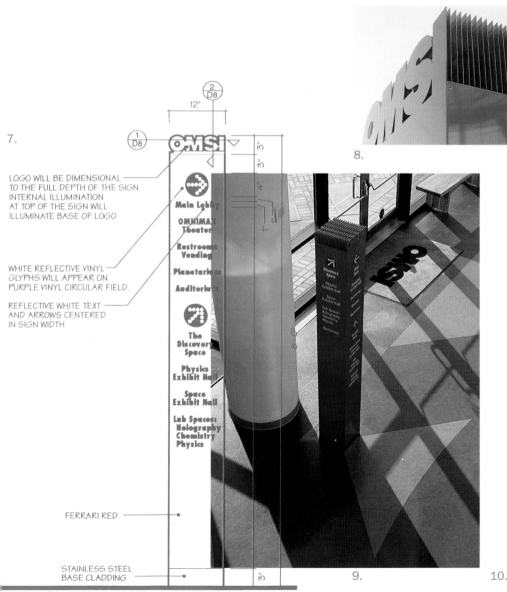

9.

10.

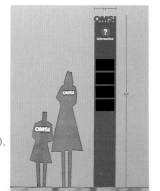

Project Facts

A four designer team spent 900 hours, some of them pro bono, on the two and a half year Oregon Museum of Science and Industry assignment. Overall project budget was approximately $200,000, of which design was $41,000 and implementation was $160,000. The scope of work included design, construction documents and contract administration for all decorative and informational graphic systems inside and outside the building — as well as the logo. The $45 million project was funded entirely by donations; every consultant donated time and suppliers donated some materials.

Technical Information

Polished aluminum letters, painted aluminum signs with concealed rivets, continuous tone painted walls were specified. Main project identity is cut and fabricated from quarter-inch aluminum, painted, and then fit into a concrete base. Logos were computer routed. Internal fluorescent and neon lighting provides illumination.

Design Details

Designers sought to make an impact and use technology; for exterior signs they worked within the constraints of a design review and green way area. The logo developed by the designers helped to guide the sign program's development.

Credits

Design Firm: Robert Bailey Incorporated, Portland, OR
Design Team: Robert Bailey, Design Director; Ian Harding, Project Manager; Carolyn Coghlan
Architect: Zimmer, Gunsul, Frasca
Fabricator: Oregon Sign, Portland, OR

1.

Wesselman Design
JOAN & IRVING HARRIS
CONCERT HALL

Signage that quietly becomes one
with the architecture

Aspen's new concert hall is located next to the Herbert Bayer Tent where the International Design Conference and the Aspen Music Festival are held. The architect wanted to respect the scale and importance of the tent by not overwhelming it with a three-story building, so he literally buried the new facility into the ground. Concertgoers enter on the top floor and descend two floors to the concert hall entrance. The architect used natural materials in their natural form — sandblasted concrete, anodized aluminum, mineral board, cherry and maple. One of the designer's goals was to integrate the signage into this quiet palette.

2.

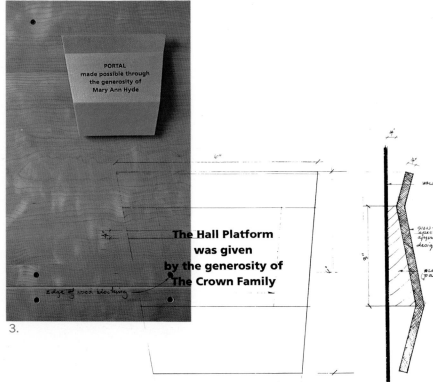

3.

M.A.A.
REHEARSAL/PERFORMANCE HALL

HARRY TEAGUE ARCHITECTS

4.

1. *Music Hall entrance gives no indication of two underground levels.*
2. *Low-key entrance sign.*
3. *Working drawing and finished, folded major donor plaque.*
4. *Architect's elevation sketch.*
5. *Donor wall folds and bends to repeat Origami - like roof.*
6. *Working drawing and actual exterior "named gift" marker.*

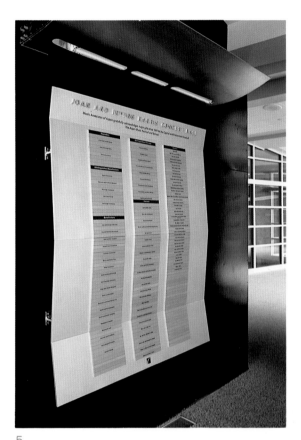

5.

sign-align with special finish approved by designer

blocking (painted black)

F.P.O.

sod

6.

Project Facts

Kathy Wesselman completed the program for the Aspen Music Festival in eight months' time. Overall project budget was $34,500, of which design was $14,500 and implementation was $20,000. Scope of work included designing, producing construction documents, contracting fabricators and supervising installation of all exterior and interior signs.

Technical Information

Aluminum and mineral board were specified. The mineral board was sandblasted for ADA signs (Americans with Disabilities Act). Aluminum was finished with a jitterbug sander for a soft, jewel-like appearance and then anodized to protect it from discoloring. Other techniques included welding and silkscreening. Fabricators were challenged to engineer the four x five foot donor wall so it could swing open to add and delete names. Entrance sign lettering is five inches tall by one inch deep, and is illuminated by spots and downlights. Courtyard and lobby sign letters are two inches tall by one-half inch deep. Named gift sign is 6 x 6 x 1/2 inches. ADA signs are 7 x 7 x 1/4.

Design Details

The concept behind the architecture was strong; it was important for the signage to complement the building in both form and materials. Context and understatement played important roles in how the designer approached the project. She chose a Frutiger typeface as a nod to Herbert Bayer. Colors are found in the architecture. The donor wall, which appears to float on the ebonized cherry wall, is actually a four by five foot piece of aluminum weighing 150 pounds.

Credits

Design Firm: Wesselman Design, Inc., Seattle, WA
Design Team: Kathy Wesselman, Design Director
Architect: Harry Teague Architects, Aspen, CO
Fabricator: Communication Industries, Denver, CO
Photo Credit: Thorney Lieberman, Boulder, CO

1.

Wayne Hunt Design
EDMUND D. EDELMAN
CHILDREN'S COURT

A self-guiding system for a child and
family-sensitive environment

Visitors to a court facility — perhaps especially one dedicated to child dependency cases — are not always well-prepared to find their way through what can seem an intimidating bureaucratic maze. Nor in the case of a new 250,000 square foot children's court for the County of Los Angeles, does the building's complex layout — and the courts' counter-intuitive numbering system — make wayfinding any easier. A front-to-back signing program for the five-floor facility, the first of its kind in the nation, addresses these concerns with clear, simple language, positive messages, color reinforcement, and pictographic information.

3.

5.

2.

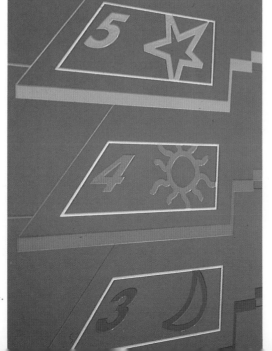

4.

6.

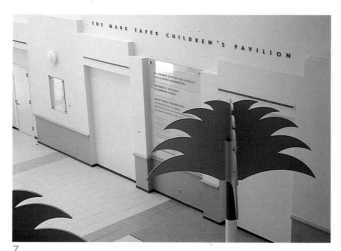

7.

Project Facts

A five designer team worked on the assignment for Los Angeles County's Internal Services Division over a two-year period. Overall sign design and fabrication budget was $520,000. Scope of work included a children's art program as well as comprehensive interior and exterior signage.

Technical Information

Materials specified include brushed stainless steel (building identification), cut aluminum (sculptural symbols), etched metal plaques decorated with glass (room identifiers), glass (displays), cut acrylic (pictograms), etched and filled plastic laminate panels edged in plate glass (elevator directories), and paint (restroom identification). For its durability, etched metal was chosen for signs required by the Americans with Disabilities Act (ADA). Official seals of the State of California were rendered in deep-carved glass. Original artwork provided by the state archivist was in such poor condition that the fabricator had to restore it based on a verbal description.

Design Details

Designers used the architect's metaphor of a house, which symbolizes a humane and welcoming environment, as a starting point for a system of icons apparent even to young children. Avoiding the temptation to make them overtly childlike, designers drew them as an artist would, not as a child would. Specific colors attached to each symbol enhance the system's efficiency. Futura and Futura Bold typefaces were chosen for legibility.

1. *Court seal designed for the project.*
2. *Early conceptual sketch of floor icons.*
3. *Colonnade of aluminum icons reinforce floor level identity.*
4. *Detail of etched and paint-filled map directory.*
5. *Cast in place concrete monument sign bisects circular planter.*
6. *Floor level identity in elevator lobby.*
7. *View of lobby showing donor recognition wall.*
8. *Oversized floor indentifiers feature flat cut-out forms, screened glass panels and dimensional numerals.*
9. *Doors to childrens rest rooms feature painted graphics.*

8.

Credits

Design Firm: Wayne Hunt Design, Pasadena, CA
Design Team: Wayne Hunt, Principal; Sharrie Lee, Associate; John Temple, Senior Designer; Katherine Go, Designer
Architect: Kajima International, Inc., Monterey Park, CA
Fabricators: Graphic Display, Glendale, CA (room plaques, exterior signs, parking garage signs) Hampton Associates, Corona, CA (lobby directories, sculptural elements) AHR/Ampersand, Los Angeles, CA (tactile signs) The Wallach Glass Studio, Inc., Sebastopol, CA (glass seals) Crystalline Images, Santa Clara, CA (glass court history)
Photo Credit: Charles Allen Photography, Pasadena, CA

9.

Tom Graboski Associates
HEALTH CENTRAL

Communicating a hospital identity with bright
colors and playful shapes

An exterior identity and wayfinding signage system for the 50
acre site of a new 200 bed hospital in Ocoee, Florida satisfies the
architect's desire for something unusual with asymmetrical design
and unexpected juxtapositions of shapes and colors — features
suggested by the building itself. Designers developed complete
exterior signage design, working drawings, location plans,
elevations and message schedules for the site, and oversaw the
program's fabrication and installation.

1.

2.

3.

4.

(19)

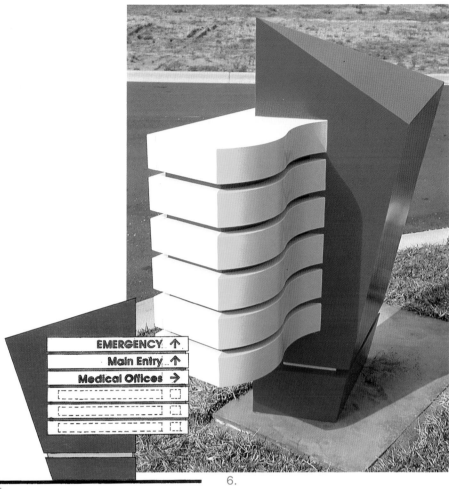

5.

6.

7.

1. Floating dimensional avant garde letters lend transparency to major sign.

2. - 3. Exterior signage emulates flamboyant architecture.

4. Presentation sketch and actual handicapped parking sign.

5. Presentation sketch of directional sign front.

6. Back view of actual directional sign demonstrates how project signage functions as sculpture.

7. Secondary directional sign.

Project Facts

Three designers worked some 500 hours on the one-year West Orange Hospitals assignment. Design budget was $11,000; implementation, $170,000.

Technical Information

Signs are welded and painted aluminum construction with internally illuminated push-through day/night text in smoked acrylic. From a distance, the fabricated aluminum sculptures resemble welded steel plate. Refining their unusual shapes required the construction of scale models. The largest sign is 17 feet high. Ground-level uplights augment its internal fluorescent and neon illumination.

Design Details

Design needed to communicate a "hospital" identity while remaining colorful and playful in context and in relationship to the architecture. Accent colors and shapes found in the building inspired an asymmetrical, sculptural solution.

Credits

Design Firm: Tom Graboski Associates, Inc., Coconut Grove, FL
Design Team: Tom Graboski, Design Director; Chris Rogers, Principal Designer/Project Manager; Mary McCormick, Designer and Production Artist
Architect: HKS, Dallas, TX
Fabricator: Federal Sign Company, Daytona Beach, FL
Photo Credit: Tom Graboski

Sussman/Prejza & Company
DENVER PERFORMING
ARTS COMPLEX

Unifying a complex with signs that perform

Denver's performing arts center is a four-building complex with a central arcade and a seven-level parking structure. Each building in turn varies greatly from the next: One is a turn-of-the-century auditorium, two are additions dating from the 1970's, and one is a current renovation. Beyond unifying the disparate elements of the complex, designers also made reference to its function by considering environmental graphics as elements of a performance. Funded by joint public and private funds, the program was implemented in phases.

1.

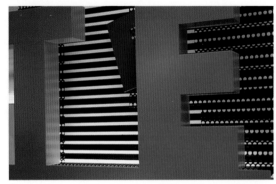

4.

2.

3.

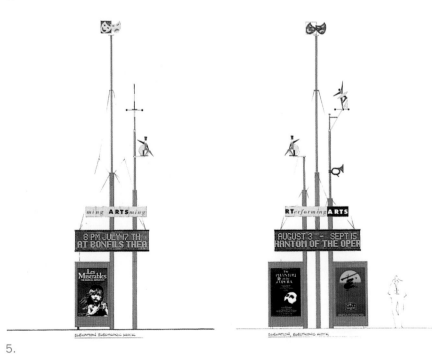

5.

6.

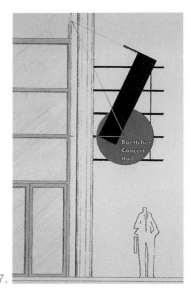

7.

1. View of covered gallery, includes event kiosk, project directory, theatre identity and project colors.

2. Early directory concept features organization of levels by musical scale.

3. Early study model of event kiosk.

4. Full size mock-up of theatre letters.

5. Final presentation board for event kiosk.

6. Gallery overview shows concert hall, identity marquee and architectural color.

7. Presentation board for concert hall identity.

8. Typical theatre level sign shows opaque panel over mesh background.

9. Masks of comedy and tragedy act as kinetic sculpture atop the event kiosk.

8.

9.

Project Facts

A team of three designers worked approximately 1,200 hours on the project for the City and County of Denver over an eight-month period. Design budget was $83,000; implementation, $300,000.

Technical Information

Materials specified include architectural and perforated aluminum, acrylic, glass, and paint. Aluminum figures on the marquee kiosks move with the circulation of air. The kiosks were difficult to detail; the use of models was very helpful. Buell Theater identification is 2 ft. 9 in. high by 86 feet wide. Kiosks, which are three-sided, are 10 feet wide by 34 feet high. Illumination is highly theatrical and varied. Kiosks use electronic message center technology as well as spots for a Klieg light effect. The Buell Theater sign is designed as if on stage and hit with stage lighting, to give an illusion of casting a dramatic shadow on the perforated aluminum "curtain" behind. The interior donor recognition wall is a fabricated aluminum frame with silkscreened sandblasted glass name panels. The entire wall is back-lit to create a dramatic, lantern-like effect. Others signs are illuminated by back-lit, interior or exposed sources.

Design Details

Designers wanted elements to engage the audience as if they are part of a performance. They introduced an underlying constructivist aesthetic that guided typography and a strong, simple color palette.

Credits

Design Firm: Sussman/Prejza & Company, Inc., Culver City, CA
Design Team: Paul Prejza, Principal-in-Charge; Scott Cuyler, Design Director; Holly Hampton, Senior Designer; Fred Hidalgo, John Johnston.
Architect: Beyer, Blinder, Belle, New York, NY; van Dijk, Pace, Westlake & Partners, Cleveland, OH
Fabricators: Sachs Lawlor Sign Division, Denver, CO; Great Panes Glassworks, Denver, CO; YESCO, Salt Lake City, UT
Lighting: Howard Brandston Lighting Design, New York, NY
Photo Credit: Peter Aaron/Esto

Gensler and Associates/Graphics
KQED BUILDING GRAPHICS PROGRAM

Distinctive signage that remains faithful to a
budget-conscious attitude

1.

Thanks to a major public fundraising effort, KQED, a San Francisco, CA public broadcasting and publishing organization, was able to consolidate its many separate facilities into a single 150,000 square foot building. In developing the exterior and interior sign program, Gensler Graphics needed to reflect the non-profit organization's attitude with a restrained use of materials and budget-conscious solutions. No elements were to seem overly extravagant, and colors, forms, and images were to appear functional and integral to the architecture. Donor recognition needed to be strong but not overbearing.

2.

1. Blade sign recalls thirties movie marquee.
2. EGD team worked with interior designers to integrate signs into the subtle interior scheme.
3. Floor embedded stainless steel disks required careful alignment to achieve a level surface.
4. Donor wall features screened glass disks.
5. - 7. Room and department identification is unified by circle (disk) motif.

3.

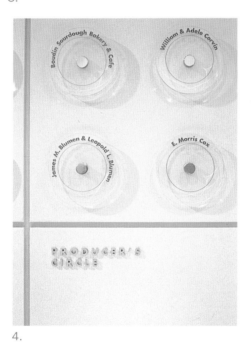

4.

5.

6.

7.

Project Facts

A team of three designers spent approximately 380 hours on the assignment, which lasted 12 months through installation. The project's overall architectural budget was $10 million. Graphic design budget was $20,000. Implementation budget was $27,000.

Technical Information

Donor recognition elements are brushed stainless steel rings, etched and infilled with epoxy enamel; and water white glass disks with silkscreened metallic ink and chromed mounting studs embedded in linoleum floor tiles. Stainless steel was chosen for luster and durability (It is commonly used on vandal-prone surfaces such as elevator doors.); water white glass for its jewel-like luster when illuminated. Epoxy silkscreen ink avoids chipping to withstand a janitor's floor buffing machine. Entry graphics are fabricated brushed stainless steel dimensional letterforms, and lacquered MDO (medium-density overlay plywood) letterforms within the reception lobby. Room and departmental identification disks are painted, multi-layer acrylic with silkscreened graphics.

Design Details

As part of the interior design team, designers were aware of the interior design direction from early schematic studies. This enabled them to develop surfaces and details that would accept signage as an integral component. Beyond its responsiveness to the architecture, the program also subtly refers to aspects of broadcasting: department ID signs reference a "focusing target," and facade fin lettering recalls a theater marquee's.

Futura was chosen. as the dominant face, with Snell Script used as a decorative background type for studio ID. Futura compliments the building's strong, modernist character and is used in KQED's corporate identity. Sign colors were derived from the interiors palette, and compliment the daylight that floods the skylighted main public space. Metals create a feeling of simple, light, natural materials.

Credits

Design Firm: Gensler and Associates/Graphics, San Francisco, CA
Design Team: John Bricker, Design Director; Tom Horton, David Lehrer, Julie Vogel
Fabricator: Thomas Swan Sign Company
Architect: Gensler and Associates/Architects
Lighting: Horton Lees Lighting, San Francisco, CA
Photo Credit: Chas McGrath, Santa Rosa, CA

Bass Yager & Associates
THE PETERSEN AUTOMOTIVE MUSEUM

A museum prepares to move in

An abandoned department store in the Miracle Mile district of Los Angeles is the site of the Petersen Automotive Museum. After developing a trademark for the future museum, designers developed the graphic treatment for a construction barricade to establish the location as an interesting destination and to build anticipation for its opening.

1.

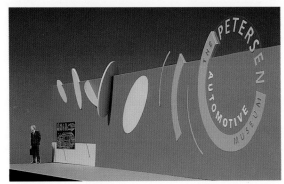

2.

3.

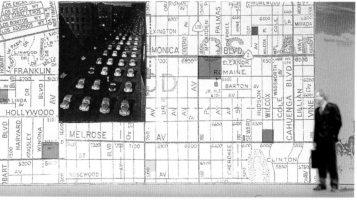

4.

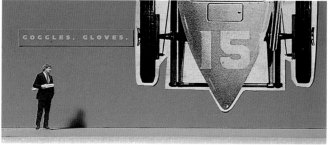

5.

1. Construction barricade study model features implied animation through abstract wheel shapes.
2. Detail showing museum logo.
3. - 5. Studies of alternative design directions.

Project Facts

The six month project for the museum, a satellite of the Natural History Museum of Los Angeles County, involved a team of three designers.

Technical Information

Painted, silkscreened, and VDC (vinyl die-cut) graphics were applied to a 12-foot high plywood barricade that included fabricated dimensional projections.

Design Details

The basic objective was to define the "automobile mystique." Designers proposed three solutions, of which the client chose the second: (a) "How the automobile changed our world," or "People, Cars, and the City" — a juxtaposition of historical images with a grid of Los Angeles, the city of the automobile; (b) geometric abstractions of motion and speed with references to Gyorgy Kepes' studies of the visual aspects of motion and Harold Edgerton's stop-motion photography; (c) fun, car parts — a whimsical look at what makes a car a car. Frutiger type was chosen for its clean, Machine Age quality; varying weights and letter spacings enhance the suggestion of rhythm and speed. Highly saturated, contrasting colors evoke emotion through tension. The graduated repetition of simple, streamlined shapes further connotes movement.

Credits

Design Firm: Bass Yager & Associates, Los Angeles, CA
Design Team: Saul Bass, Design Director; Jennifer Bass, Project Designer; Marry Ellen Buttner, Assistant Designer; Pamela Meadow, Account Manager

Lorenc Design
PALMETTO INTERNATIONAL EXPOSITION CENTER

Reuniting the parts of an expanded exhibit hall

After two decades of expansion, an 800,000 square foot expo complex covering four city blocks of Greenville, South Carolina, was a maze of spaces and appendages. The addition of a new conference center was intended to reunite the overall center with a focal point; the accompanying sign program helps to bring the project together with a dynamic color scheme and powerfully simple cubic architectural elements. The overall design team collaborated through a series of charettes to develop a font, color and material palette that would be fully cohesive with the architecture and interiors.

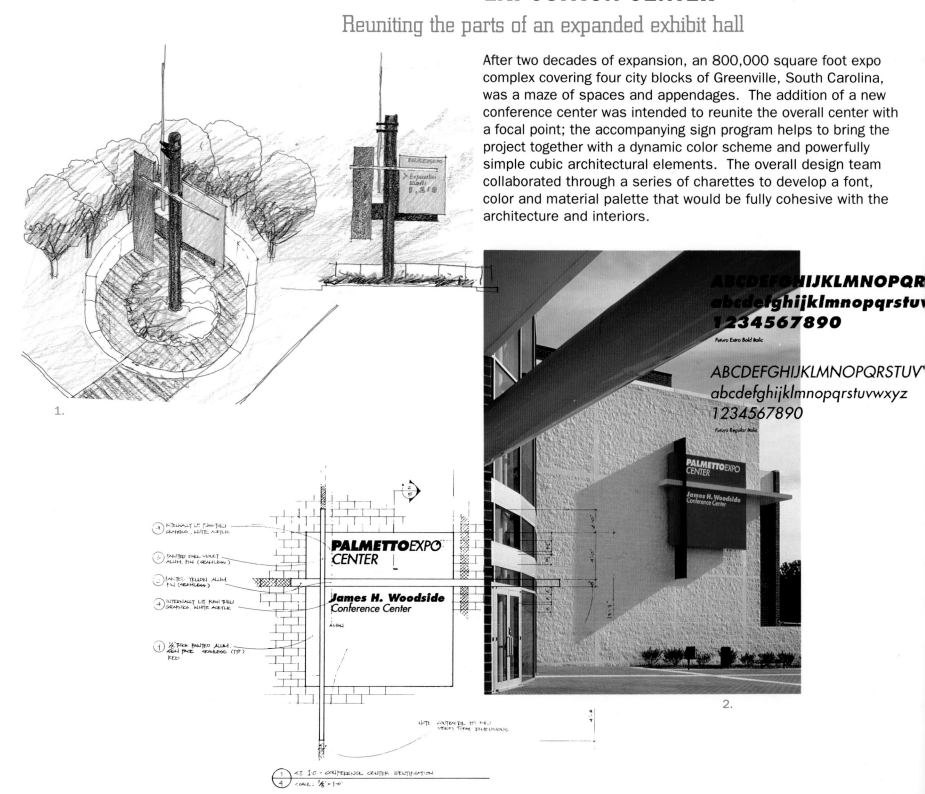

1.

ABCDEFGHIJKLMNOPQR
abcdefghijklmnopqrstuv
1234567890

Futura Extra Bold Italic

ABCDEFGHIJKLMNOPQRSTUV
abcdefghijklmnopqrstuvwxyz
1234567890

Futura Regular Italic

2.

3.

4.

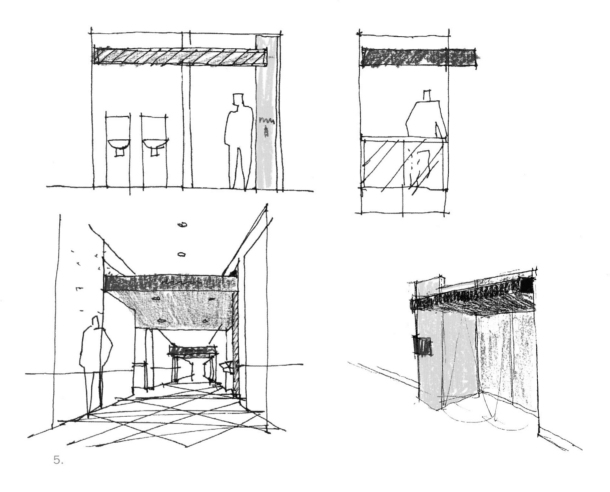

5.

6.

1. Early axonomteric sketch details elements used in finished signs.

2. Working drawing and typography presentation culminates in actual exterior project identity sign.

3. Bright colors enhance visibility in a monumental space.

4. Interior directional sign.

5. Conceptual sketches showing use of soffits as sign program elements.

6. Soffit used as sign at information desk.

4.

1. Exterior identity sign picks up line of architectural detail.

2. Plaques meet ADA requirement with Braille consistently located on yellow bands.

3. Architectural color is used as a wayfinding element.

4. - 5. Room identity plaques.

6. Working drawing of directional overhead sign.

7. Life safety signs are included and work effectively in the sign system.

8. Early presentation sketch.

9. Yellow is used for area designation in color system.

1.

2.

5.

3.

6.

7.

8.

9.

Project Facts

The two-year first phase of the ongoing five year assignment for Textile Hall Corporation involved three designers working a total of some 800 hours. Overall project budget was $280,000, of which $80,000 was design, $200,000 was implementation.

Technical Information

Aluminum, acrylic and sheet rock were specified. Fabrication techniques included welding, chemical bonding, etching and silkscreening. Signage is a part of the architecture, with soffits and small plaques intersecting the wall. Plaques meet ADA (Americans with Disabilities Act) requirements with Braille consistently located on a yellow horizontal band. Constant coordination between the general contractor and architect was essential to insure a tight fit for all elements. Interior plaques are lit by ceiling-recessed cans. Soffits contain fixtures to accent portals, which provide a human-scale transition into the exhibit hall's huge volumes.

Design Details

Design involvement began as the interiors were beginning to be designed; aesthetics developed through the overall design team's brainstorming sessions. Ultimately, intersecting bands recall the dynamic interweaving of textiles, a reference to the center's strong ties to the exhibition of textile equipment. The color system uses red for information, yellow for area designation portals (soffits), and purple and blue for accents.

Credits

Design Firm: Lorenc Design, Atlanta, GA
Design Team: Jan Lorenc, Design Director; Chung Youl Yoo, Steve McCall
Architect: CRSS Architects, Greenville, SC
Fabricator: Architectural Image Manufacturers (AIM),
Photo Credit: Jan Lorenc; Ron Rizzo/Creative Sources

Dennis S. Juett & Associates
DONOR RECOGNITION SYSTEM, ART CENTER COLLEGE OF DESIGN

A donor wall for a design school

The Art Center College of Design's donor recognition wall began as an assignment for a small group of graphic design students in an experimental exhibit design class. Criteria called for an easily updated system that would uphold the school's reputation. Dennis Juett's winning design uses a pencil as the vehicle for meeting these criteria. After refining the design and developing a budget over the following 14-week term, he completed the wall and gifts after graduation, in time to celebrate the successful completion of a $25 million fundraising campaign. Since then, the program has attracted new gifts and created interest and rivalry among donors.

1.

1. Overview of donor recognition wall.
2. Gift given to major donors echoes the colors and materials of wall display.
3. Side view detail of display cases.
4. Actual showcases.

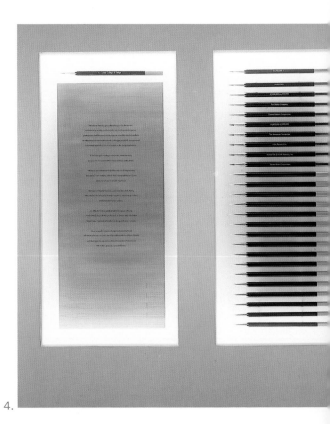
4.

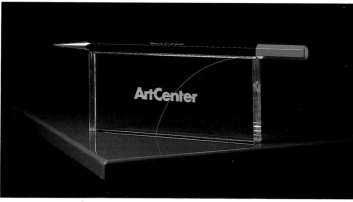

2.

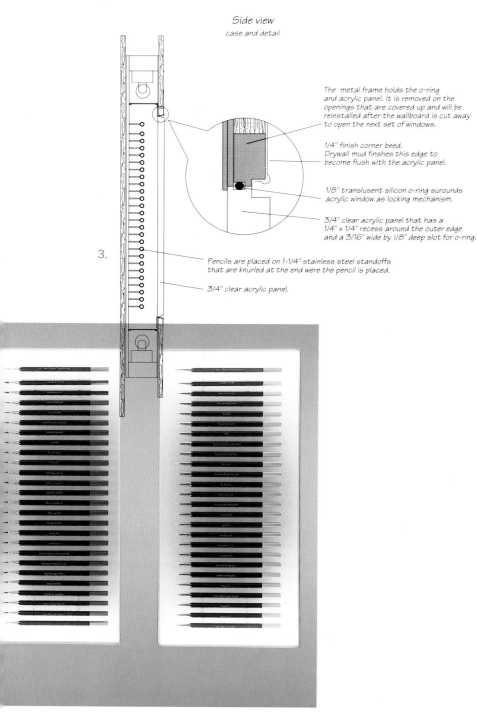

Side view
case and detail

The metal frame holds the o-ring and acrylic panel. It is removed on the openings that are covered up and will be reinstalled after the wallboard is cut away to open the next set of windows.

1/4" finish corner bead.
Drywall mud finshes this edge to become flush with the acrylic panel.

1/8" translusent silicon o-ring surounds acrylic window as locking mechanism.

3/4" clear acrylic panel that has a 1/4" x 1/4" recess around the outer edge and a 3/16" wide by 1/8" deep slot for o-ring.

Pencils are placed on 1-1/4" stainless steel standoffs that are knurled at the end were the pencil is placed.

3/4" clear acrylic panel.

3.

Project Facts

The designer worked on the Art Center College of Design (Pasadena, CA) project over a nine month period. Donor wall construction, without cases, was part of a new school addition. The system was a turnkey program for the school, with the designer managing all aspects of the fabrication, assembly and installation.

Technical Information

The wall consists of four metal cases with 20 vertical display units, internal lighting, evenly spaced standoffs to hold pencils, and a plaque with a brief history of the school with acknowledgment of key donors. The gift consists of a wood box, insert foam, acrylic pedestal with Art Center logo and silkscreened symbol, pencils, leads, holders, used lead removal rods, instructions and thank you cards. Materials include steel, aluminum, acrylic panels, wax, dry pigments, fluorescent lighting, electrical wiring, auto-motive paints, metal plating, etching, wood, foam and silicon. Pencils were fabricated out of woods, acrylics and metals to explore sizes, weights and appear-ances. Computer outputs were made to explore type-face legibility, and different etching processes were used to explore the appearance of donor names on pencils. A prototype case was fabricated to study the lighting, standoff length for the pencils, and acrylic window locking device. A small custom candle maker was located to blend wax to mix with dry pigments for pencil leads. The mixture was critical; if the wax was too hard it broke, and if too soft it would bend.

Design Details

The designer settled on the pencil as the pro-ject icon after briefly exploring a concept relating to the school's architecture. He selected Futura type for the pencils, plaque, and gift pedestals, and a combination of Futura and Goudy for the gift's instruction card and thank you note. Futura is used for the Art Center logo-type and some school communications; Goudy's style and character compliment the Futura. Pencil lead and end cap colors designate different levels of giving. The pencil body is anodized black so the donor name can be etched into the aluminum for readability.

Credits

Design Firm: Dennis S. Juett & Associates, Inc., Pasadena, CA
Designer: Dennis Scott Juett

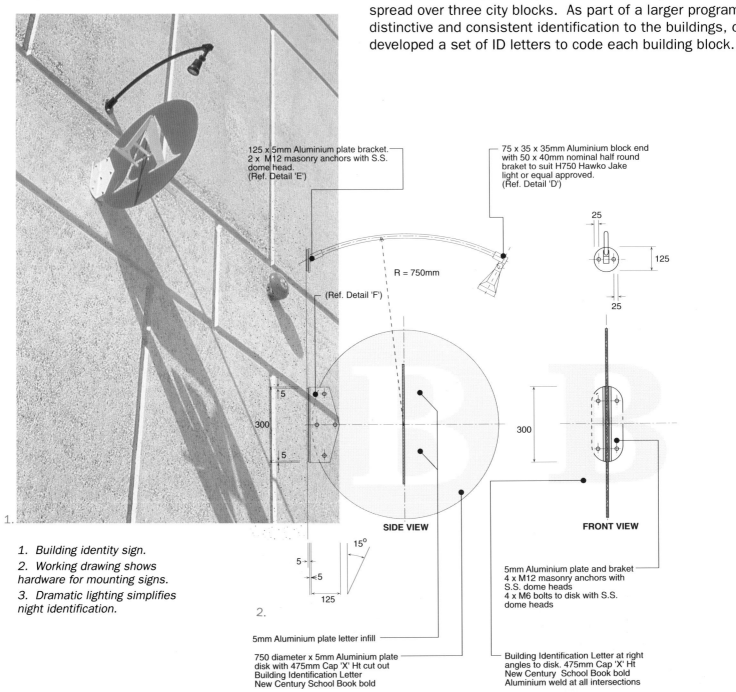

Dot Dash Pty. Ltd.
SOUTH BRISBANE TAFE PRECINCT

Distinctive identification for college
building blocks An inner city technical college in South Brisbane, Queensland consists of a series of disparate new and recycled buildings spread over three city blocks. As part of a larger program to bring distinctive and consistent identification to the buildings, designers developed a set of ID letters to code each building block.

125 x 5mm Aluminium plate bracket.
2 x M12 masonry anchors with S.S.
dome head.
(Ref. Detail 'E')

75 x 35 x 35mm Aluminium block end
with 50 x 40mm nominal half round
braket to suit H750 Hawko Jake
light or equal approved.
(Ref. Detail 'D')

R = 750mm

(Ref. Detail 'F')

25

125

25

5

300

5

SIDE VIEW

300

FRONT VIEW

15°

5

5

125

1. Building identity sign.
2. Working drawing shows hardware for mounting signs.
3. Dramatic lighting simplifies night identification.

5mm Aluminium plate and braket
4 x M12 masonry anchors with
S.S. dome heads
4 x M6 bolts to disk with S.S.
dome heads

5mm Aluminium plate letter infill

750 diameter x 5mm Aluminium plate
disk with 475mm Cap 'X' Ht cut out
Building Identification Letter
New Century School Book bold

Building Identification Letter at right
angles to disk. 475mm Cap 'X' Ht
New Century School Book bold
Aluminium weld at all intersections

1.

2.

Project Facts

Two designers spent approximately 150 hours over a six-month period developing the system for the client, Q Build Project Services. Design budget was approximately US $10,000.

Technical Information

Signs are made of welded aluminum plate. The relative smallness and scarcity of points of contact made connecting the elements more complicated than usual. The 2 ft. 6 in. diameter signs are spot lit.

Design Details

The design objective was to develop signs that would be distinctive and "curious" in the land-scape. Lighting was used to illuminate signs and to increase their impact by casting shadows on the wall.

Credits

Design Firm: Dot Dash Pty. Ltd., Brisbane, Queensland, Australia
Design Team: Mark Ross, Design Director; Max O'Brien, Designer
Architect: Spence Jamieson, Brisbane, Queensland,
Fabricator: Plastic Products & Signs, Brisbane, Queensland, Australia
Lighting: Steven Giddings, Brisbane, Queensland,

3.

Wieber Nelson Design
UCSD MEDICAL CENTER

An integrated approach to wayfinding for
a medical center's facilities

The multi-block University of California, San Diego (UCSD) medical center is a fifteen-minute drive from the main university campus, where two new medical center facilities were recently completed. Despite their disparate locations, all have an atrium as an architectural focal point in common, and designers were inspired by the qualities of light and materials that create these environments to develop an integrated approach to wayfinding. The extensive use of sandblasted and airbrushed glass is unusual for a medical project of this size.

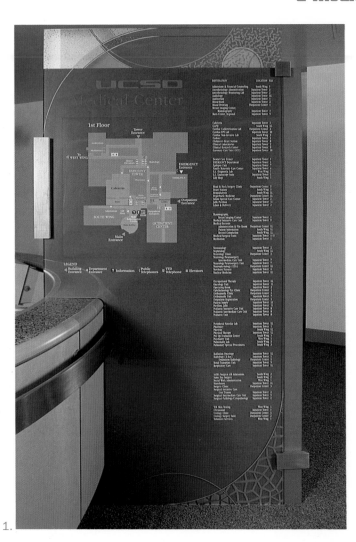

1.

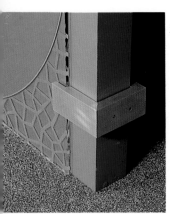

2.

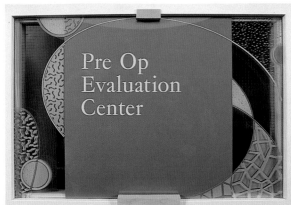

3.

4.

1. Map directory is attached to information counter.
2. Detail of aluminum set bracket.
3. Room identity plaque of sandblasted, tempered glass and acrylic.
4. Primary directional sign.
5. Destination identity detail.
6. Working diagram of typical wall-mounted signs.
7. Destination identity motif on signs refer to the building rotunda in plan view.

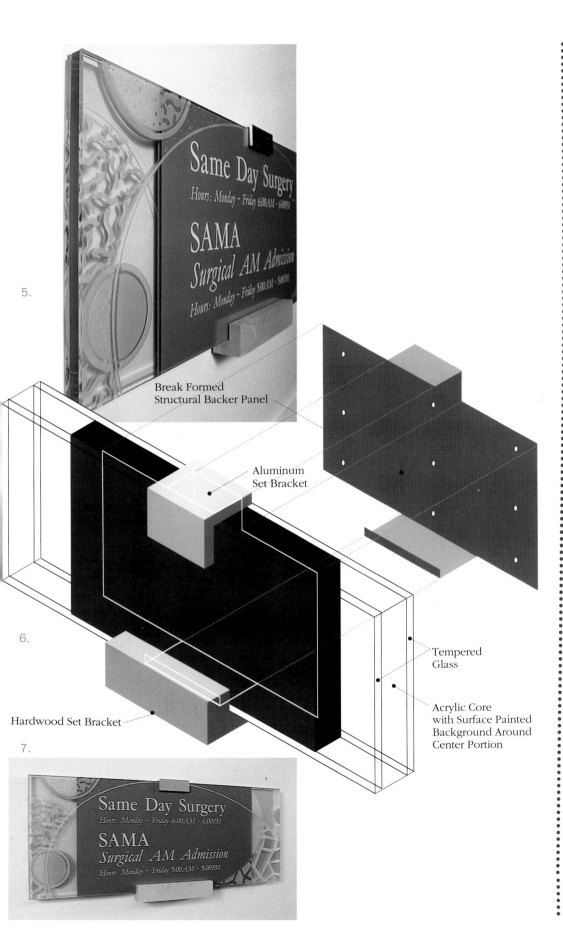

5.

6.

Break Formed
Structural Backer Panel

Aluminum
Set Bracket

7.

Hardwood Set Bracket

Tempered
Glass

Acrylic Core
with Surface Painted
Background Around
Center Portion

Project Facts

Three designers worked approximately 350 hours over a seven-month period on the University of California, San Diego assignment. Fabrication budget was $145,000. Overall building construction cost was $20 million.

Technical Information

Typical sign construction consists of a front and back layer of 1/4-inch tempered glass with a core panel of half-inch acrylic. The acrylic is first painted with the field color. Both layers of glass are sandblasted and infilled with three airbrushed colors. Glass layer designs and color applications are slightly different to create interplay. Due to the weight of the glass, determining the right structural component was critical; designers specified top aluminum and bottom white maple brackets to hold the three layers in place. Copy is second surface vinyl on the front layer of glass and is easily changeable by UCSD's in-house sign shop. Fabricators were challenged to achieve even airbrushing as colors gradated, and needed to exercise extra care in sandblasting to achieve the desired depth. Primary elements range in size from 36 x 18 inches to 36 x 48 inches.

Design Details

Designers were guided by the university medical system's new master plan of excellence for the year 2000. Type styles and field colors (cream and teal) are used consistently in each facility for continuity while the graphic pattern changes at each location. For the medical center in the San Diego neighborhood of Hillcrest, a contemporary asymmetrical geometric represents the new rotunda in plan view with the intersecting arc of the mezzanine. Pattern and color variations between the front and back layers of glass create an interplay and motion as the viewer passes by the signs. The sandblasted pattern for the Hillcrest facility was airbrushed with three colors; other facilities will be different traditional patterns with infilled accents in gold leaf. Variations in the patterning distinguish directory, directional and destination sign types.

Credits

Design Firm: Wieber Nelson Design, San Diego, CA
Design Team: Harmon O. Nelson III, Design Director; Cindy Wieber
Collaborator: Carol Kerr Graphic Design, San Diego, CA
Fabricator: Karmen, Ltd., Canoga Park, CA

1.

Mayer/Reed
COLUMBUS CONVENTION CENTER

Forsaking traditional graphic systems for
complexity and variation

Architects who won a national design competition for a new
530,000 square foot convention center in Columbus, Ohio set out
to explore new forms of codifying space using volume, form, and
juxtaposition. In creating a seamless extension of the architects'
work, designers had to create a solution void of any expression of
material or connections. They also chose to replace "a traditional
emphasis on *graphic systems*, with their rigid and repetitious
elements," with a program that is "'de-sanitized' and rich with complexity and variation." Architectural forms were so complex that the
project could not be understood from drawings, and designers flew
to New York to study an interior model of the concourse. Afterwards,
they worked via fax between Portland and New York.

2.

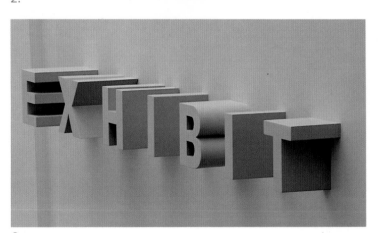

3.

1. Informational monument sign.
2. - 3. Dimensional aluminum
letter create provocative shadows.
4. Interior signs are applied to
architectural volumes.
5. - 6. Front and back of
eccentrically shaped information
kiosk, side of kiosk includes
video monitors.

4.

5.

6.

Project Facts

Four designers spent approximately 2,400 hours on the three-year project for the Franklin County Convention Facilities Authority. Overall project budget was $347,000, of which design was $82,000 and implementation was $273,000. Scope of work included project identity, interior and exterior wayfinding, interior kiosks with maps and video monitor information displays, and an identification system for building areas and rooms.

Technical Information

Materials specified include painted aluminum, acrylic, photopolymer, and medium-density fiberboard. Twelve-foot kiosks are constructed from seamless, welded aluminum with concealed hinges for 5 x 8 foot aluminum doors. The interior kiosk form was based on two interlocking cubes, each with one non-parallel side, and rotating them four to six degrees on both the x and y axes — a difficult accomplishment. Matching sign colors to architectural colors was critical and complex; a single sign type might include multiple shades in five color families. Colors were often borderline in meeting the ADA (Americans with Disabilities Act) 70 percent contrast requirement.

Design Details

All components express the relationship of building forms, volumes and colors created by the interplay and transfer of moving parts. Extruded text breaks through the skin of walls. Information kiosks are juxtaposed monolithic volumes twisted to reveal the tension of the space between. In part academic exercise, the program could not be fully realized because of budget constraints: A laser light system intended to further codify areas of the building was eliminated, and the budget did not allow for uniquely different kiosk forms at each of five intersections along the concourse.

Credits

Design Firm: Mayer/Reed, Portland, OR
Design Team: Michael Reed, Design Director; Debbie Fox Shaw, Chris Ingalls, Kathy Murray
Architect: Trott/Eisenman Architects (Eisenman Architects, Richard Trott & Partners), New York, NY
Fabricator: Andco Industries Corporation, Greensboro, NC
Photo Credit: D.G. Olshavsky/ARTOG, Columbus, OH

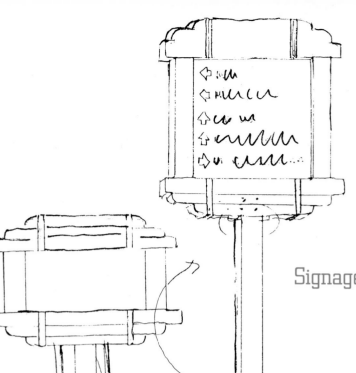

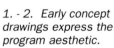

2.

Patricia Newton Design Studio
LAS ENCINAS HOSPITAL

Signage for a Craftsman-style hospital campus

The Early 1900's Craftsman-style architecture of Las Encinas Hospital in Pasadena, California is set amidst the winding, wooded paths of a 27-acre botanical garden. After surveying the area and determining how best to direct patients, visitors and employees to the various small buildings and bungalows on the hospital campus, the designer introduced a system of directional signs that complements the architecture and preserves the serene garden setting. Since building uses change often, she also developed an easy-release system for changeable messages.

5.

1. - 2. Early concept drawings express the program aesthetic.

3. - 4. Presentation rendering and actual directional sign.

5. Detail of peened aluminum strap evokes craftsman style.

6. Working drawing of hidden fastening system.

7. Directional sign features removable redwood slats.

8. Map directory and concept sketch.

9. Directional signs feature sandblasted and paint filled letters.

3.

4.

108

FASTENING SYSTEM

Wood Plug

3/16" thick Aluminum

1/2" thick Plexiglass

3"x3" Redwood post

6.

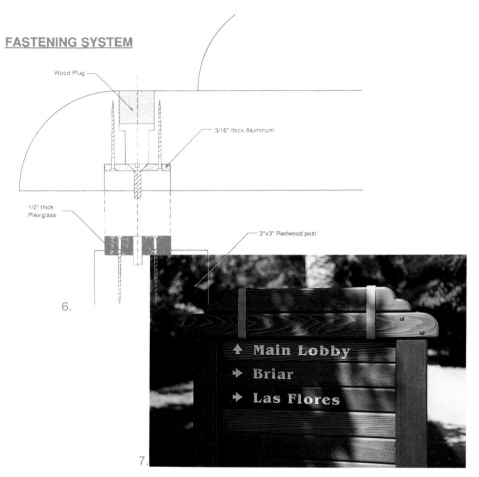

↟ Main Lobby
↦ Briar
↦ Las Flores

7.

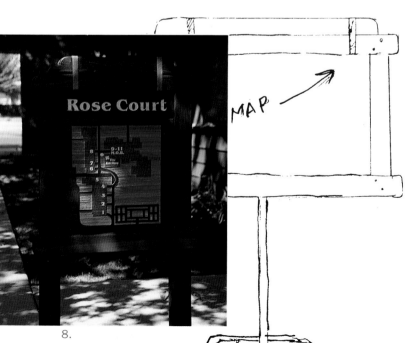

Rose Court

MAP →

8.

←Shipping
←Receiving

9.

Project Facts

Lasting ten months from bidding through installation, the project involved a single designer who worked approximately 225 hours. Overall project budget was $38,000, of which $14,000 was design and $24,000 was implementation.

Technical Information

Signs were fabricated from redwood with sandblasted and filled copy. The wood was stained and coated with oil/resin exterior finish and installed on bases of river rock and brick. A hydraulic jack was used to form the aluminum straps around a special jig before they were peened. Signs incorporate a totally hidden, easy-release fastening system for the removal of changeable slats.

Design Details

The foremost aesthetic consideration was to theme the signs to the Craftsman style architecture in its wooded, garden setting. Signs were to be easily located yet integrated into their surroundings. To avoid creating focal points and obscuring views, sign height was limited to five feet. Benguiat Bold was chosen for its period feeling, and soft, muted colors were used to blend with the tranquil setting. Each sign was designed to use, or appear to use, typical Craftsman detailing: wood edges softened with a quarter-inch roundover; mortise and tenon or stub tenon joints secured with wooden pegs; and peened metal straps.

Credits

Design Firm: Patricia Newton Design Studio, Pasadena, CA
Designer: Patricia Newton
Fabricator: T.F.N. Architectural Signage, Inc., Santa Ana, CA

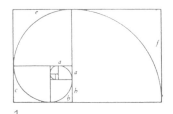

1.

The Office of Michael Manwaring
CHILDREN'S DISCOVERY MUSEUM
& OPERA SAN JOSE

When a building is an unforgettable
sign in its own right

The City of San Jose, California, is experiencing an urban renaissance. Several civic projects have been designed by acclaimed architects, among them a building by Mexican architect Ricardo Legorreta to be shared by the Children's Discovery Museum and the offices and rehearsal space for Opera San Jose. Surrounded by bright green lawn, the building's strong geometric volumes and intense violet color give it a pure, object-like quality — a sign in itself, the designer argued, that would suffer from the addition of still more signs. The San Jose Redevelopment Agency agreed: all that was needed was to identify the two organizations at the street with freestanding human-scaled signs.

2.

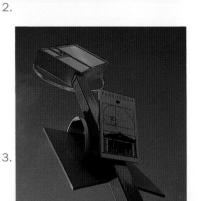

3.

4.

1. The Golden Section, a mathematical proportion system, used for centuries as the basis for "ideal" proportions and suggests the spirit of discovery.

2. Freestanding identity sign, placed at curbside, so that it does not compete with architecture.

3. Rear view of sign suggests its object like quality.

4. Sign detail.

5. Six foot treble clef is the main element of the Opera San Jose identity sign.

6. Sign detail.

7. - 8. Early presentation models.

5.

6.

7.

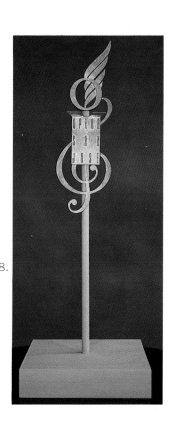

8.

Project Facts

Michael Manwaring completed the signs for the San Jose Redevelopment Agency in five months' time.

Technical Information

Both signs are fabricated of aluminum and mounted to square steel columns. Recessed lighting in the pavement illuminates the signs at night. Dimensional spirals based on the Golden Section were used to link the museum identity's front and back sign panels. Graphics on the back panel, which show the relationship of the Golden Section to the Parthenon, were acid-etched into a half-inch thick aluminum plate and filled with black enamel. The museum sign is 24 feet high.

Design Details

For the museum identity, designers wanted to express the idea or spirit of discovery. After sketching their way through symbols such as question marks and lightning bolts, they decided on a dimensional representation of the Golden Section, a mathematical proportion system invented by the ancient Greeks and used for centuries by artists and architects as the basis for "ideal" proportions.

For the opera, musical elements formed the basis of the design direction; a six-foot treble clef and shield with dimensional letters make up the large motifs, while an "O" for Opera and a musical note become smaller motifs — and a wing shape makes lighthearted reference to Wagnerian imagery. The form and thickness of the various components give the sign a dimensionality that makes it recognizable from all angles.

Credits

Design Firm: The Office of Michael Manwaring, San Francisco, CA
Design Team: Michael Manwaring, Design Director
Fabricator: Thomas Swan Signs, San Francisco, CA

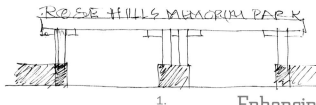

Follis Design
ROSE HILLS MEMORIAL PARK

Enhancing a memorial park's long-lasting image

For all their appeal to timelessness, memorial parks must also periodically review their image programs. For a 2,500-acre facility in Whittier, California, designers developed a sign program that brought a contemporary dimension to a long-lasting image while preserving the tranquil setting.

2.

3.

1. - 2. Thumbnail sketches and color ideas.

3. Finished monument sign incorporates restrained and dignified lettering and colors.

4. Concept studies for monument sign.

5. Presentation board of vehicular directional sign.

6. - 7. Secondary entry monuments.

8. White is used as a field for directional and informational signs.

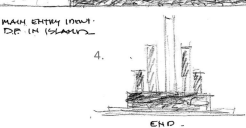

OPTION WITH OUT ROSE.

TYP. GATE NO.   MAIN ENTRY IDENT. D.E. IN ISLAND

4.

END.

5.

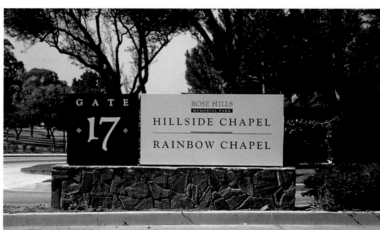

6.

7.

8.

Project Facts

The two-year assignment for Rose Hills Memorial Park involved three designers. The scope of work included complete exterior and interior signing using the existing logotype and symbol.

Technical Information

Cast concrete, aluminum and bronze were specified. The client also requested that designers incorporate the use of stone based on the existing main entrance. Installers needed to dig very carefully near grave sites.

Design Details

The designers' objective was to provide a conservative, contemporary image appropriate to the nature of the park's business. Dark blue is used as a field for entry monuments; white is used for directional and informational signs.

Credits

Design Firm: Follis Design, Pasadena, CA
Design Team: Grant Follis, Design Director; Dick Petrie, Harjanto Sumali
Fabricators: AHR/Ampersand, Los Angeles, CA; JKB Construction, Fullerton, CA

Tom Graboski Associates
ARC BROWARD

A working and learning environment
for mentally challenged individuals

ARC Broward is unlike most other education and training facilities: Its clients are retarded citizens ranging in age from young children to adults. The lively, upbeat identity program and signage system that designers created for the five-acre Sunrise, Florida development avoids an institutional look yet remains highly functional — and fits within the charitable organization's limited budget.

1.

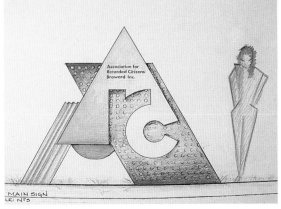

2.

3.

4.

1. Monument sign is a dimensional treatment of the school logo.

2. Concept presentation board of monument sign.

3. Lobby identification sign of metal and acrylic.

4. Exterior building identification sign.

5. Donor recognition wall features screening on marble panels.

6. Colorful wall graphics create a bright happy atmosphere for the learning impaired.

7. Complex directory features zig-zag pedestal.

8. Classroom identification.

5.

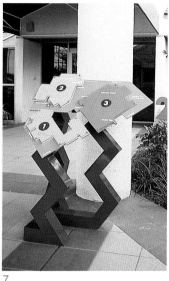

7.

6.

8.

Project Facts

Two designers worked a total of 320 hours, some of them pro bono, on the five-month project for ARC Broward. The $6,000 design budget included print design and specifications. Signage implementation budget was $22,000.

Technical Information

Signs are fabricated using a variety of materials and techniques including painted and polished welded aluminum, stainless steel, marble, glass, subsurface silkscreened acrylic and vinyl. Door plaques are 7 x 7 inches; major identity sign is five feet high.

Design Details

Designers sought to create a singular working and learning environment. They used colorful graphics and unusual, often sculptural juxtapositions of shapes and materials help to foster an imaginative atmosphere. The letters of ARC's logo become massed dimensional components of the center's main identity.

Credits

Design Firm: Tom Graboski & Associates, Inc., Coconut Grove, FL
Design Team: Tom Graboski, Design Director; Molly Murphy
Architect: Moritz Salazar Associates
Fabricator: Mark Johnson Associates, Pittsburgh, PA
Photo Credit: Patricia Fisher, Tom Graboski

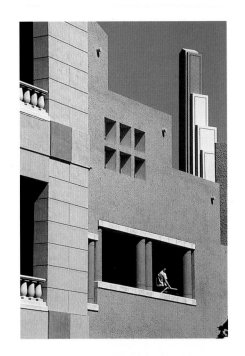

DEBORAH SUSSMAN
Color

Color is a companion to structure, and it is always affected by and, in turn, affecting light. It can express the dynamics of a building's structure. It can also perform a provocative and challenging role when interacting with structure, massing, and volume. There can be irony in the use of color in architecture. In practical terms, color often plays a role by identifying architectural components as well as by helping users find their way around. Manipulation of color in a practical manner can be studied and learned.

However, the experience of color (reactions to and selection of it) is very personal. Almost everyone seems to dislike certain colors and love others — unanimity is out of the question.

As Josef Albers taught, color is relative: Relative to what is around it, how big it is, how much of it is used (a question of scale), what material it is put on. Also, one's memory of color while moving through an environment affects the perception of color. In other words, time plays as much a role as space, light, volume, quantity, and all the other factors that influence perception of color.

To be able to manipulate color as fully as possible as a mature designer, the student should feel free and adventurous when experimenting. Applied colors are infinite in number, whereas colors of natural building materials — stone, metal, wood, brick, and so on — are limited. The juxta-position of both "manufactured" and "available" colors can yield the joy of discovery forever. It is interesting to consider the use of color throughout history and observe how radically it can differ in different hands at various times, and how valid such radically different approaches can be. Consider the "absence" of color in the work of Mies van der Rohe and in the International Style he pioneered, versus the personal, cultural, and emotive-colored statements of the Mexicans Barragan and Legorretta. In each case, color is part of what the architecture is about. In simplified terms, Mies is about clarity of structure and abstract universal form. Color is a by-product of structure and is handled similarly anywhere in the world. By contrast, the Mexican architects use color to speak about their particular culture and their personal statements as architects and as artists. In each of these cases, the palette is fairly consistent over time.

In working with many architects for several decades, I have dealt with an interesting and provocative range of attitudes. Some deal with color largely as an adjunct to structure, avoiding any reference to history, building type, or "story." Others embrace the emotive, graphic, or evocative qualities of color. Many look to cultures where color plays a major role in the urban fabric. Color can be so integral to a city that its very name is inseparable from its origin, as in "Siena."

Finally, what matters when working with color is conviction, the knowledge that one has engaged with it as fully as possible, that one has emerged from the creative struggle with a feeling of "rightness." Then one's choices have the power to move others.

Deborah Sussman is a principal of Sussman/Prejza & Company, Inc. in Culver City, California, which she founded in 1968. She is a member of the Alliance Graphique Internationale, former national board member and founder of the Los Angeles chapter of the American Institute of Graphic Arts, Fellow of the Society for Environmental Graphic Design, and Honorary Member of the American Institute of Architects, which awarded Sussman/Prejza Institute Honors, the highest recognition given to an allied profession.

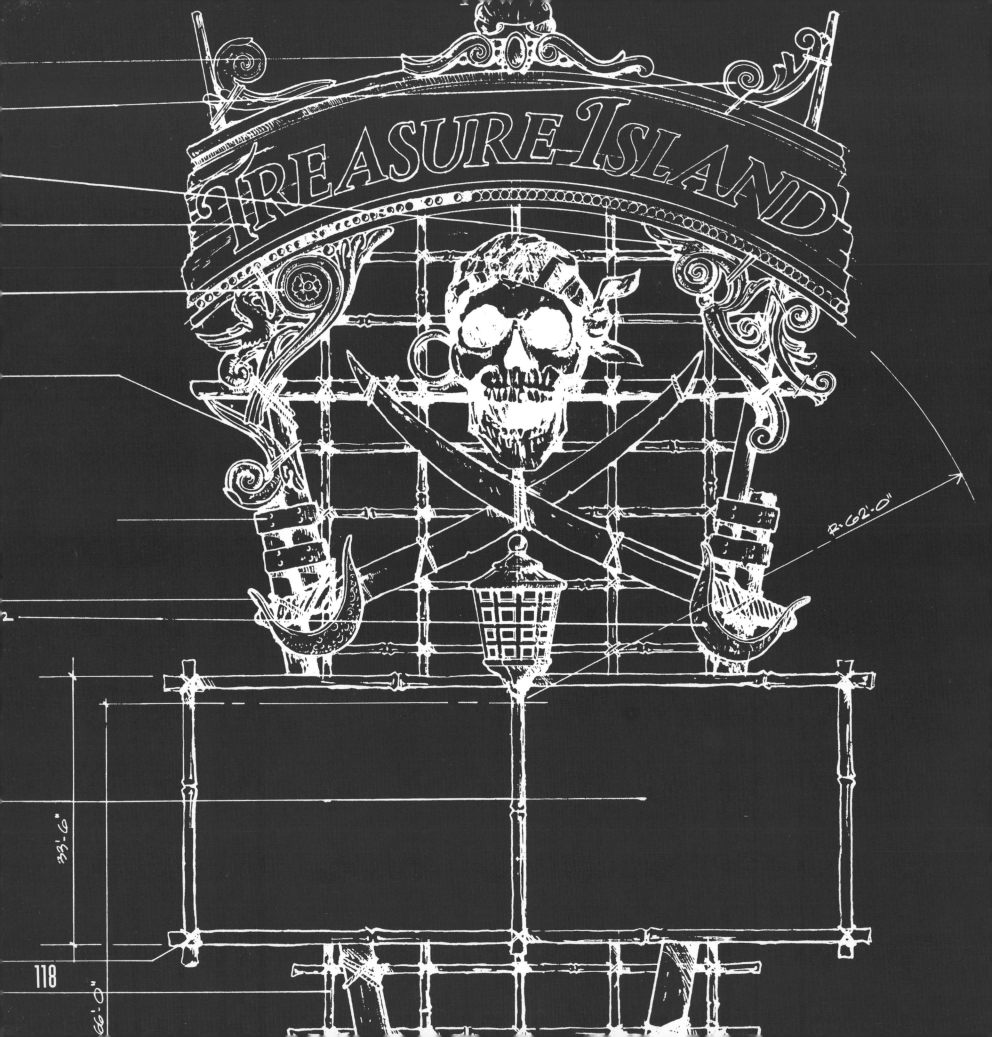

Leisure Environments

Dynamic graphics and signage have emerged as integral parts of the entertainment venue.

The Office of Michael Manwaring
SAN JOSE ARENA

A new arena makes a strong impression

For a 20,000-seat sports and entertainment facility in San Jose, CA, designers wanted, above all, for the impact of the graphics program to leave visitors with a strong, clear and positive image of the new arena long after an event was over. The building is concrete and steel — a relatively neutral environment that not only cleared the way for a strong approach, but demanded it.

1.

2.

3.

4.

1. Overview of concourse showing a variety of graphic elements.

2. Information desk introduces the signature stripe.

3. Neon outlined figures punctuate space. Oversized, striped restroom signage is visible from a distance.

4. Neon figures illustrate the activities that take place at the arena.

5. Model study for electronic sign.

6. Sculptural city seal is fabricated of fiberglass with metallic finish.

7. - 8. Model study and actual parking entrance structure.

9. Oversize arrows become elevator marquee.

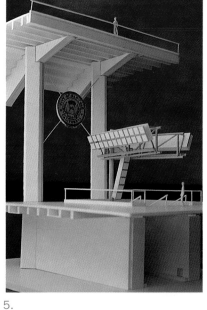

5.

7.

8.

6.

9.

Project Facts

Two designers worked on the project for the San Jose Redevelopment Agency and San Jose Sharks over a three-year period. Scope of work included exterior identificaiton signage; parking directional signage; interior directional and concession signage; consultation on exterior and interior color ; and advertising.

Technical Information

Arena entrance identity columns are fabricated from steel, stainless steel, fiberglass, gold leaf, and paint. Fiberglass, aluminum leaf and steel supports were specified for city seals. For "M" and "W" letterforms, fabricated aluminum and paint. For neon silhouettes, fiberglass, paint and neon. Arena entrance identification columns are 36 feet high. City seals are 12 feet in diameter by three feet thick. "M" and "W" letterforms are 8 feet by 3 feet thick. Neon silhouettes are five inches thick and range in height from 8 to 14 feet.

Design Details

Designers chose stripes as the unifying motif; they are formally dynamic, hence appropriate for a sports and entertainment facility; and they are easy to implement, an important consideration in a program with numerous and varied components. Univers-series type was chosen because, like the architecture, it is modern. Its plainness was also important; complexity would come from the sheer number of visual components — signs, vendor stands, advertising panels — not to mention 20,000 casually and comfortably dressed Californians.

Credits

Design Firm: The Office of Michael Manwaring, San Francisco, CA
Design Team: Michael Manwaring, Design Director; Jeff Inouye
Architect: Sink Combs Dethlefs, Denver, CO
Fabricators: Heath & Company, Los Angeles, CA; Marketshare, Milpitas, CA;
Thomas Swan Signs, San Francisco, CA; Nordquist Sign Company, Minneapolis, MN

Landmark Entertainment Group
STARQUEST

Signing strengthens the futuristic theme of an
ambitious World Expo pavilion

The Starquest pavilion at World Expo '93 in Taejon, Korea, invites
visitors from around the world to "Experience the Wonders of
Space." Conceived as an 11-story space station in the year
2093, the pavilion includes signage for show, exhibit and operational areas. Unlike most pavilions designed for the Expo,
Starquest is earmarked as a permanent attraction for a post-Expo
science theme park. Therefore, the sign program required lasting
power in both design and materials. Working extensively in metal,
designers explored a space-oriented high-tech theme. To translate
and lay out Korean language messages for the bilingual signs, the
team retained a special consultant and used special computer
software and hardware. The result is a delicate visual balance of
both languages.

1.

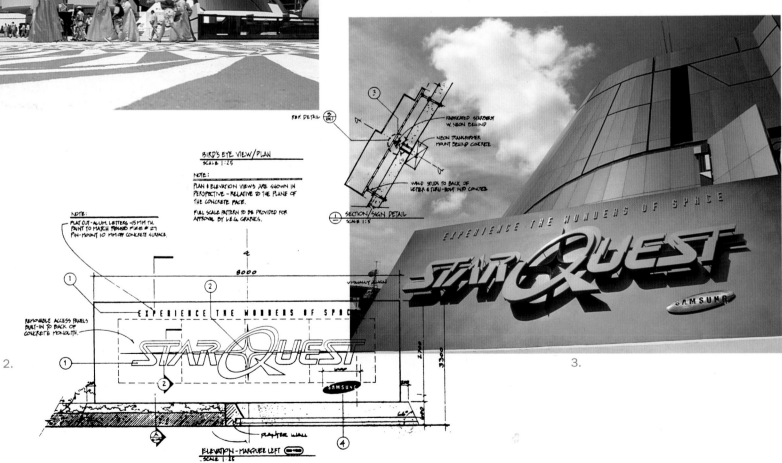

2.

3.

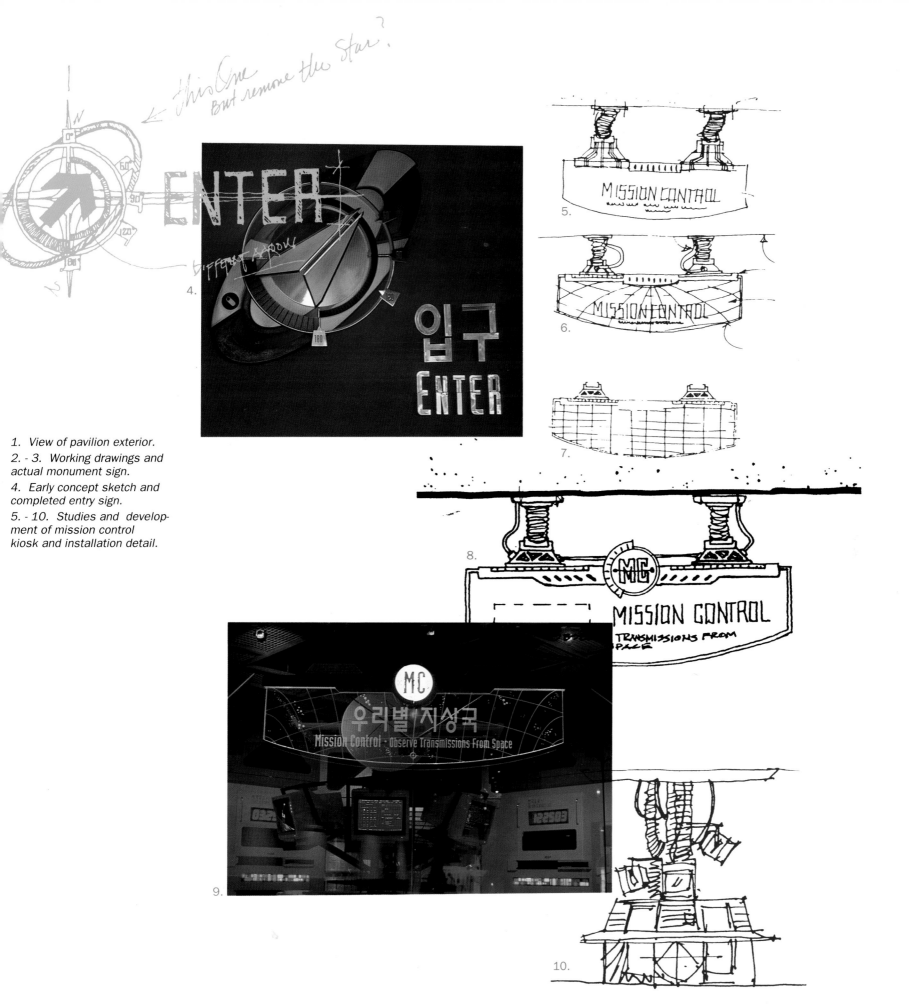

1. View of pavilion exterior.

2. - 3. Working drawings and actual monument sign.

4. Early concept sketch and completed entry sign.

5. - 10. Studies and development of mission control kiosk and installation detail.

입구
ENTER

MISSION CONTROL

MISSION CONTROL

MISSION CONTROL
TRANSMISSIONS FROM SPACE

MC
우리별·지상국
Mission Control · Observe Transmissions From Space

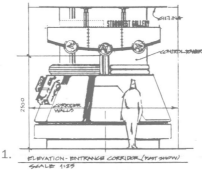

1. ELEVATION - ENTRANCE CORRIDOR (POST SHOW)
   SCALE 1:25

2.

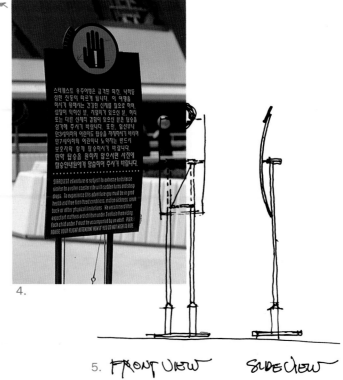

4.

5. FRONT VIEW   SIDE VIEW

1. Early study for retail kiosk.

2. Project overhead signage.

3. Working drawing and installed planet plaque.

4. - 5. Safety disclaimer sign is treated with the same attention to detail that characterizes the pavilion.

6. Custom numerical alphabet was developed to express the futuristic theme.

7. Working drawing showing proposed men's room sign.

8. Design detailing extends to operational signs.

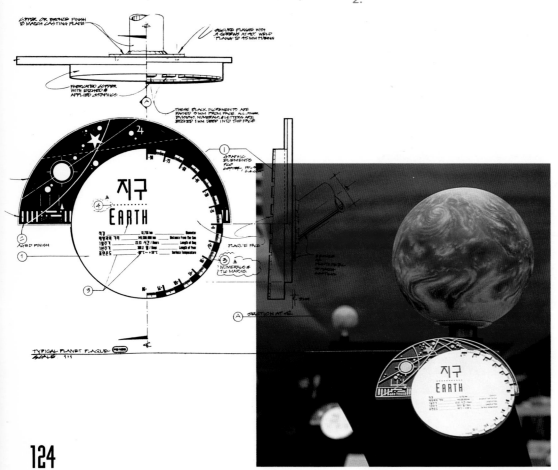

3.

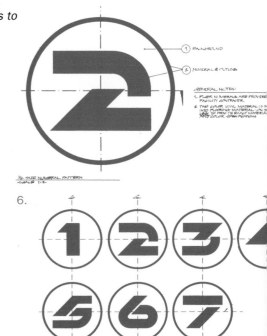

6.

124

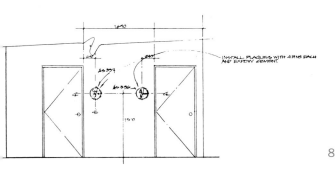

8.

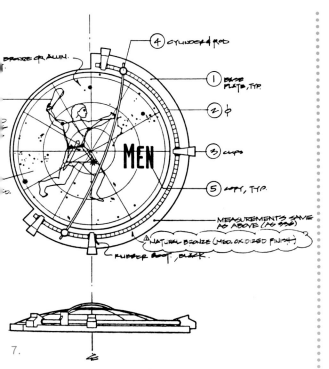

7.

Project Facts

On the seven-month assignment from Samsung Pacific (La Mirada, CA) & Cheil Communications for the Samsung Group, a four-designer team logged approximately 2,800 hours. Overall signage budget was $215,000, of which $175,000 was implementation and $40,000 was design. (Total cost for the pavilion was $40 million.) Five categories of sign types comprising 60 unique designs and a total of 190 signs were designed, manufactured and installed. Contract documentation was complete and issued for bid within 14 weeks after planning commenced.

Technical Information

Sign materials include copper, Muntz metal, brass, stainless steel, aluminum, cast bronze, sign foam, acrylic and vinyl. The design approach called for a mixture of decorative and functional components. For cost effectiveness, smaller parts were fabricated from precision milled metal and many larger surfaces were finished in metal particle paint to achieve a rich appearance.

Fabrication techniques included precision mill work, carving, casting, multiple depth etching, formed and built up metal fabrication, sandblasting and edge illumination. Three-color infilling on etched metal work as well as metal forming and bending to compound measurements posed special challenges. Fabrication was divided between sign manufacturers based in Seoul, Korea and Los Angeles, and was completed jointly in eight weeks.

Larger elements range from 2.5 to 3 meters in overall height or width; some elements are as small as 30 centimeters in diameter. Due to space constraints and availability of color choices, neon was specified for all back lighting, edge lighting and halo illumination applications.

Design Details

In keeping with the space station concept, signage and graphics needed to border on industrial design. They had to reflect a sense of aerodynamics and the "mechanics of progress." Compound curves and arcs draw an association to the charting of space. Perhaps the most significant recurrent form, however, is the circle or sphere, which represents timelessness and beauty, and characterizes the solar system. An "Industria" typeface was chosen for its mechanical appearance. Several letterforms were reconstructed on the computer to better adapt to the project's aesthetics. The lunar cycle recurs as a graphic element to separate Korean and English text. A special project arrow resembling an aerodynamic shape was created for use on all directional applications. Each sign component was treated as a sculptural object of functional, technical and aesthetic significance.

Credits

Design Firm: Landmark Entertainment Group, North Hollywood, CA
Design Team: Marc Romero, Design Director; Scot Moss, Carlos E. Lopez, Tetsuo Kadonaga
Pavilion Design: Landmark Entertainment Group, North Hollywood, CA; Chuck Cancilier, Design Director
Architect: Sam Woo Architects & Engineers, Seoul, Korea
Fabricators: Sign Colors Inc., Los Angeles, CA; Signpac, Costa mesa, CA; Master Metal Works, El Monte, CA; Gasser/Olds Company, Inc., Vernon, CA; Korean Sign Manufacturing, Seoul, Korea
Special Consultants: Jun Lee, Los Angeles, CA (translator and CIS specialist)
Don Harmon, Manhattan Beach, CA (fabrication designer)
Marc Carsten, Pacoima, CA (fabrication designer)
Global Tech Alliances, Reseda, CA (Hungal software)
Photo Credit: Gary Krueger, Los Angeles, CA

Beck+Graboski Design Office
MIRAMAR SHERATON HOTEL

A new look for a landmark hotel

The stately 400-room Miramar Sheraton Hotel is one of the oldest hotels in Southern California. As part of a multimillion dollar renovation to upgrade it to five-star status, the hotel has received a new interior and exterior signing and environmental graphics program, as well as a new identity and logo. The symbol was designed using elements of the original "Miramar" identity from the 1890's, when Senator J.P. Jones, Santa Monica's founder, owned the land where the hotel now stands. As a focal point for arriving guests, designers created a 15-foot diameter granite compass with bronze details set flush in the driveway. A series of 24 custom designed and fabricated light bollards of polished bronze and copper blends into the landscaping and light the path to the hotel entrance.

1. - 4. Existing gate, with applied name and address plaque and working drawing.

5. Huge terrazzo compass greets guests at main automobile entry.

6. Working drawing and completed exterior directional sign.

7. Daily event directory is finely detailed.

8. Uplit glass lobby counter sign exeplifies the richness of the project.

9. Directional sign with interior illumination.

10. Typical directional sign.

5.

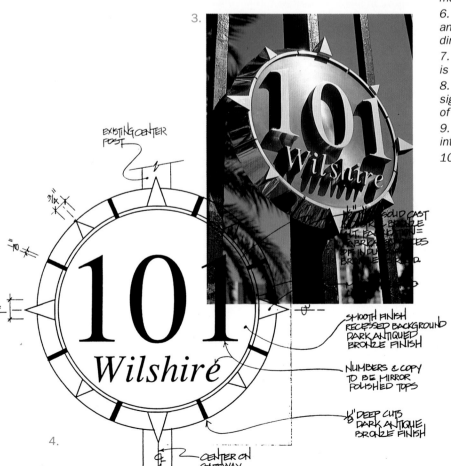

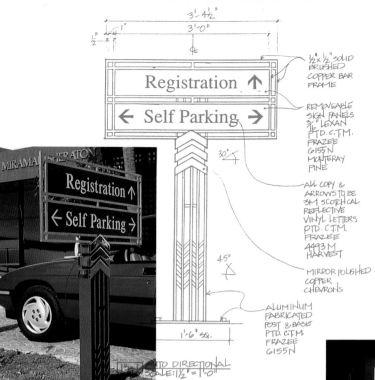

3'-4½"

3'-0"

Registration ↑

← Self Parking →

½" x ½" SOLID
BRUSHED
COPPER BAR
FRAME

REMOVEABLE
SIGN PANELS
¾" LEXAN
PTD. C.T.M.
FRAZEE
6155N
MONTERAY
PINE

ALL COPY &
ARROWS TO BE
3M SCOTCHCAL
REFLECTIVE
VINYL LETTERS
PTD. C.T.M.
FRAZEE
4493 M
HARVEST

MIRROR POLISHED
COPPER
CHEVRONS

ALUMINUM
FABRICATED
POST & BASE
PTD. C.T.M.
FRAZEE
6155N

30°

45°

1'-6" SQ.

AUTO DIRECTIONAL
SCALE: 1½" = 1'-0"

6.

7.

8.

← 157~162
↑ 163~174
↗ 175~194

9.

10.

Project Facts

A two-designer team logged "hundreds" of hours on the continuing three-year assignment for the Futica Corporation U.S.A. Implementation budget is $200,000+. The new program includes signing for the completely renovated lobby and public areas, electronic directory and meeting room signs as well as pedestrian, auto directional and project identification signs. Also included are life safety and code signing with ADA compliant room numbers. At the project's outset, four construction barricades were designed to shield guests from the work in progress.

Technical Information

Specified materials included copper, bronze, Japanese glass, milk glass crystal, granite and computer directories. Granite and bronze were used for a custom compass sent into the driveway; all parts needed to fit together with a high degree of accuracy. Installers exercised care to work within an operating hotel without disturbing guests. Signs vary in size, the smallest being 6-by-6 inch room numbers. Directional signs are illuminated by low-voltage incandescent lighting. Computer directories have LED screens.

Design Details

Quality rather than budget was the key factor in meeting a mandate to create an elegant environment. A Frank Lloyd Wright-inspired chevron motif appears on light fixtures, sign bases and other signing elements throughout the project. Copper and bronze were left with their natural finishes, to develop rich patinas as they age and to eliminate the constant maintenance that bright polished metals require.

Credits

Design Firm: Beck+Graboski Design Office, Santa Monica, CA
Design Team: Terry P. Graboski, Design Director; Constance Beck, Creative Director
Architect: Solberg & Lowe Architects, Santa Monica, CA
Fabricators: Ampersand, Los Angeles, CA; Windsor Displays, Los Angeles, CA; Cornelius Architectural Products, Pittsburgh, PA; Wallach Glass Studio, Sebastopol, CA; Morrow Technologies, Largo, FL; Hatch Masonry, Los Angeles, CA
Lighting Consultant: LSI, Cincinnati, OH
Photo Credit: Jim Simmons, Annette del Zoppo, Michael Garlander, Terry P. Graboski

Olio
TREASURE ISLAND AT THE MIRAGE

Designing a pirate village

Treasure Island is the centerpiece of the Mirage resort hotel and casino in Las Vegas. In designing and art directing its 1,000-foot pirate village set with a lagoon, pair of full-sized 18th Century sailing ships, and the world's largest Jolly Roger pirate sign, Olio was challenged to create a detailed themed environment that was "believable and not cartoonish." Resort elements such as guard rails, signage, a patio bar and second floor restaurant had to be incorporated into the scheme without destroying the illusion created by the set. Time was the designers' biggest constraint; budget and other considerations were secondary in comparison.

1.

3.

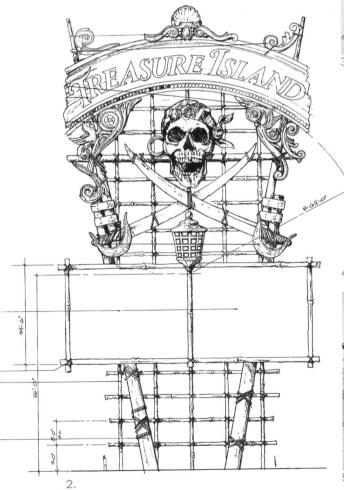

1. Overview of pirate village, with hotel/casino in background.

2. Working drawing for streetside marquee. Note heroic 150 foot height.

3. - 5. Concept studies for the pirate village.

6. Presentation model of the pirate village.

7. Night view of marquee. One of the owner requirements prevented the use of neon - making it different from neighboring signs.

2.

4.

5.

6.

7.

Project Facts

Olio's team of six designers worked with several architectural designers from the Jerde Partnership, for whom they provided conceptual design and consultation for the pirate village; they provided art direction for Atlandia Design (a division of Mirage Resorts International). In addition to designing special artwork such as paintings, themed signage, sculptures for the casino interior and exterior, Olio designed the two ships and all the sculpture on them, as well as actors' costumes. Designers were also asked to create a smiling Jolly Roger sign that would stand out on the Las Vegas strip; the project required the team's full-time involvement over a two-year period.

Technical Information

Almost all scenic elements were specially created by set fabricators. Many items were sculpted out of foam or clay and cast in fiberglass and painted. Architectural scenic elements such as balconies, windows and shacks were fabricated in Burbank and shipped to Las Vegas. Special mechanical show elements such as the ships had to be engineered to withstand repeated shows and were built in Las Vegas.

Design Details

Design parameters were established by owner Steven Wynn, who was personally involved in all design decisions. His desire to build the most authentic themed environment since Disneyland and his business knowledge guided all aspects of the project. For designers, illustrating what pirate architecture might look like proved the most difficult problem. They took the position that pirates would not actually build a village, but would take over an existing one. A plausible "history" for the village was created as a guide for the design. The buildings were inspired by indigenous seaport architecture from around the world.

Credits

Design Firm: Olio, Venice, CA
Design Team: Charles White III, Design Director; Bob Bangham, Alison Yerxa, Rowena Macaraeg, Robert Jew, Ray Goudy
Architect: The Jerde Partnership, Venice, CA
Fabricators: Showtech USA, Las Vegas, NV (ships and interior sculptures); Lexington Scenery & Props, Burbank, CA (scenic set pieces); Two Cat Studios Moonlight Molds, Los Angeles, CA(interior sculptures)
Artists: Jay Fisher, Los Angeles, CA (scenic painting of pirate village) Martin Smeaton, Los Angeles, CA (ship sculptures) Kent Jones, Los Angeles, CA Jose Fernandez (sculptures) Cam DeLeon(main sign skull)

1.

2.

3.

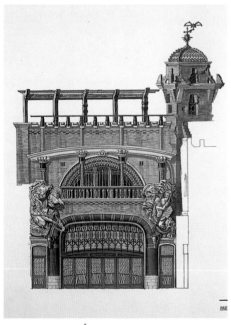

4.

5.

6.

7.

1. - 3. Rendering and actual ships. These ships actually sink, after a pyrotechnic battle, 6 times daily.

4. - 5. Concept rendering and detail of hotel/casino entry.

6. View of pirate village from pedestrian bridge.

7. Hotel registration lobby - note the skull chandelier detail.

Pentagram
HOUSTON ZOO SIGNAGE

Creating a consistent look for expanded
zoo facilities When the Houston Zoological Gardens added new facilities, designers turned to existing print materials for direction in developing new and redesigned existing signage. A limited budget demanded creative use of inexpensive materials.

1.

2.

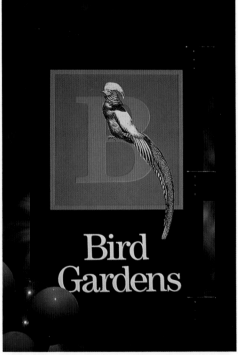

3.

1. Rhinoceros exhibit sign in context.
2. Early concept sketches.
3. Final design solution combines letters of the alphabet and animal illustrations.
4. Signs are cantilevered from posts with simple welded brackets.
5. - 6. Colorful design approach creates appropriate contrast with the natural environment

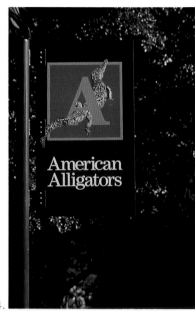

4.

Project Facts

Three designers worked approximately 200 hours over a three-month period on the project for the Zoological Society of Houston. A percentage of the design fees was donated.

Technical Information

Signs were fabricated from basic sheet metal and steel plumbing pipes, which served as supports. Messages were silkscreened. Typical signs measure 3 x 5 feet.

Design Details

In keeping with the style and colors established for print materials, signage was friendly and casual, with animals as the central focus.

Credits

Design Firm: Pentagram Design, San Francisco, CA
Design Team: Lowell Williams, Design Director; Bill Carson, Lana Rigsby, Designers
Fabricators: Cantrell, Stafford, TX

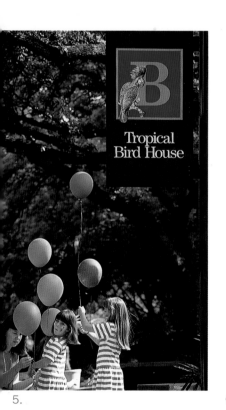

5.

6.

Clifford Selbert Design
AVALON

A nightclub's icon serves as a landmark in an urban setting After creating a new identity for Avalon, a nightclub in Boston, designers expressed the club's logo as a towering three-dimensional sculpture visible from the nearby Mass Pike.

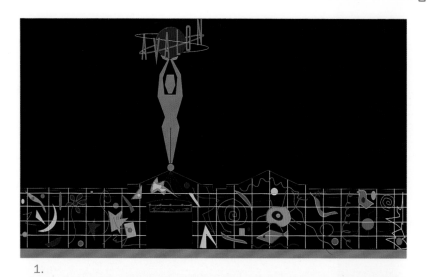

1.

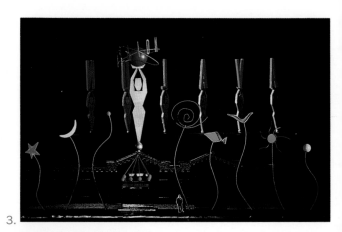

3.

2.

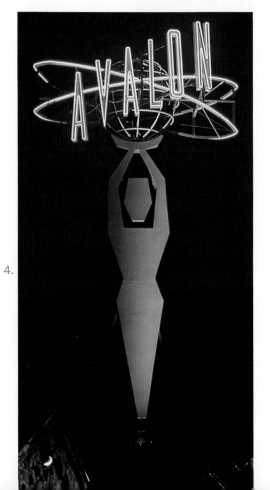

4.

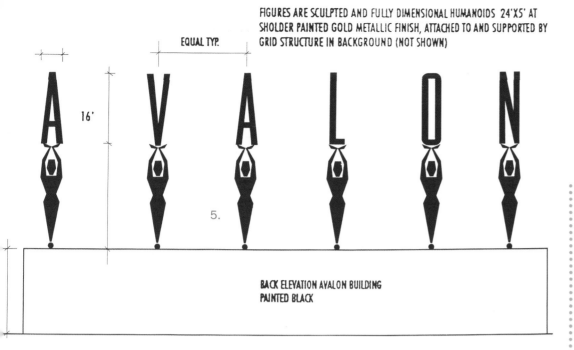

EQUAL TYP.

16'

5.

BACK ELEVATION AVALON BUILDING
PAINTED BLACK

1. - 2. Computer generated design
studies show alternate approaches.
3. Model of near-final design.
4. Detail of 28 foot humanoid
figure supporting sculptural
neon identification.
5. Proposed alternate signage for
view from Massachusetts Turnpike.
6. Identification sign towers
over streetscape.

6.

Project Facts

One designer completed the project for
Lyons Management Group (Boston, MA), working
approximately 100 hours over a six-month period.

Technical Information

Materials include a new welded steel support
and structure, wood frame, fiberglass overcoat on the
figure, and neon lights. The 1,200-pound sculpture is
six feet deep, 28 feet high, and 13 feet wide.

Design Details

Inspired by the club's name, that of the other-
worldly realm of Arthurian legend, designers created a
logo based on an androgynous figure suggesting
allure and mystery. Additionally, larger than life flowers
with stalks of metal tubing were developed to curve
up the building's facade and give the suggestion of an
undulating undersea bower. These would have been
installed in the sidewalk. To further identify the building to motorists on the turnpike, an identity was also
planned for the rear facade: a series of 10-foot cut-
out metal letterforms supported by tiny figures and
spelling out "Avalon." Due to budget constraints,
these elements ultimately weren't built.

Credits

Design Firm: Clifford Selbert Design, Boston, MA
Design Team: Robin Perkins, Design Director
Fabricators: Alternative FX, Waltham, MA; Neon
Jungle, Worcester, MA

Wayne Hunt Design
LAKE ELSINORE DIAMOND

A minor league baseball stadium hits
a home run with graphics

The all-American sport of baseball is enjoying a resurgence in small-town markets, and a new multi-purpose stadium built for the California town of Lake Elsinore exemplifies the trend. Designed with 6,000 seats, the brick structure can be expanded to 8,000 and doubles as a concert venue for the growing town of 25,000. The architectural concept, layout and steel building details are based on traditional turn-of-the-century ballparks, a return to familiar forms and a nostalgic stadium vocabulary inspired in part by the success of new major league venues like Orioles Park at Camden Yards and Caminsky Park in Chicago.

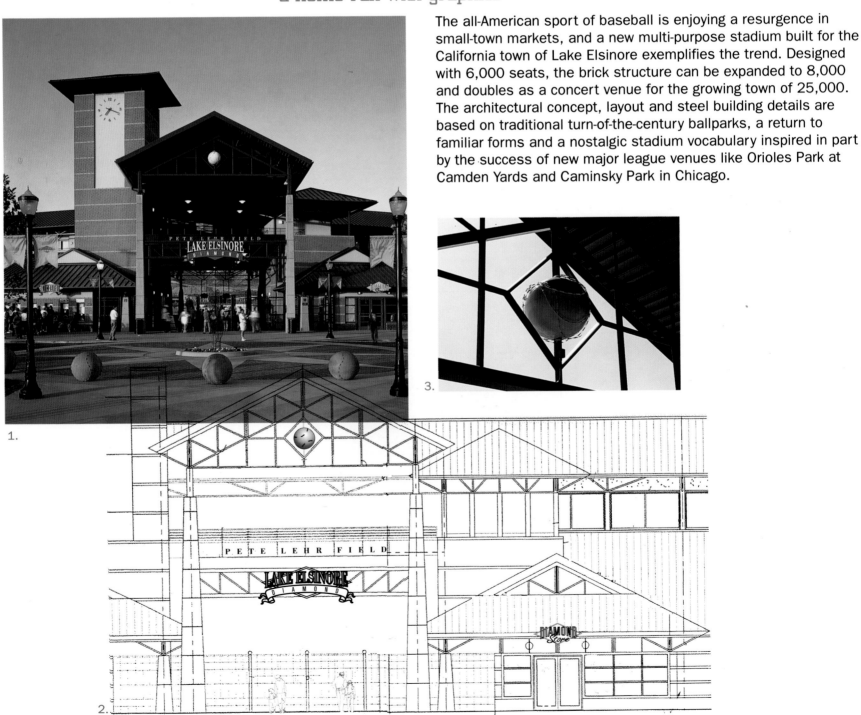

1.

3.

2.

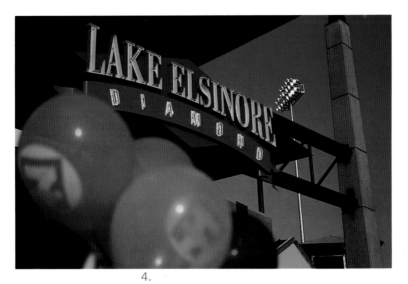

4.

5.

6.

1. - 2. Working drawing and
elevation of stadium entrance

3. Three foot baseball is 3
step animated neon that creates
illusion of pitched curve ball.

4. - 5. Marquee sign features
traditional open channel letters
with exposed neon.

6. Thematic diamond shape provides continuity for stadium signs.

7. Non-structural glass wall would
not support a traditional sign.
The solution was to use light-weight
sign foam. This 8 foot sign weighs
25 pounds.

7.

SECTION
122

SECTION
109

SECTION
107

BOX
11

3rd
B A S E
G A T E

1. Exterior view from parking.

2. - 3. Suspended section number signs add color and rhythm to colonnade.

4. Six inch plaques identify private boxes.

5. Secondary gate identification sign.

6. - 9. Concession areas are enlivened by overscale nostalgic food images and neon detailing.

6.

7.

8.

9.

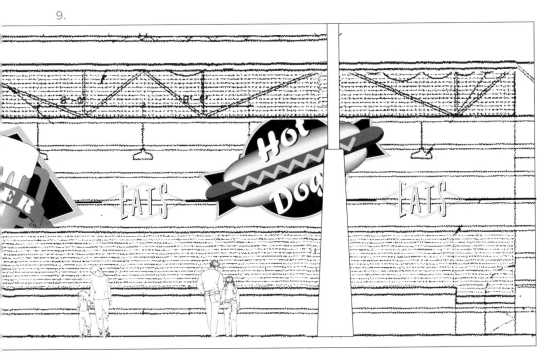

Project Facts

Three design firm staff worked on graphics for four months prior to award of the contract to the signage vendor. The building was well underway at this time, forcing a rush schedule but allowing for visits to the site to see actual sign locations, materials and context. Graphic design and implementation budget was about $150,000.

Technical Information

In keeping with the architectural concept of tradition, simple, familiar technology dominates the signage palette: large aluminum marquees with exposed neon; cut-out diamond sign shapes of aluminum and foam with a painted finish; gold leaf letters; and bronze plaques. For concession areas, large food and drink graphics were painted directly onto the brick concourse wall and "aged" back for a softer look. Additional techniques included silkscreening and photopolymer.

Design Details

The stadium name, the shape of a baseball field, and the nostalgic shell building led to the selection of a diamond shape as a major design motif. Simple "baseball" typography over diamonds and squares underlines the designs. Colorful section markers add punctuation and rhythm to the colonnade. Exposed neon completed the "aged" graphics at the concession counters. Colors were drawn from the architecture, and are dominated by dark green with light yellow and red accents.

Credits

Design Firm: Wayne Hunt Design, Pasadena, CA
Design Team: Wayne Hunt, Principal; John Temple, Senior Designer; Christina Allen, Dinnis Lee
Architect: HNTB, Kansas City, MO
Fabricator: Brilliant Signs, Orange, CA
Lighting: Howard Brandston Lighting Design, New York, NY
Photo Credit: Jim Simmons, Annette Del Zoppo, Culver City, CA; Wayne Hunt

Wesselman Design
HOTEL DORAL TELLURIDE

Non-traditional hotel signage expresses
a magical sense of place

At 9,500 feet above sea level in the Colorado Rockies, the Hotel Doral Telluride is spectacularly set amidst rugged mountains, deep valleys and starry night skies. Extremes of climate as well as a complex layout combined to make developing a sign system for the 365,000 square foot building a challenge. Exterior signs needed to withstand dramatic weather conditions and temperature shifts. Inside, signs needed to lead people easily to a variety of facilities contained under one roof — hotel suites, penthouses, spa, restaurants, daycare center and golf clubhouse as well as back-of-house areas. Besides satisfying routine city and county regulations, the designer also worked with restrictions imposed by the design review board for the mountain village.

1.

2.

3.

4.

7.

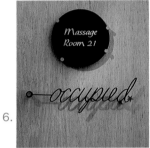

5.   6.

8.   9.   10.

1. Early concept sketches. Note unusual top view, which indicates animation.

2. Final rendering of proposed monument sign.

3. - 4. Front and back views of completed sign.

5. - 6. Massage room sign showing movable metal script "occupied" message.

7. Etched operation sign is attached to wall at three points.

8. - 9. Sketch and completed directional sign.

10. Movable message sign provides a "twist" with unusual base.

Project Facts

Wesselman spent approximately 570 hours on the project for Doral Hotels & Resorts Management Corporation (New York, NY). Project duration was one year, four months. Overall project budget was $180,000, of which $45,000 was design and $135,000 was implementation. Scope of work included development of a comprehensive interior and exterior sign program from concept to installation supervision. The program consists of over 500 signs.

Technical Information

Stainless steel, French brown patined bronze and anodized aluminum were the materials specified. Patterns were etched and die cut. Fine art techniques — the pattern applied to the stainless steel base, the patina on the bronze, and etching — were applied to a commercial project. Fabricators were challenged to achieve a consistent patina on several hundred individual signs. Also, due to the monument sign's cantilever, an internal structural support system was needed. At the same time, the sign's disk was internally illuminated and lighting needed to be carefully planned around the structure.

Design Details

The client left the designer free to develop the concept and aesthetics, which were inspired by the environment's "top of the world" feeling, the designer's interest in sculpture, and her desire to take a less commercial approach. To complement the designs and materials, Wesselman chose a Garamond typeface for the hotel's public areas and hand lettering for the less formal, more relaxed spa. The use of bronze and the French brown patina were also chosen to give a more human-made versus machine-made feel. Etched and die-cut patterns in the sign faces refer to the constellations, reminding people where they are and enhancing the signs' tactile quality. A unique "occupied" sign in the spa area swings up and rests on an anodized button when rooms are in use.

Credits

Design Firm: Wesselman Design, Inc. , Seattle, WA
Design Team: Kathy Wesselman, Design Director
Architectural Consultant: Anthony Pellecchia
Fabricators: Sign Systems Inc., Denver, CO;
Independent Signs, Denver, CO; Metal Letters, Lehi, UT
Special Consultant: J.R. Harris Engineers, Denver, CO
(monument sign)

141

1.

Richardson or Richardson
STONECREEK, THE GOLF CLUB

Signing a golf course with stones

After developing the image and theme for a renovated 200-acre golf development in Phoenix, Arizona, designers turned next to its golf course signs. For tee signs that would be truly unique yet within the established budget, they re-created large boulders. The hand-built artificial rocks mimic the stone components of the trademark.

2.

3.

1. Golf course logo applied to golf ball.

2. Selection of sketches, color chips and research photographs.

3. Unusual fairway diagrams are cast into mock boulder.

4. Silica based concrete boulders under construction.

5. Typical details of fairway maps.

6. Distance marker is made of the same concrete material.

4.

142

5.

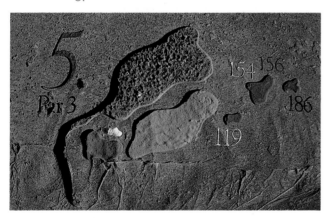

6.

Project Facts

The one-year project for Westcor Partners (Phoenix, AZ) involved four designers who spent approximately 200 hours on design and consulting, and 150 hours on coordination and fabrication. Overall project budget was $75,000, of which $35,000 was design. Stones for tee signs cost $1,500 apiece.

Technical Information

Using a real boulder from a nearby creekbed as a model, fabricators built 18 boulders from fine grade, silica-based concrete, each with a somewhat flattened area for sandblasting maps and graphics. Graphics were hand-cut in thick rubber masking, which was difficult to adhere to the stones' rough concrete surface. Stones are approximately six feet long and weigh 900 pounds. Installing the rocks proved difficult; the course was already planted and access was limited to the seven-foot wide cart paths.

Design Details

The course was designed with an arroyo meandering through it; thus the name and concept for "Stonecreek" emerged. Designers wanted to create signs that didn't look like signs; they would be part of the golfscape and unlike anything golfers had ever seen before. Goudy, originally chosen for the trademark, was extended to the signs, for which it was copied over and over to give it a rough appearance. Each tee stone is slightly different; the variations enhance the suggestion of naturalness. Yardage plaques flush with fairways are also artificial stone.

Credits

Design Firm: Richardson or Richardson, Phoenix, AZ
Design Team: Forrest Richardson, Design Director; Valerie Richardson (naming), Rosemary Connell (trademark), Jim Bolek (fabrication)
Architect: Arthur Hills and Associates, Toledo, OH
Fabricator: Original Rock of Arizona, Scottsdale, AZ
Project Manager: Resort Management of America,
Photo Credit: Alexander Stocker, Phoenix, AZ

Knott's Berry Farm
Design & Architecture
INDIAN TRAILS IDENTITY SIGN

A Native American-themed sign that strives to avoid stereotyping

At Knott's Berry Farm in Buena Park, CA, a free-standing sign made from Northwest Coast drfitwood and draped with a hand-painted leather skin identifies a Native American themed area. The designers' solution intelligently addresses a classic problem of themed signing: how to be sensitive to the representation of a culture and not resort to stereotypes.

1.

2.

SUPPORT BRACKET "BRANCH".

SIGN PANEL

WOOD SUPPORT POLE. SEE ◯.

1. Finished sign in theme park context.

2. Side detail showing foreshortened branch bracket.

3. Front elevation working drawing showing leather connection detail.

4. - 5. Presentation sketches for individual signs.

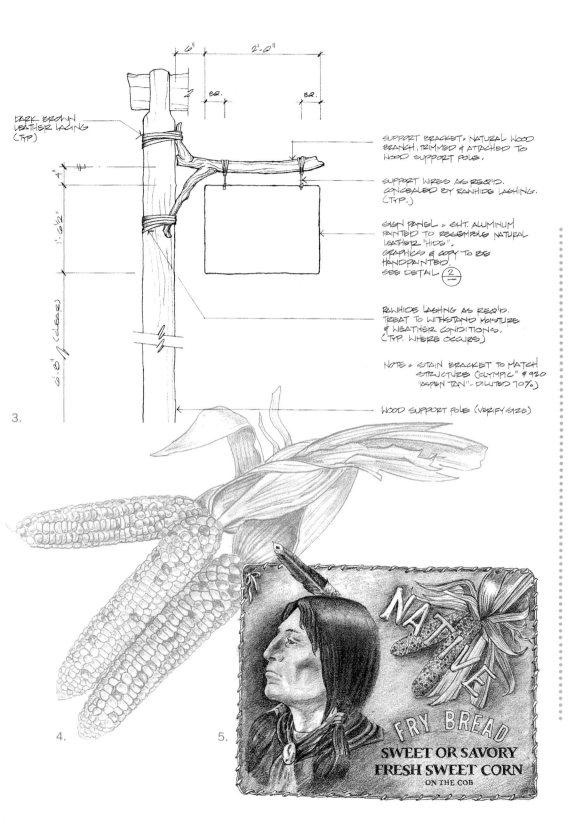

Project Facts

Two in-house designers developed signage for the themed area over a five-month period, spending about 30 hours on the identity sign itself. Overall area signing budget was $60,000.

Technical Information

The two-sided sign is made from aluminum, leather, and a driftwood branch. Leather was hand-painted and laced together. Installers were challenged to keep reinforcements and hardware supporting the branch arm concealed.

Design Details

While working without specific up-front parameters, designers sought to find natural materials and designs indigenous to Native American cultures, and to use "natural" looking typefaces — which proved difficult to find. The headline was hand-drawn.

Credits

Design Firm: Knott's Berry Farm Design & Architecture, Buena Park, CA
Design Team: Robin Hall, Design Director; Tracy Caviola, Designer
Fabricator: Knott's Graphic Arts (in-house); Bruce Humphrey, sign painter
Special Consultant: Bob Loza, Burbank, CA (fabrication design consultant)

Tom Graboski Associates
M.S. SOVEREIGN OF THE SEAS

Elegant signage for a floating resort

In developing a complete wayfinding and environmental graphics system for the world's largest cruise ship and its sister ships, the Miami-based Majesty of the Seas and Monarch of the Seas, designers must reckon with conditions that include constant use of the facility, corrosive salt air, and strong Caribbean sunlight with high levels of ultraviolet light. Understandably, signs must be made from high-quality, low-maintenance materials. The assignment has an international character: Signs are fabricated and installed in France, and designers work with a team of seven architects from five nations. How many passenger-area signs are needed for a floating resort 880 feet long and 106 feet wide that carries 2,400 passengers and 827 crew? About 10,000.

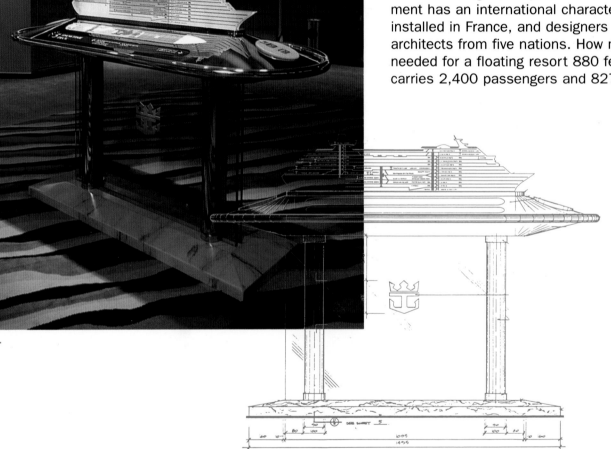

1.

1. Pedestal based ship directory features hand-rail and interior illumination.

2. Working drawing of suite sign.

3. - 4. Working drawing and actual deck level directory.

5. Working drawing and actual deck directory & information plaques

2.

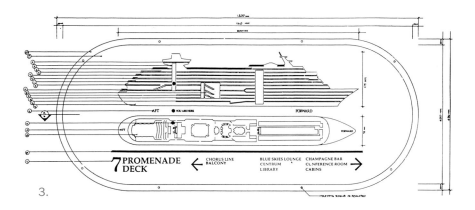

3.

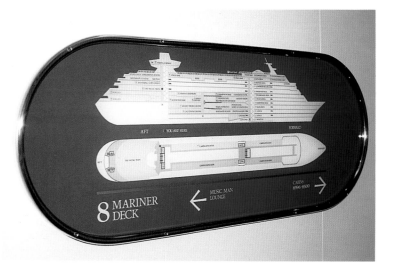

4.

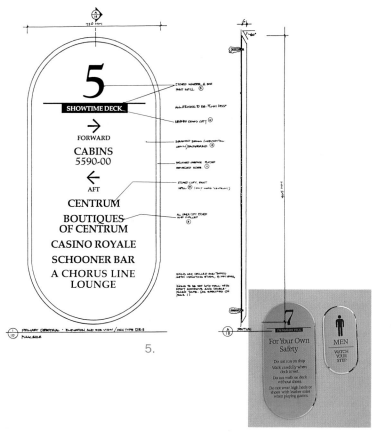

5.

Project Facts

A six-designer team logs some 2,500 hours on each Royal Caribbean Cruises Ltd. ship. Each assignment has a two-year duration. Overall construction budget for each ship is $300 million; for signage and graphics, $120,000 is spent on design and $400,000 on implementation. The system includes directional, informational and life safety signage.

Technical Information

Sign materials include sub-surface silk-screened acrylic, polished metals, brass and chrome. Brushed brass signs have chrome-plated edges. A wide range of fabrication techniques were used. Signs range in size from 10 by 30 mm to 1,500 by 3,500 mm. In addition to signage, designers also created an edge-lit ship's model (cutaway) on a glass pedestal directory. The directory is internally illuminated by fluorescents, including elevator call buttons.

Design Details

All elements were presented to and approved by a 25 to 35 member steering committee that met every eight weeks. The committee included the company's chief executive officer, president and operations managers as well as all architects and interior designers. Design objective was to provide effective wayfinding with an elegant, understated sign system. Typeface was a corporate standard. Messages needed to be legible to an older population.

Credits

Design Firm: Tom Graboski Associates, Inc., Coconut Grove, FL
Design Team: Chris Rogers and Cindy Reppert Ault, Project Managers; Lorraine Franc, Keith Oliver, Mary McCormick, Les Smerek, Remy Francis
Fabricator: Boscher Gravure, Nantes, France
Photo Credit: Tom Graboski, Chris Rogers, Tom Elliott

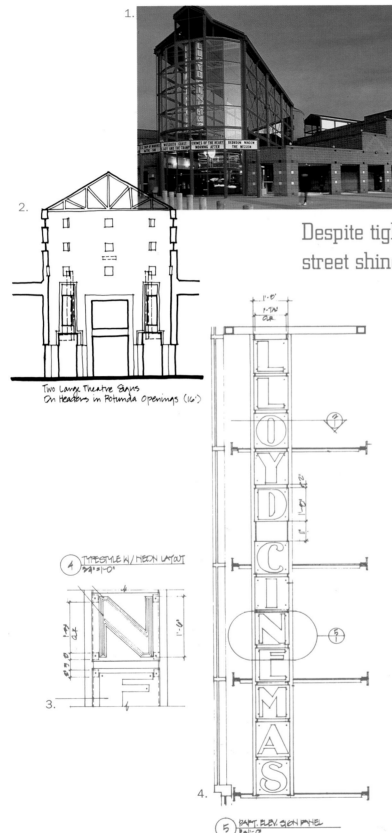

1.

2.

Two Large Theatre Signs
On Headers in Rotunda Openings (16')

3.

4. TYPESTYLE W/ NEON LAYOUT
4

5. PART. ELEV. SIGN PANEL

The Design Offices of Robert Bailey
LLOYD CINEMAS

Despite tight sign controls, a theater
street shines bright A "little Broadway" neon extravaganza provides information, graphic
color and lighting ambiance for ten combined theaters covering
two city blocks in downtown Portland, Oregon. Design intent was
to create a theater street with large-scale marquees "to lure movie
viewers away from their VCR's and back to the theater." Easier
said than done: The cinema is in a sign control zone, with one
side facing an interstate highway. To overcome these constraints,
designers placed identity signs inside the building, where size
restrictions don't apply.

5.

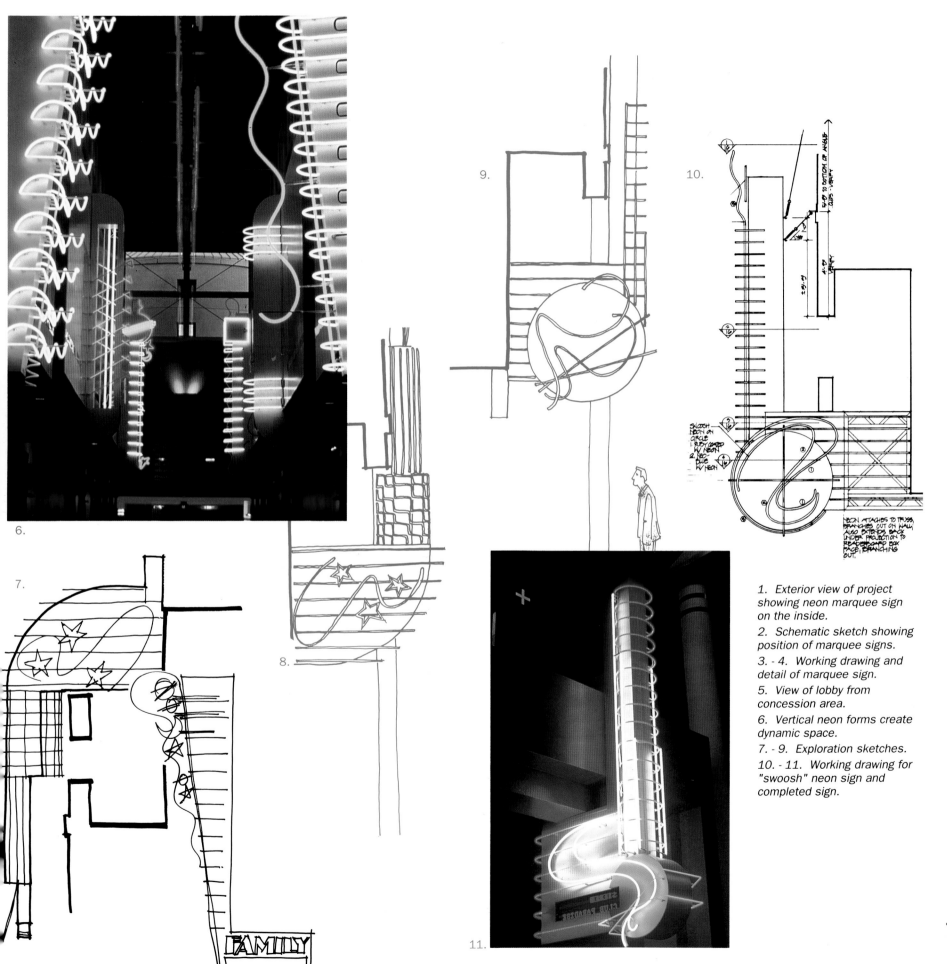

6.

7.

8.

9.

10.

11.

1. Exterior view of project showing neon marquee sign on the inside.

2. Schematic sketch showing position of marquee signs.

3. - 4. Working drawing and detail of marquee sign.

5. View of lobby from concession area.

6. Vertical neon forms create dynamic space.

7. - 9. Exploration sketches.

10. - 11. Working drawing for "swoosh" neon sign and completed sign.

1.
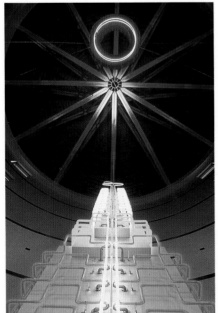

2.

1. Neon structure calls attention
to ceiling detail.

2. View from theaters looking
out shows grand scope of project.

3. View of rotunda from balcony.

4. View of lobby corridor.

5. Neon detail.

6. Working drawing of neon
marquee sign.

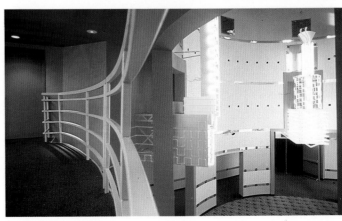

3.

4.

5.

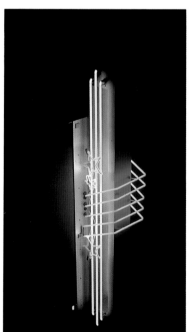

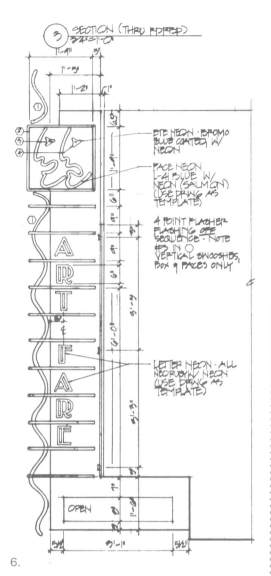

6.

Project Facts

Three designers spent approximately 500 hours over a year and a half period developing the program for Moyer Theaters (Portland, OR). Overall signage budget was $300,000, of which $27,000 was design and $273,000 was implementation. Project cost was approved as designed, even though bids came in higher than initial budget. Scope of work included design for all decorative and informational graphics outside and inside the building, construction documents, and contract administration.

Technical Information

The extravaganza is fabricated from multi-color neon in highly reflective, hand-finished aluminum cases. Joints are flush to conceal fasteners. Typical elements are 2 by 12 feet.

Design Details

Designers recognized a special opportunity to make environmental graphics a part of the theater experience. Taking the position that "signing should always combine with architecture as one," the cinemas' signs become the projects excitement, color, lighting and informational devices. All type was custom-designed. Colors were selected from commercially available neon colors. Chrome accents throughout the interior reflect the neon light and add to the active atmosphere.

Credits

Design Firm: The Design Offices of Robert Bailey, Inc., Portland, OR
Design Team: Robert Bailey, Design Director; Cynthia Nease, Carolyn Coglan
Architect: Broome, Oringdulph, O'Toole, Rudolf, Boles & Associates, Portland, OR
Fabricator: Meyer Sign, Seattle, WA

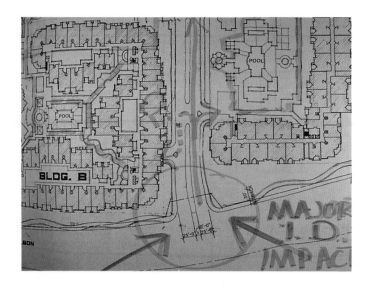

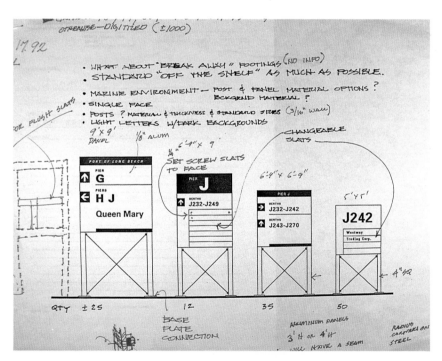

WAYNE HUNT

Basic Principles of Wayfinding

Wayfinding is about getting places and organizing the tools to get you there. The origin of the term is indefinite, but its use by environmental graphic designers has made wayfinding into a distinct and definable component of signage programs. Designers now often represent themselves as wayfinding experts, as opposed to sign or sign system specialists.

What is wayfinding?

Finding your way has never been more important. Getting places on time, with minimum stress, is more valuable than ever. Easy accessibility to services, from medical to transportation, whether on foot, by public transit, or by automobile, is not just a matter of courtesy and common sense. It is an economic necessity. At times it can be a matter of life and death.

In office complexes, a trend towards fewer staff and receptionists results in more posted messages and self-guiding systems. In addition, built environments — both public and private — are increasingly complex. Mixed-use developments, for instance, contain an array of amenities and sub-destinations, with residential units sharing floor space with retail, office and commercial uses. Airports have taken on elements of retailing, while hotels have added complex meeting facilities. In most cases, too, first-time users and frequent or regular visitors are thrown together, and in all cases many steps and decision points stand between visitors and their destinations.

From the designer's perspective, wayfinding consists of creating the tools to help visitors find their way to and through buildings and other spaces. These tools can be highly diverse (landscape and planting, seasonal, architectural, color, etc.), but more frequently they are signs and other graphics, placed in useful locations with informative messages and designs, to guide visitors to their destinations. Wayfinding is the science of organizing and defining a sequence of posted messages to make a building or space as self-navigable as possible.

Systems of wayfinding are a common part of our familiar environments and daily routines: street address systems, airport concourses and gates, freeway signs, numbered aisles at the supermarket. A typical trip from your home to an airplane seat may expose you to between 75 and 100 wayfinding elements.

CHALLENGING FACILITIES

Many environments are naturally self-guiding. Things are where you expect them. The sequence of spatial components unfolds in a logical way. The hierarchy of a building's floor plan, sight lines and visual cues makes finding your way an easy, linear process.

Unfortunately, constraints on cost, land, aesthetics, renovation and practicality — not to mention our own lack of awareness — preclude making wayfinding a priority in the building planning or architectural design process.

Tradition, experience, common sense, and most of all human

nature provide the basis for self-guiding. We know that entrances have a certain scale or look. We know that the first floor is on the ground level (in the United States, at least). We know that Aisle A precedes Aisle B, and that Room 404 is probably on the fourth floor. As visitors to buildings and other spaces, we carry these and many other assumptions and bits of information with us. But if this information is denied or substantially altered, we cannot guide ourselves. When a plan, building, department, entrance or pathway is located inconsistently with our experience or expectations, wayfinding breaks down.

LIMITATIONS OF WAYFINDING

Even the most logical layout and the best organized and sequenced signage system won't be understood or cannot be used by a percentage of the population. Some people cannot respond even to simple signs. Some can't read, or don't speak the language. Still others will be prevented from understanding by cultural, experiential and cognitive factors, or by their attitude or purpose. Some individuals are unable to understand maps. Still others simply do not choose to use signs, insisting instead on asking a human being for even the most obvious direcitonal information. The result? Some of us will always get lost. Signs alone are not enough to create foolproof self-guiding systems.

Physical barriers aren't alone in making self-guiding difficult. Confusing, inappropriate and obscure names and numbering systems are also impediments to natural wayfinding. These are the psychological barriers to self-guiding, and they are a common occurrence in complex built environments.

In the Los Angeles County Court system, for example, all dependency hearing rooms have numbers in the 400s, regardless of their location. Imagine going to court for the first time with a notice to appear in Department 404, only to discover by default that your destination is in fact on the second floor.

The importance of logical, familiar and descriptive names cannot be overestimated. Environmental graphic designers frequently influence these aspects of building projects by numbering gates in airports and piers at ports, renaming discontinuous streets, and providing meaningful names for buildings, departments, neighborhoods, and even entire projects.

DETERMINING AN APPROPRIATE SYSTEM

In principle, visitors can find any destination the owner, developer or architect wants them to find. Since, however, neither architects nor environmental graphic designers can actually make everything equally accessible, we prioritize. Each type of building or space tends to have unique destination priorities. In theme parks, for example, restrooms are always just inside the main gate and are usually well labeled. In office buildings, where priorities are different, restrooms are virtually hidden. As a result, in complex spaces designers can't always tell you how to get everywhere.

Good wayfinding balances the imperative of getting visitors to their destinations against the need to protect the overall visual integrity of the building or site. Huge signs with large, bold messages will probably get patrons to the Ferris wheel quickly, but do operators want utilitarian highway signage degrading their amusement parks? Elegant letters sandblasted into granite may point the correct way to the hospital emergency room, but in critical situations, clear, large, high-contrast, well-placed signage is all that matters — aesthetic refinements are low on the priority list.

The balance between efficiency and aesthetics changes depending on the situation, from life-or-death contexts (emergency services) to concerns for safety (highway systems) to courtesy (retail). In some cases — executive offices, for instance, - signs might not be needed at all.

Factors to consider when determining an appropriate system include:
- percentage of first-time visitors
- urgency of need for the services sought
- quantity of destination choices
- emotional and mental condition of visitors
- complexity of the route
- level of ambient distraction

ORIENTATION FIRST

Visual orientation is the first requirement of wayfinding. In other words, we have to know where we are to find our way to somewhere else. When we enter a train station or other large building, we lose the cues that keep us oriented outdoors (vistas, terrain, building shapes, light and shadow). Distinctive entrances can build these cues back into the environment, as can signs, names, colors, artworks, landscaping, and even sound. (In a large parking structure in Los Angeles, theme music from different favorite movies helps visitors to recall their parking level.)

Anyone familiar with Walt Disney Imagineering will instantly recognize the colorful term "big weenie," which refers to Oscar Mayer's 1950's hot dog-shaped trucks, as an important part of the Disney design process. Disney wanted to give his visitors large-scale icons that could command their attention from a distance and draw them through a space. In Disneyland, Cinderella's Castle is the quintessential big weenie. In retail environments, clock towers, fountains and colorful or oversized graphics serve the same purpose. In more mundane environments the concept still applies: the weenie can even take the familiar shape of the next sign down the hallway, pulling you along the path.

GETTING THE MESSAGE

Information of any kind is most easily used when broken down into small units, and never is this truer than in wayfinding. We can generally view, read, comprehend and act on only one step of a sequence at a time. If a single sign is used to tell visitors to turn left, go to the end of the hall, and then turn right, one might as well post a stack of paper directions at the entrance and let visitors peel off a page to carry with them.

Good wayfinding usually seeks the fewest signs using the fewest words. Simple, clear language and short, familiar words make the most effective signs. Verbs are often dropped, sentences truncated. Signs should be simple statements or commands.

Wayfinding particulars often change, depending on whether signs are for motorists or pedestrians. Drivers generally read signs on the move, and need information in advance of decision points. Pedestrians generally stop to read even simple signs, and need them at decision points; they want to see their destination (or the next sign) before they make a decision. In parking garages, drivers and walkers share the same space. The driver needs to know where to park and, later, where to exit. The pedestrian needs a safe and clear route to the elevator and a way to remember where the car is. Keeping these purposes clear and distinct is one of the keys to good garage graphics.

MAP DIRECTORIES

Map directories, though often necessary, are overrated as a self-guiding tool. Using them requires a particular skill of perceiving and processing information that some people don't have. In addition, maps that are fixed in place require memorizing and recall.

The following tactics can increase a map's effectiveness:
• portraying information pictorially or literally
• providing drawings in perspective
• mounting the map horizontally and orienting it to the compass
• enabling viewers to look from a map's landmarks to its real counterparts
• placing limits on remote legending (although usually necessary, it inhibits comprehension)

COLOR CODING

Color coding, more accurately called *color reinforcement*, is often one of the most misunderstood and least effective wayfinding tools. Individual colors have very little intrinsic meaning. In wayfinding systems, therefore, colors must be assigned meanings (yellow means Building A, blue means the second floor, etc.), which users must then memorize for each location they visit. For this reason, color is best used in conjunction with other visual and verbal tools (numbers, words, names, etc) to *reinforce*.

For colors to be truly useful in coding, visitors must be able to name them. Beyond basic red, yellow, blue and green (and maybe orange), verbal and visual continuity fall off. Purple, for instance, is often called violet or lavender.

HIGHWAY SIGNS: UGLY DUCKLINGS, GOOD WAYFINDING

Necessity has led to a remarkably efficient wayfinding system on our nation's highways. Traveling at 65 miles per hour, motorists need exactly the right sign message at exactly the right time in a highly visible and understandable format.

The modern highway sign is the ultimate wayfinding tool. Developed many years ago by the Federal Highway Administration and refined by individual state agencies such as Caltrans in California, this language of typefaces, colors, rules of placement, size and display is a straightforward, unambiguous signage system unfettered by subjective aesthetics.

FHWA principles might sound extreme, but may prove useful in your own wayfinding situation:
• *Prioritize messages.* In a disciplined victory over sign clutter, highway signs are used only where needed and with logically sequenced messages. The sequence is: 1) advance warning sign, 2) lane assignment for exits, 3) off-ramp directional sign.
• *Limit messages or destination to two per sign.* Any prospective third message is placed on a separate sign some distance away.
• *Use space generously.* Unused space between letters and words and around entire messages plays the same role as white space in good page layout; it provides clarity and elegance, and allows the reader to focus on the message.
• *Maximize the legibility of type.* The classic FHWA Series E letterform remains the ultimately legible letter style, even if it is overdue for research and refinement.

CONCLUSION

These points are really about the pre-design or programming issues of sign systems, which is what the term wayfinding has come to mean: the functional, planning phase of our work — where signs should be placed and what they should communicate.

However, the best wayfinding plan is only as good as the actual sign design. Materials, colors, typography, shapes and sizes as well as architectural context, lighting, viewing distance and other factors are all ingredients of successful sign design. Combining good wayfinding with good sign design is the real secret to accessible, appropriate, and successful environmental graphics.

Wayne Hunt is president of Wayne Hunt Design, Inc. in Pasadena, California. He is on the faculty of Art Center College of Design, where he teaches courses in environmental graphics and corporate systems, and is on the Board of Directors of the Architectural Foundation of Los Angeles and the Society for Environmental Graphic Design. A past President of the Art Directors Club of Los Angeles, Mr. Hunt has been a guest critic at the USC School of Architecture and a juror for the AIA Foothill Chapter Honors Program.

Civic Spaces

Colorful, informative graphics bring identity
and a sense of pride to cities and towns.

1.

Cloud and Gehshan Associates
UNIVERSITY CENTER

A new identity for a newly-named district

A 121 acre urban district in the heart of Baltimore that had always suffered from a lack of character was given a strong new identity with a system of exterior signs and environmental graphics ranging from a sidewalk paving pattern and construction fence to banners and a "life science achievement award trophy." A recurring aluminum spiral symbolizes the double helix of DNA, in reference to the district's many institutions dedicated to the life sciences. A large, complex group of constituents included the University of Maryland, University of Maryland Medical System, Veterans Administration Hospital and two residential neighborhoods.

2.

1. Presentation rendering.

2. Scale model showing family of sign types.

3. - 4. The banner program, showing an example of the decorative double helix inspired streamer.

5. Campus directional sign acts as street sculpture.

6. Automobile directional sign.

7. Address plaque. The cut out twist translates well at all sizes.

8. Typical campus building identification sign.

9. - 10. Model and actual campus construction barricade.

3.

4.

5.

6.

7.

8.

10.

Project Facts

The two year project involved three designers from Cloud and Gehshan Associates. A $200,000 design budget for the first of a two phase program included $100,000 from the University of Maryland and $100,000 from the University Medical System, a group of hospitals affiliated with the university. Doctors in district medical office buildings contributed an additional $16,000 for a banner program around their buildings.

Technical Information

Designers specified aluminum with a non-directional sanded finish and anodizing. The bending of the twist in half-inch aluminum proved difficult to achieve; the metal tended to crimp where it was held. Letters were applied to the aluminum using a special weather resistant vinyl adhesive.

Design Details

Designers were encouraged to use symbols and metaphors from the life sciences for the medically oriented "Neighborhood of Discovery." They were also asked to create a program with a "high-tech" look, which they interpreted to mean clean and contemporary. They presented three different concepts in model form; the client chose the least conservative. A Frutiger typeface, considered to have more personality than other sans serif faces such as Helvetica or Univers, supports the contemporary look. Signs also needed to be human in scale; pedestrian directionals were installed in sidewalks.

Credits

Design Firm: Cloud and Gehshan Associates, Inc., Philadelphia, PA
Design Team: Jerome Cloud, Virginia Gehshan, Ann McDonald
Fabricators: Nordquist Signs, Minneapolis, MN (signs) Haxel, Baltimore, MD; National, Philadelphia, PA (banners) Belsinger Signs, Baltimore, MD (neon) Jed Wallach Studio, Santa Rosa, CA (glass award)

Downtown
MANHATTAN BEACH

1.

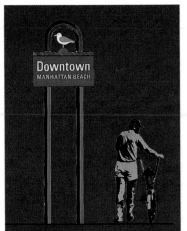

2.

Follis Design
DOWNTOWN MANHATTAN BEACH

Graphics help revitalize a beach community's
business district

Designers gave an older business district in the coastal Southern California city of Manhattan Beach more than its own identity. Using only the existing public right-of-way, they also found the means to heighten its visibility without sacrificing the community's small town feel. Because of the district's proximity to the beach, signs needed to be made of materials durable enough to withstand coastal weather and corrosive sea air.

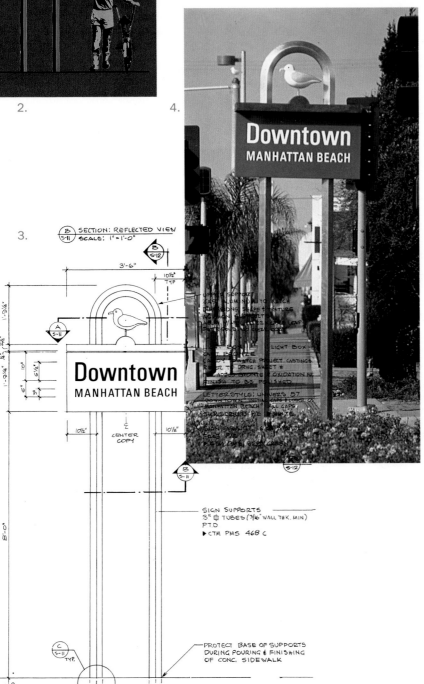

4.

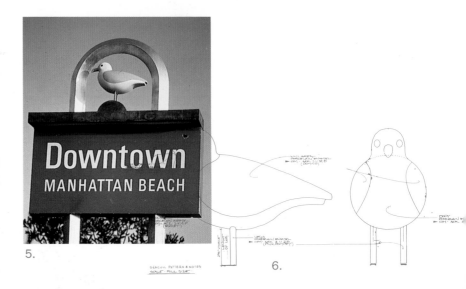

5.

6.

7.

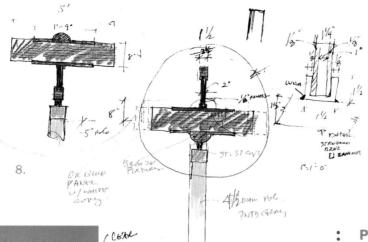

9.

10.

1. Project logo.
2. - 3. Presentation board and working drawing for gateway sign.
4. Gateway sign, though monumental, allows view of businesses through posts.
5. Gold leafed arch frames sculptured seagull, the project icon suggested by the community.
6. Diagrammatic working drawing for interpretation by sculptor.
7. Pedestrian walkway identification signs.
8. Color concept sketches for street signs.
9. - 10. District makeover extends to often ignored street and transit signs.

Project Facts

A team of three designers worked on the improvement project for the City of Manhattan Beach over a one-year period. Signage for the 12-block area was part of a larger redevelopment program; designers worked in conjunction with a landscape architect. The city chose the sign fabricator.

Technical Information

Signs were fabricated from porcelain enamel, cast bronze, stainless steel, gold leaf, hot dip galvanized steel, and cast concrete. The seagull perched on the main identity is cast aluminum with a porcelain enamel finish. The main identity is front-illuminated; other signs are non-illuminated. The simultaneous addition of new sidewalks made sign installation easier.

Design Details

Design elements reflect a beach community's attitude: The use of a seagull for a district identity was suggested at a public meeting. Distinctive pedestrian walkway signs superseded charming but low-visibility concrete posts. Colors and typestyle are clean and contemporary. A condensed typeface accommodates sometimes lengthy messages.

Credits

Design Firm: Follis Design, Pasadena, CA
Design Team: Grant Follis, Design Director; Dick Petrie, Lisa Langhoff
Landscape Design: Erikkson Peters Thomas, Pasadena, CA

1.

Anderson Krygier
JAPANESE AMERICAN HISTORICAL PLAZA

If stones could speak

In 1942, thousands of Oregon citizens of Japanese descent were forced to abandon their homes and move to confinement camps for the duration of the Second World War. A two-block waterfront park and memorial along Portland's Willamette River acknowledges the tragedy of their internment and serves as a tribute to the Bill of Rights. The designers who created the memorial's graphic elements were part of a team that included landscape designers, writers, and other artists.

2.

4.

1. Overview of project.
2. Detail of project showing "talking stones."
3. Marker for Bill of Rights.
4. Japanese haiku stone
5. Fabricator sandblasts stone.
6. "Mighty Willamette" talking stone.
7. Standing stone with sandblasting matte.
8. Standing stone with list of Japanese-American internment camps.

JAPANESE AMERICAN HISTORICAL PLAZA

BILL OF RIGHTS

3.

5.

6.

7.

8.

Project Facts

The Oregon Nikkei Endowment (Portland, OR) allocated $500,000 to the project overall. Elizabeth Anderson and John Krygier logged approximately 200 hours in developing the environmental graphics. Project duration was three years.

Technical Information

The curved wall is sandstone and Columbia River basalt; "talking stones" are granite from the North Cascade Range; pavers are also granite; plaques displaying the Bill of Rights and letters from Congress are cast bronze. The "talking stones" were hand-set under the direction of a traditional stonesetter from Japan and sandblasted on site. To enhance legibility, colors were sprayed into the letters while sandblasting mattes remained on the stones. Because designers wanted to retain the irregular, coarse and often mossy surfaces of the natural stones, sandblasting presented a unique challenge for the fabricator.

Design Details

The design philosophy embraces classic American landscape design and the traditional values of Japanese gardens. In both, understated graphics are integrated into the natural environment. "Talking stones" are a key feature of the memorial garden. Landscape architect Robert Murase selected the stones individually from the slopes of the Cascade Mountains. He viewed them with an astute eye and felt an affinity for each stone he brought back to Portland. Each stone is unique in size, shape, volume and texture — qualities that contribute to an individual temperament and "voice." Designer Elizabeth Anderson also "listened" to these qualities and, with graphics, carefully added the voices and writers to each of the stones. Preliminary layouts were made on computer; final placement was determined at the site. Classical proportions, full forms and asymmetrical serifs of Stone Informal Semibold convey the poems' feelings and withstand sandblasting on irregular surfaces. Trajan Bold is used for more formal applications.

Credits

Design Team: Elizabeth Anderson, John Krygier
Landscape Architect: Murase Associates, Portland, OR
Fabricator: Vancouver Granite, Vancouver, WA
Sculpture: Jim Gion, Portland, OR
Stonemason: Masatoshi Izumi, Japan
Poetry: Lawson Inada, Ashland, OR; Hisako Saito, Portland; Shizue Iwatsuki, Hood River, OR

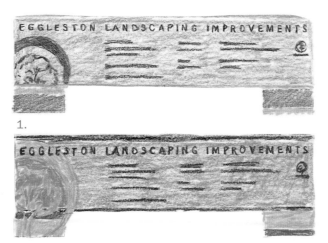

1.

2.

City of Cincinnati, Office of Architecture, Graphic Design Studio
SITE SIGNS FOR CITY PROJECTS

A city brings excitement to its projects

Cincinnati maintains an ongoing, citywide effort to provide project and site signs for its municipal projects. The graphics studio of the city's architectural office designs signs not only to announce projects and list the agencies and politicians involved, but to help create excitement for new buildings and site improvements as they are taking shape.

3.

7.

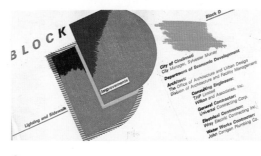

6.

4.

5.

1. - 3. Concept sketches and landscaping project billboard.

4. - 5. Computer generated layout and installation photograph shows changes from concept to actual sign.

6. - 7. Color study and finished billboard.

8. - 10. Explorations of district symbol and type and finished sign.

11. - 12. Concept sketches and finished double paneled sign.

MAIN STREET

8.

Main

S T R E E T

Main
S T R E E T

9.

10.

FIFTH
STREET
SKYWALK

BLOCK E
PHASE II -
PUBLIC IMPROVEMENTS

HAVE ONE
PERSON
MOVING
IN OTHER
DIRECTION

11.

12.

Project Facts

One art director and one designer spend a total of about eight hours on each sign for projects varying in duration from one month to one year. Signs typically cost about $1,200 apiece. Half of this cost is implementation, the other half is design. The fabrication budget is routinely included in the overall project contract, and the general contractor chooses from a list of approved fabricators.

Technical Information

Disposable signs are plywood, paint and cut vinyl letters. They are nailed to braces, hung on chain link fences, or mounted on posts. On average, they measure 4 x 8 feet. Portability is a key to their construction and installation; they may be moved frequently throughout a project's duration. Change-ability is another key; vinyl lettering can be removed easily with a heat gun and replaced if project information changes.

Design Details

Each project gets its own unique sign. Designs are suggested by memorable project features — a neighborhood logo, for instance, or the architectural details of a building. In the past, when signs were hand-painted, lettering incorporated a wide variety of typestyles and colors. Relying now on computer generated vinyls, designers keep typefaces simple and achieve a desired look with greater consistency.

Credits

Design Organization: Graphic Design Studio, Architecture Division, Cincinnati Department of Public Works Design Team: Marcia McGinnis Shortt, Design Director; Laura Martin, Lucy Frueh, Laura Curran, Mary Beth Cluxton

Sussman/Prejza & Company
DIRECTION PHILADELPHIA

Philadelphia gets a citywide vehicular
signing system

Designers worked with a large group of shareholders (including institutions, government agencies, and the city's convention and visitors bureau) to develop one of the few citywide signing systems in the country. The scope of work also included a criteria manual for phased implementation. In all, 12 districts will be signed, district by district, as funding becomes available. Direction Philadelphia works in conditions ranging from Colonial neighborhoods with narrow streets and abundant trees to urban settings dense with visual information.

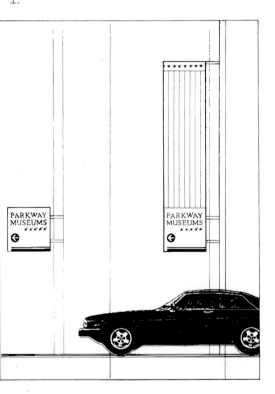

1.

4.

2.

3.

1. Presentation board showing sign family.

2. - 3. Early conceptual studies for automobile and pedestrian directional signs.

4. Signing program in urban context.

5. Area identification sign shows attention to detail. Note sculptured post, finial and distinctively shaped panel.

5.

Project Facts

Collaborating closely with the city's non-profit Foundation for Architecture, a staff of four designers spent approximately 3,000 hours on the project. Three years were required to complete the design, and an additional two years to fabricate and install proto-types. Design budget was $300,000.

Technical Information

Signs are aluminum panels on steel poles with painted faces. Reflective vinyl die-cut letters illuminate when struck by vehicle headlamps. To achieve highly accurate letterspacing, designers used a custom spacing table developed with the Signus System, a computerized vinyl lettering machine. Aluminum fasteners were specially designed to be vandal-resistant — vandals steal aluminum hardware to trade in at recycling centers. On average, signs are 12 feet high and panels measure 3 x 4 feet.

Design Details

The signage system needed to fit the city's rich history and small-scale streets while being large and bright enough to be noticed and read. The variation on a red, white and blue palette refers to Philadelphia's historic role as the cradle of the American Revolution and home of the flag, a reference reinforced by deco-rative details. Some of the type refers to early colonial layouts used by Philadelphian Ben Franklin. Color coding distinguishes *district* directionals from *destination* dirèctionals within districts. Messages are limited to no more than three per sign, the most a motorist can easily read.

Credits

Design Firm: Sussman/Prejza & Co., Inc., Culver City, CA
Design Team: Paul Prejza, Principal; Debra Valencia, Design Director; Tom Carr, Jennifer Bass, Corky Retson
Sign Fabricators: Adelphia Graphics Systems, Phil., PA
Architectural Graphics, Inc., Virginia Beach, VA
Planners: Kise Franks & Straw, Philadelphia, PA
Photo Credit: J.B. Abbott, Philadelphia, PA

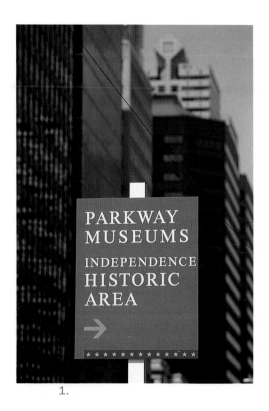

1.

2.

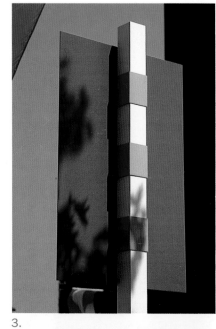

3.

4.

5.

6.

1. - 2. Area identification signs and destination ID signs show hierarchy of information.

3. Color and distinctive brackets on back of signs, clearly identify this identification system.

4. Variation of color and symbol is used to identify park signs.

5. Typical pedestrian directional sign within park scheme.

6. Icon for historic residence shows folk art influence

7. Park trailblazer.

8. Full-size prototype, of actual materials, photographed on site.

8.

7.

Environmental Image
SAN JOSE HISTORY WALK

A walking tour that won't get passed up

To develop signage and graphics for a self-guided walking tour in the city of San Jose, California, designers began by following the tour route themselves. The discoveries they made changed the direction of their original assignment; a series of bronze wall plaques no longer seemed appropriate. In many instances, they could find nowhere suitable to install a plaque. For example, a glass curtain wall building occupies the site where an adobe house once stood. They also discovered that San Jose was already covered with bronze historical plaques, most of them unnoticed. After reviewing these discoveries with their client, they decided to make the plaques freestanding, so they wouldn't depend on the suitability of wall surfaces, and highly visible, so people would see them and stop to read.

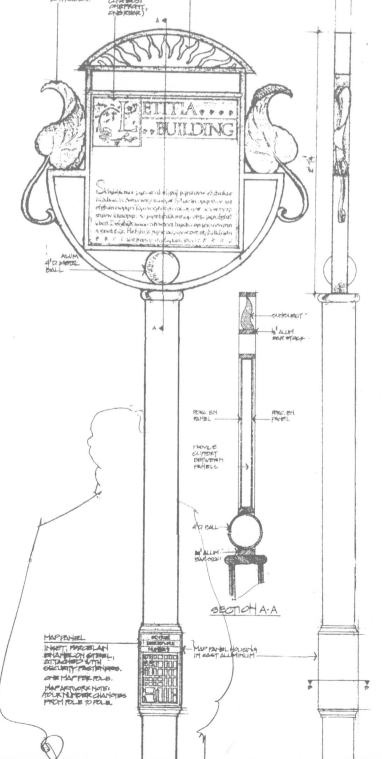

3.

2.

1. - 2. Working drawing and actual historical marker.

3. Detail showing cast aluminum leaf.

4. History walk identification sign.

5. Sign panels are porcelain enamel on steel and gold leaf.

6. Each sign post incorporates locater map of history walk.

4.

5.

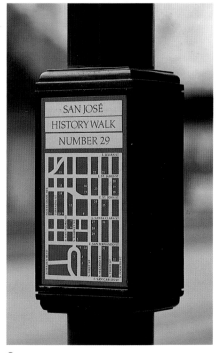

6.

Project Facts

Two designers worked on the San Jose Redevelopment Agency project for its two-year duration.

Technical Information

The pole and harp are aluminum; bases are granite; graphic panels are porcelain enamel on steel, gold leaf, and paint. To keep unit cost of the 38 markers as low as possible, ornamental elements were sand-cast aluminum. Designers experimented with clay sunbursts and leaves in their office to find a form for each that could be easily sand cast. Typical markers are 32 by 4 inches, and are 10 ft. high. A full-scale mock-up enabled designers to evaluate their solution at actual tour sites. They watched how people read and reacted to the mock-up, making sure it could be read by older people as well as children.

Design Details

To make the markers symbolically reflect the history of old San Jose and the spirit of new San Jose, designers decided to frame plaques in a meaningful, appropriate way. Their first studies focused on agricultural symbols, since agriculture was the early cornerstone of San Jose's economy. They also studied high tech iconography referring to the city's Silicon Valley fame. Concerns that such imagery might look dated after a short time led them back to their first direction. Plaques were raised above eye-level to be visible above parked cars. A rectangular panel displaying the entire walking tour is located halfway up columns.

Credits

Design Team: Michael Manwaring, Design Director; Patricia Thornton; Paul Chock
Fabricator: Thomas Swan Signs (San Francisco, CA)

Gottschalk+Ash International
PATH, TORONTO
UNDERGROUND WALKWAY

A wayfinding program organizes a city's vast underground network.

With 8.7 kilometers of enclosed walkway, Toronto's Path System is the largest pedestrian network of its kind in North America. It links transit and commuter systems with indoor concourses that include hundreds of stores, restaurants and entertainment destinations, and provides access to the city's commercial and financial services. Despite its importance, people were constantly getting lost in it or finding themselves facing blank walls in dead end tunnels: The system's maze-like rambling and lack of above-ground reference were compounded by widely varying ceiling heights, corridor widths, colors and finishes. A lack of coordinated signing only added to the confusion. In communicating wayfinding information in a creative way, the design team developed a hybrid of methods to address the Toronto system's unique conditions - considering its projected growth as well as its marketing - as a tourist destination and shopping alternative.

1.

2.

3.

4.

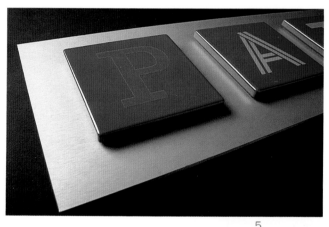
5.

1. - 2. Typical directional signs showing color coded arrows.

3. Overhead signs indicate exit to street.

4. Directional signs at intersections.

5. Detail showing porcelain enamel on steel.

6. Sign system features map which documents entire downtown walkways.

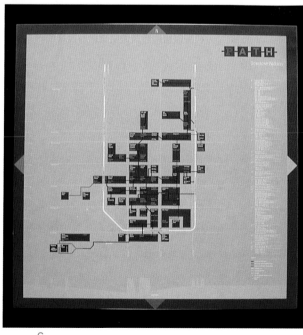
6.

Project Facts

The project began in earnest in 1988 when the City of Toronto retained a full-time coordinator and design team. The team currently numbers six designers from two firms and four project coordinators. A design concept had been developed and approved by building owners by 1989. From 1989 to 1991 the city negotiated with owners to plot an installation plan for each of 36 buildings, and the design concept was refined. Fabrication began in 1992. The first signs were installed in 1993; installation is ongoing. Total budget over seven years is approximately $2 million: $400,000 was spent on coordination; $500,000 on design, $100,00 on legal, trademarking and promotional expenses; and $1 million on implementation.

Technical Information

Signs are porcelain enamel on steel. The system applies to connected concourses only; it does not extend to other concourse levels. Focus is placed on *transition spaces*, the tunnels between buildings, as comprehensive information stations. A consistent level of directional information throughout the system includes the next closest destination and limits the amount of information provided at any one time. Specific information to find a destination within a complex is also given. The design team has also proposed compatible supplementary building signage and local area maps for individual destinations.

Design Details

The schematic design of the system map is the cornerstone of the design concept. In addition to showing the overall system's expanse as well as Path links between and through buildings, the design also functions as a directory. An analysis of the Path System helped to define locations within the system where signage must be placed. Design and location of signs reflects corporate standards and the desire of building owners not to over-sign. Each property within the system is treated with the same level of importance — all property owners are represented equally.

Credits

Design Firm: Gottschalk+Ash International, Toronto, Ontario, and Keith Muller Associates Design Consortium, Toronto, Canada
Design Team: Gottschalk+Ash International: Stuart Ash, Principal; Diane Castellan, Katalin Kovats, Keith Muller and Associates: Keith Muller, Principal; Randy Johnson, Merritt Price
Fabricator: King Products, Mississauga, Ontario

Dot Dash Pty. Ltd.
THE CLIFFS BOARDWALK

Identifying a recreational walkway with sculpture and signs

In the center of Brisbane, a historic quarry cliff face along the Brisbane River is a popular recreation destination. For a new 1.5 mile urban pedestrian path and cycleway along the river, designers developed signage and paving design. They also sourced maritime artifacts to reference the historical nature of the site as well as a series of sculptures entitled "Man & Matter" to add liveliness and serve as colorful beacons — all on a limited budget and a fast-track schedule.

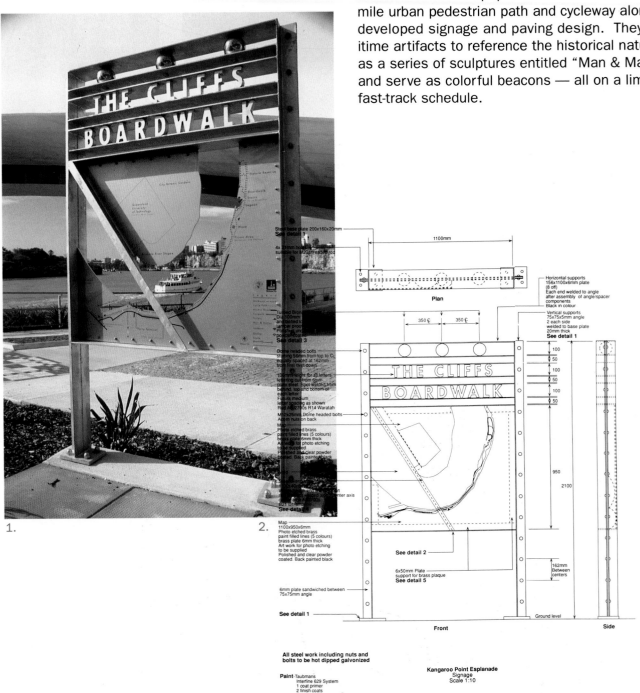

1.

2.

Kangaroo Point Esplanade
Signage
Scale 1:10

All steel work including nuts and
bolts to be hot dipped galvonized

Paint-Taubmans
Interline 629 System
1 coat primer
2 finish coats

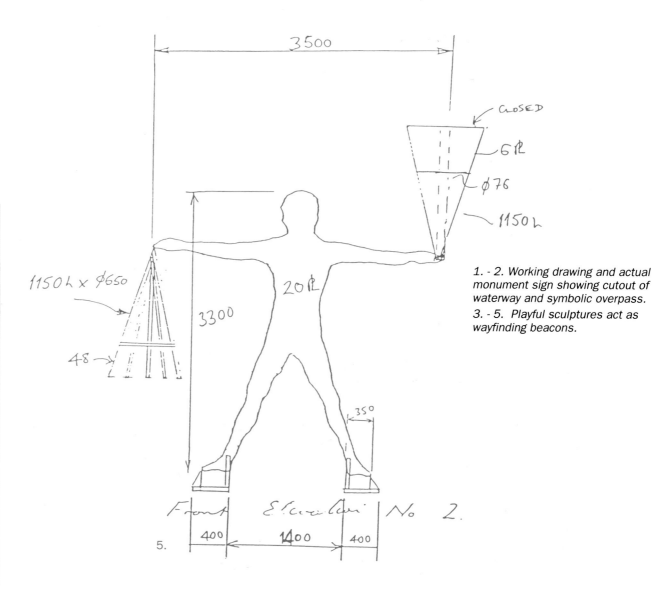

3.

5.

Front Elevation No. 2.

1. - 2. Working drawing and actual monument sign showing cutout of waterway and symbolic overpass.
3. - 5. Playful sculptures act as wayfinding beacons.

4.

4.

1.

Side elevation No 11

2.

Front Elevation No 11

1. - 3. Sculptures are galvanized steel, powder coated and reference their waterway site.

4. Flat sculpture of running figure holding helm sits atop sculptured concrete base.

5. Project scope extended to tile paving design.

6. - 7. Sculptures recall navigational instruments

8. Construction drawings.

3.

5.

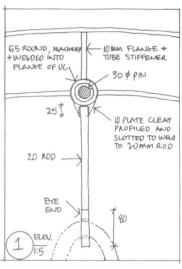

1 ELEV. 1:5
65 ROUND, MACHINED + WELDED INTO FLANGE OF UC
10MM FLANGE + TUBE STIFFENER
30 ⌀ PIN
25
10 PLATE CLEAT PROFILED AND SLOTTED TO WELD TO 20MM ROD
20 ROD
EYE END
80

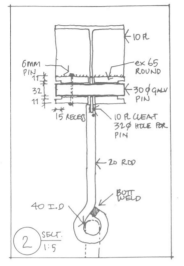

2 SECT. 1:5
10 PL
6MM PIN
32
11
15 RECESS
ex 65 ROUND
30 ⌀ GALV PIN
10 PL CLEAT 32⌀ HOLE FOR PIN
20 ROD
40 I.D
BUTT WELD

6.

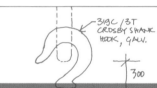

3 ELEV. 1:5
319C/3T CROSBY SHANK HOOK, GALV.
300
240 SW

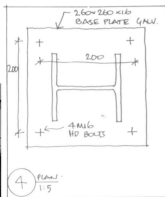

260x260x16 BASE PLATE GALV.
200
200
4 PLAN. 1:5
4 M16 HD BOLTS

7.

8.

Project Facts

A team of three logged some 600 hours on the eight month project for Q Build Project Services. Overall walkway/cycleway budget was $4 million (Aust.). EGD design budget was $35,000; implementation, $35,000. In addition to design, the scope of work included documentation, construction and installation supervision.

Technical Information

Signs are made of hot dipped galvanized steel (including nuts and bolts) and turned solid brass. Steel letters of the main identity were oxygen cut and individually spot welded from behind; brass map was photo etched and paint filled, polished and clear powder coated.

Design Details

Shipbuilding construction techniques were used for strength and durability of the outdoor program as well as to reflect the history of the site, in keeping with nautical references — a rudder, buoy, and semaphore signaler. An outdoor sculpture conservator was consulted regarding installation and preservation of the sculpture series. Futura type was chosen for clarity and compatibility with the ship-related imagery.

Credits

Design Firm: Dot Dash Pty. Ltd., Brisbane, Queensland, Australia
Design Team: Mark Ross, Design Director; Max O'Brien, Kim Hawker
Architect: Spence Jamieson, Brisbane, Queensland,
Fabricators: Q Build Project Services, Brisbane, Queensland, Australia; Roderick Bligh Structures, Fortitude Valley, Queensland, Australia
Special Consultant: Peter D. Cole (sculpture artist), Brisbane, Queensland, Australia

Environmental Image
DOWNTOWN PLAZA

Using color, pattern, and form to create outdoor civic "rooms"

With architectural graphics and building ornament, designers created a series of four articulated public spaces in a six-block area of downtown Sacramento, California, where only relatively undefined space existed before. Signage, color, ornament and patterning include large letterforms integral to the architecture and jewel-like free standing pole signs.

1.

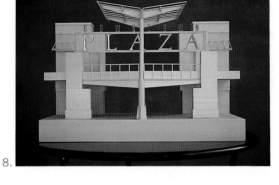

2.

3.

4.

5.

6.

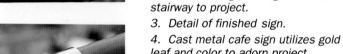

7.

8.

1. Early model for totem.
2. Freestanding pole sign in front of stairway to project.
3. Detail of finished sign.
4. Cast metal cafe sign utilizes gold leaf and color to adorn project.
5. - 7. Details of decorative handrail ornaments.
8. Study model for main entry.
9. Detail of actual main project identity.
10. Model for directory.
11. Bronze orientation plaque is embedded in terrazzo.
12. Jewel like ornamentation tops directory.

Project Facts

The four-year project for the Hahn Company (San Diego, CA) required a team of four designers. The project employed a joint public and private approval process.

Technical Information

A wide variety of materials was specified, including stained GFRC and concrete; etched stainless steel; cast bronze; spun fiberglass; painted metal; gold, silver, copper and aluminum leaf; and anodized aluminum. Techniques ranged from hand-work to the use of digital milling machines. Most of the fabricators, chosen by the client, had not created these kinds of graphics before. Elements range in size from 2 x 3 in. (etched stainless steel handrail brackets) to 13 x 70 ft. (major roadway and identity signs). Exposed neon, low voltage quartz halogen and fluorescent were used to light various elements.

Design Details

From the outset, designers worked with the understanding that all elements would be seen against the sky or the plaza's buildings. Working with an architectural language of steel frames and other industrial elements, they used rich colors and leafed surfaces to act as "jewelry" for buildings. Taking advantage of the open-air nature of the project, they chose materials that would develop a pleasing natural patina.

Credits

Design Firm: Environmental Image
Design Team: Michael Manwaring and David Meckel, Design Directors; Tim Perks
Architect: The Jerde Partnership, Venice, CA, David Rogers, Architect.
Fabricators: Federal Sign Co., Oceanside, CA; Street Graphics, Oakland, CA; William Kreysler Associates, Pengrove, CA; South Bay Bronze, San Jose, CA; Doublet Flag & Banner, San Francisco, CA
Sculptor: Jacquelyn Giuffré (Pengrove, CA)

10.

9.

11.

12.

The Sheila Studio
BIDDY MASON: TIME & PLACE

Honoring a woman who made a difference

1.

An 80 ft. long narrative wall chronicles and celebrates a pioneering African-American woman who came to Los Angeles in the mid-Nineteenth Century and became a leader in her community. No woman of African descent had been so honored in the city before, in spite of the major presence of African Americans in the city since its beginnings. The designer chose the site within a garage-to-be, decided upon the form and content of the memorial, conducted the research, and selected all vendors. The designer needed to make sure the needs of the African-American community were met while engaging in support of the developers. Says deBretteville, "The project can provide hope and serve as a model for how to survive severe adversity and be creative and generous to all people in your city."

2.

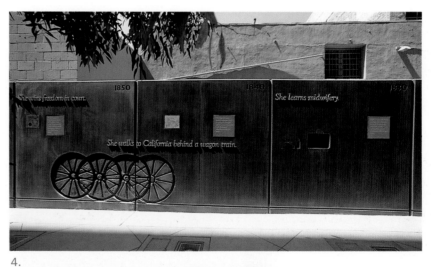

4.

5.

3.

7.

6.

8.

Smith transports
slaves to California,
a free state, where
Judge Hayes declares
Biddy Mason's family
entitled to freedom
and free forever,
1856.

Project Facts

Sheila Levrant de Bretteville completed the
project for Systems Parking, Inc. and the Los Angeles
Community Redevelopment Agency (CRA) over a
three year period. Overall project budget was
$60,000, of which design was $5,000 and implementation was $55,000.

Technical Information

The memorial is made of concrete, slate,
granite, and steel. Granite was etched as in cemetery
monuments. "Live" materials such as agave leaves
were pressed into 8 ft. x 6 in. deep concrete forms.
A test panel helped the designer to determine what
materials could be easily picked out of the concrete.

Design Details

The designer allowed herself to be guided
by her own identification with Biddy Mason's story;
she too came to Los Angeles and tried to make a
difference through her work. To represent the city's
diversity, no specific colors were chosen. Various
typestyles were used.

Credits

Gensler & Associates/Architects
DOWNTOWN DENVER GUIDE SIGNS

Strategic signage guides visitors to a city's
downtown attractions

A wayfinding system of directional signs helps motorists find their way from major thoroughfares to Denver's four square mile central business district and its major attractions. Working extensively with interest groups that included the Auraria Higher Education Center, Lower Downtown Business District, Colorado Historical Society, Denver Art Museum, Denver Mint, Denver City Planning Office, Downtown Retail Association, and state and federal highway regulatory agencies, designers provided destination analysis, graphic signage design and construction documentation. They conducted extensive interviews with a variety of agencies and inspected designated areas to assess the city's and county's signage needs.

1.

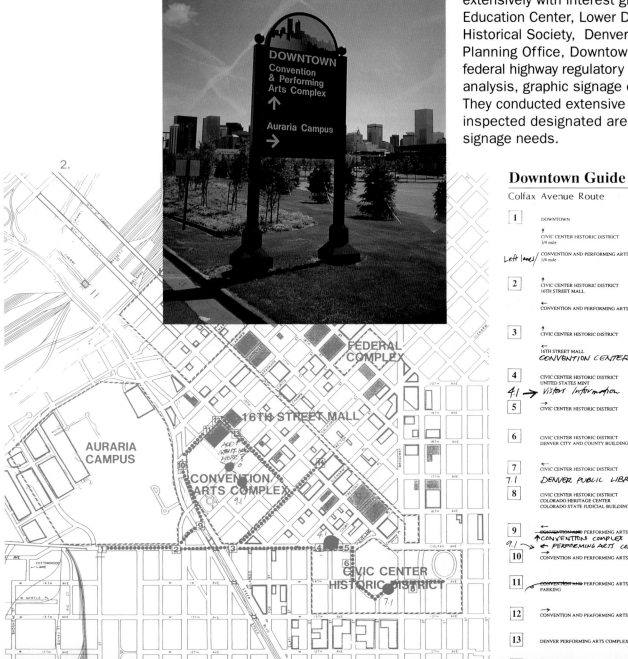

2.

3.

Downtown Guide Signs

Colfax Avenue Route

1	DOWNTOWN
Left lanes	↑ CIVIC CENTER HISTORIC DISTRICT 3/4 mile CONVENTION AND PERFORMING ARTS COMPLEX 1/4 mile
2	↑ CIVIC CENTER HISTORIC DISTRICT 16TH STREET MALL ← CONVENTION AND PERFORMING ARTS COMPLEX
3	↑ CIVIC CENTER HISTORIC DISTRICT ← 16TH STREET MALL CONVENTION CENTER
4	CIVIC CENTER HISTORIC DISTRICT UNITED STATES MINT
4.1 →	Visitors Information
5	→ CIVIC CENTER HISTORIC DISTRICT
6	CIVIC CENTER HISTORIC DISTRICT DENVER CITY AND COUNTY BUILDING
7	← CIVIC CENTER HISTORIC DISTRICT
7.1	DENVER PUBLIC LIBRARY
8	CIVIC CENTER HISTORIC DISTRICT COLORADO HERITAGE CENTER COLORADO STATE JUDICIAL BUILDING
9	~~CONVENTION AND~~ PERFORMING ARTS COMPLEX ↑ CONVENTIONS COMPLEX
9.1 →	← PERFORMING ARTS COMPLEX PARKING
10	CONVENTION AND PERFORMING ARTS COMPLEX
11	~~CONVENTION AND~~ PERFORMING ARTS COMPLEX PARKING
12	CONVENTION AND PERFORMING ARTS COMPLEX
13	DENVER PERFORMING ARTS COMPLEX

4.

1. Footed vehicular directory sign.
2. Map showing sign system programming.
3. Union Station icon marks signs in historic downtown district.
4. - 5. Color and silkscreened pictogram featuring capitol indicates civic center historic district.

5.

Project Facts

Working for the City and County of Denver's Department of Transportation, one designer completed the project in four months' time. Overall project budget was $300,000. The system numbers more than 180 signs.

Technical Information

Simplicity in design and materials were a key project objective. Signs consist of sheet aluminum, reflective vinyl, steel posts, and concrete footings and incorporate silkscreened "pictograms" of Denver architectural icons. Installation was coordinated with regard to downtown utility systems and historic landmark considerations. Three sizes of sign panels were used: 11 x 6 ft., 6 x 4 ft., and 3 ft. 6 in. x 2 ft. 6 in.

Design Details

The designer's goals were to develop a friendly, colorful and inviting sign system that would be unique to Denver and, above all, would make the city's downtown more accessible. Anxiety is reduced by reassuring visitors at strategic points that they are still on the right track. Designers presented two color schemes. The first was based on the colors of the Colorado flag; the second, which was accepted, on a simple green and white palette.

Credits

Design Team: Christopher Nims, Design Director; David Baker; Robert Karn (The Denver Partnership)
Architect: Gensler & Associates/Architects, Denver, CO
Fabricators: Young Electric Sign Company, Denver, CO
Communication Industries, Golden, CO (mock-ups)
Structural Engineer: Martin/Martin, Denver, CO

Clifford Selbert Design
SEVEN HILLS PARK

Transforming a mundane park into a community landmark

A new park, even if it's only three-quarters of an acre, is an important enhancement to the land-poor city of Somerville, Massachusetts. Design of the park and its graphics went to Clifford Selbert Design, which had already completed the adjacent linear park. After meeting with community groups to determine what the new park should have, the team considered elements that would provide visibility and refer to the city or the site, a former railroad right-of-way. Researching local history, designers discovered the city was originally built on seven hills, each used for a different purpose. These became the basis for the new park's identity, with seven giant "weather vane" sculptures referring to them. Besides environmental graphics and signage, the design team's unusually wide-ranging scope of services extended to master planning and landscape architecture.

1.

2.

3.

1. Park overview.

2. - 3. Progression from concept sketch to working drawing to actual "weather vane" sculpture.

4. Detail of three of the seven icons.

5. Color sketch of clock icon.

6. - 7. Sculptures are constructed of high density foam over metal armatures.

8. Concept sketch for icons.

9. Porcelain enamel plaque is mounted on a brick and granite base. Hill identification is carved in granite.

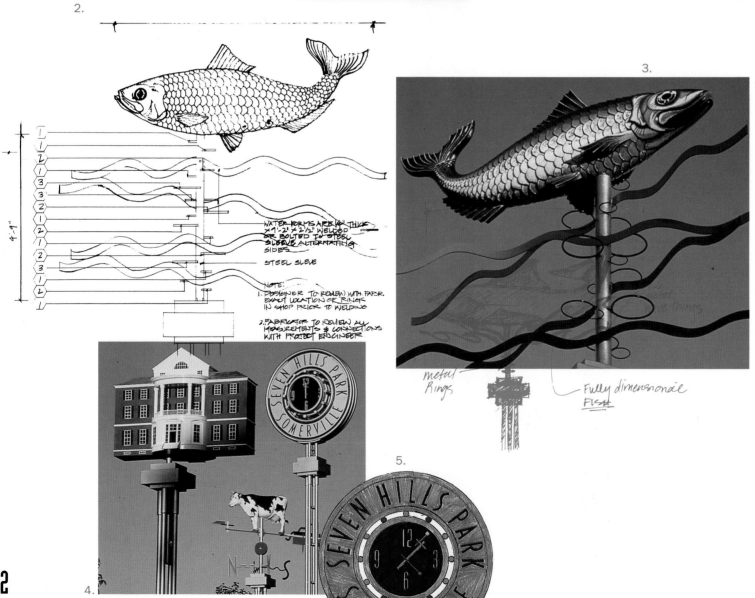

4.

5.

6.

7.

9.

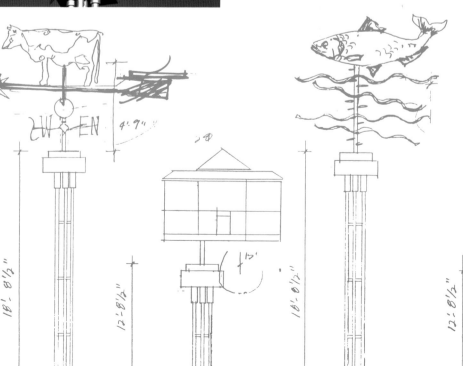

Project Facts

A team of two designers and one landscape architect completed the project for the City of Somerville. Almost two years passed from the time designers began work to the park's opening, including a five-month idle period while financing was secured. Sculptures and graphics cost $100,000.

Technical Information

Sculptures are made from high-density foam, which weighs less than wood and is more durable, with internal steel structures. Measuring 8 x 12 feet on average, each "weather vane" weighs between 1,000 and 2,000 pounds. Designers consulted structural engineers to insure the monuments could withstand high winds. Except for the clock, all sculptures — or elements of them — turn in the wind. Support poles and turning mechanisms are made of weather resistant steel. Porcelain enamel plaques are mounted on 12 foot brick and granite bases, to discourage vandalism of poles. Installers needed to exercise care in mounting plaques to the uneven brick surfaces: Plywood nailed into 3/8 inch reveals, cut into the brick, shaped itself to the brick. Additional shims were required for signs to fit their housings.

Design Details

Shapes and colors of weather vane sculptures were inspired by American folk art. Designers worked with local historians to determine which events of local importance would be most suitably expressed as symbols. Matrix Wide was selected as a body typeface; initial capitals are an art deco Casablanca Light Condensed, which designers scanned into their computers from an old book and then modified. Designers opted for yellow copy against a turquoise background after examining mock-ups at the site, for ease of reading outdoors and to reflect colors in the sculptures.

Credits

Design Firm: Clifford Selbert Design, Boston, MA
Design Team: Clifford Selbert and Robin Perkins, Design Directors; Ruth Loetterle, Landscape Architect
Fabricators: Amidon & Company, Sandwich, MA; Cornelius Architectural Products, Pittsburgh, PA; Enameltec, Langly, BC
Structural Engineer: Joan Rumbaugh Engineering, MA
Photo Credit: Anton Grassl, Cambridge, MA

Bruce and Susan K. Burdick are principals of The Burdick Group in San Francisco, California. The Burdick Group specializes in applying the disciplines of industrial design, interior architecture, graphic and interactive media design to public experience projects for clients worldwide. Bruce and Susan Burdick have lectured nationally and internationally, including participation in conferences at the American Center for Design and with Design Station, Tokyo and Herman Miller, Japan.

BRUCE BURDICK

The Interpretive Environment as an Active Public Resource

It is difficult to describe the design of most expositions, in the sense that a piece of architecture can be described as *designed*, since, unfortunately, most exhibits aren't designed but *written*. What results is something like a book or an assemblage, a sort of super wallpaper that bleeds through three-dimensional space, divided into chapters formed by rooms. In this "exhibit as book" approach, objects — and physical objects are what museums are all about — almost disappear within walls of contextual graphics.

This leads to the unfortunate assumption that exhibits, constructed along a storyline narrative, are meant to be seen only once, in the same way that a book is usually read once. In fact, an exhibit can be a unique information resource capable of being revisited again and again.

It should be obvious that an exhibit is not a book or a film. With the latter, the reader (or viewer) is locked within a linear method of communication by the author (or director). Page by page or frame by frame, the individual is more or less obliged to *sit there* as information passes by. An exhibit is different. Three-dimensional space provides the designer with an opportunity to create a very large interactive device, and the viewer is free to move forwards or backwards in physical space. Exhibits are the only communication medium you can physically enter and inhabit.

Interpretive environments make of use every form of communication: objects, graphics, typography, photographs, film, and electronic media. It is a daunting design challenge to bring together this abundance of media within the richness of opportunity three-dimensional space provides.

Charles Eames was the first exhibit designer to understand the critical difference between "exhibit-as-communication-resource" and "exhibit-as-linear narrative." Few exhibit designers recognize this difference even today. In addition to being a wonderful furniture designer and filmmaker, Eames developed a new dynamic between three-dimensional objects and two-dimensional photographs and graphics. His exhibits were filled with discovery and could be revisited repeatedly. *Mathematica*, an exhibit he built for IBM in 1961, is still fresh today.

Interpretive environments *do* need communication goals. And goals need to be flexible enough to change when examined within the context of available objects. In exploring goals, one should concentrate on the advantages of three-dimensional space in relation to objects, choosing and developing those objects for display that provide the best opportunity for visitor exploration. If the designer follows a story-like script instead of developing a goal-oriented plan, it is all too likely that typography, photographs, and multimedia will end up dominating the exhibit and "real stuff" will play only a supporting role.

A case in point: A prominent history museum prepared an exposition about one of our founding fathers. Unfortunately, the staff used scripting to define the order of display and neglected to ask essential questions about the three-dimensional material such as "Is this the best use of these objects?" and "What can the objects communicate?" The result was a series of objects *hooked* into a lifeless history story propped up by words and photographs.

The museum's director, viewing the pedantic result of this approach with concern, asked us to develop an adjacent exhibit that would bring this historical person to life. By *listening to* the objects the curators had passed over instead of using a storyline, we were able to design an exhibit that revealed much more about this individual (and about Americans in general).

An exhibit is a "self-agenda" device for visitors to select what interests them. Planning communication goals for an exhibit is analogous to designing information for a magazine or a newspaper: the reader can start on the last page or in the middle. An exhibit *will* have an entry point — as a magazine has a cover — but visitors are free to turn right or left or double back, ignoring large chunks of information and selecting what interests them. For visitors to have this experience, one has to create the physical metaphor of a magazine or newspaper, a *structure* that provides freedom of movement for and an understanding of where related information can be found.

To achieve this type of *information structure* for the Philips Corporate Museum in the Netherlands, we constructed a number of armatures, each illustrating a Philips product innovation. The visitor, in motion, can intercept an armature at many physical points. Each illustrates an act of innovation that contributed to a particular product. Taken together, the armatures depict the finished product, but each armature can also stand on its own.

Such information *structuring* is both aggregative and fractal in nature — illustrative details and overarching ideas are inherent in any one element. Each armature tells the story of the synergism Philips achieves from its various groups to invent a product; the larger story of Philips is also inherent in each. Each armature is a resource of data, methods and approaches that can be viewed casually or in depth; their total is an understanding of the Philips creative process. It's an understanding that grows richer with each return visit.

Interpretive Environments

Well-organized and compellingly displayed three-dimensional information educates and inspires visitors.

1.

Joseph A. Wetzel Associates
BIRMINGHAM CIVIL RIGHTS INSTITUTE

Depicting segregation in America and
the movement that strove to break it down

2.

For a 12,000 square foot permanent exhibit funded by the Birmingham Civil Rights Institute and the City of Birmingham, Alabama, designers were given a powerful, moving storyline to work with. After focusing the narrative on Birmingham's role in the movement and coming to terms with a building plan that dictated flow, they sourced as much production and fabrication as possible through minority firms. Original artifacts include a 1960 vintage Greyhound bus that was purchased and burned for an exhibit and the door of the jail cell in which Martin Luther King, Jr. wrote his famous "Letter from Birmingham Jail."

4.   3.

5.

1. *Typical photo identification panel.*
2. *Collage of printed ephemera complements dimensional displays.*
3. *Dramatically lighted historical vignettes employ full sized cast figures.*
4. *Changing projected images add animation to static wall display.*
5. *Simple corner vignette makes powerful contribution to storyline.*
6. *Cutouts are used to illustrate secondary story points.*

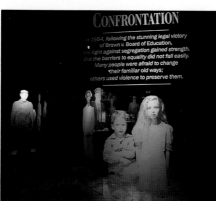

6.

Project Facts

The two phase project for the Birmingham Civil Rights Institute and the City of Birmingham involved one architect, one industrial designer, and one graphic designer with up to five other designers assisting. The team worked a total of 15,393 hours over the course of the project's three year first phase and year and a half second phase. Implementation budget was $2.6 million.

Technical Information

To capture the time period and setting of the exhibit program, designers tried to use as many period artifacts as possible. When originals weren't available, accurate reproductions were substituted. Throughout the exhibit, care was taken to employ building and finish materials that complemented the program. In one gallery, Bomanite, a flooring material that can be molded and colored, was used for sidewalks, curbs and asphalt to emphasize the "road to freedom" theme. Oak flooring, cinder block, wired security glass, rusted iron, shattered glass, period wallpaper, furniture and fixtures are all part of the materials palette. They are illuminated by an array of floods, spots, washes and pin lights mounted on suspended track.

Design Details

While period artifacts drove the aesthetic, designers attempted to immerse the visitor in the story through attention to detail. A tense moment occurred when the time came to shatter a $1,000, 450 pound piece of safety glass for the mini-theater's intro wall. The glass needed to shatter perfectly; designers had no backup. The drop was successful and the lamination between layers held the glass together. A monochromatic color palette of reddish-gray recalls the city's iron ore past and seems to have settled on the exhibits like a fine dust. Typefaces were inspired by newspapers of the 1960s: Bodoni Bold Condensed, Times Roman, and Franklin Gothic.

Credits

Design Firm: Joseph A. Wetzel Associates, Inc., Boston
Design Team: Howard Litwak, Principal-in-Charge; Gail Ringel, Project Manager; Sherry Proctor, Project Designer; Chris Danemayer, Project Graphic Designer
Architect: Max Bond Associates, New York, NY
Fabricators: 1220 Exhibits, Nashville, TN; Madison Davis Lacy, New York, NY; Reel Deal, New York, NY; Donna Lawrence Productions, Louisville, KY; Dave Schuster, Southboro, MA; AV Associates, Storrs, CT; C. Brown Systems Design, Berkeley, CA

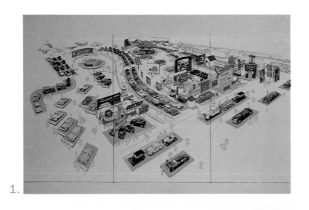

1.

Albert Woods Design Associates
"THE AUTOMOBILE IN AMERICAN LIFE"

An exhibit on the automobile launches
a museum's redesign

A 60,000 square foot multimedia exhibition on the development of the automobile and its impact on American life for The Henry Ford Museum in Dearborn Michigan was the initial project in implementing the designers' master plan for the museum's eventual total redesign. Over 100 automobiles are organized into thematic areas and supported by vintage motion picture footage to show them in action as well as by artifacts, manuscripts and memorabilia to enrich their presentation. Designers not only needed to develop a visual approach unique to the exhibit and to make full use of the museum's large volume, but to anticipate the relationship between this exhibit and those to come.

For more information about a designer, touch his picture.

2.

3.

1. Color perspective rendering of exhibition.
2. Interactive video display.
3. Reproductions of historic billboards punctuate display spaces.
4. Autos of the future add counterpoint to highway of antique cars.
5. Period roadside signage enlivens display.
6. Auto parts of historic cars show changes in technology.
7. An important part of this immense exhibit is the highway of history which flows through it.

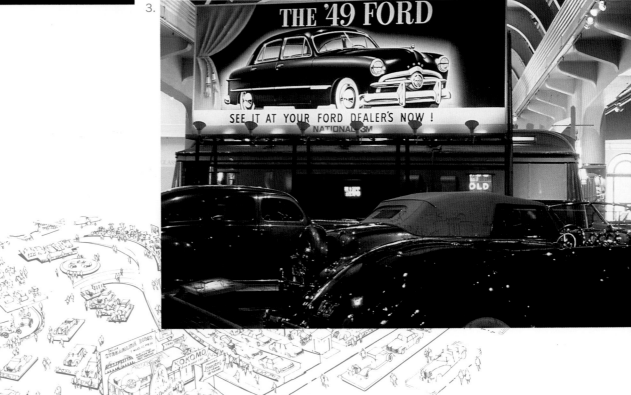

4.

5.

6.

7.

Project Facts

The permanent exhibition involved 16 designers. Design and construction lasted one and a half years. Overall project budget was $6 million, of which $3 million was implementation. Scope of work included research, design, specifications, supervision and production of all audiovisual components.

Technical Information

Varied fabrication techniques were used. For a "seamless" highway and barrier, a special continuous pebble texture was wet-applied to the 250 foot roadway and platform surfaces, and a cast aggregate process was used to form curbs and rail supports. Billboards are 24 feet high. A flexible overhead track system illuminates the exhibit.

Design Details

The exhibit needed to provide a suitable framework for the museum's automobile collection and to have its own materials palette. Beyond enriching and bringing the collection to life, design needed to allow free circulation among the displays, which include a drive-in theater and a serpentine multi-level highway.

Credits

Design Firm: Albert Woods Design Associates, New York
Design Team: Albert H. Woods, Design Director; Tomas Ancona, Ileana Truneanu, Heather Cook, Masahiro Ogyu, Peter Galperin, May Liu, Katherine McKenna, Alexis Cohen, Nikolai Buglaj, Patrick McCabe, Hank Whittemore, George Kanelba, Bettina Bottome, Fred Karp, Mary Lance, Eric Breitbart Lighting; Donald L. Bliss, Maywood, NJ

Wesselman Design
"THE ART OF ARCHITECTURE -
DENVER ART MUSEUM RECONSIDERED"

Educating the public about a museum

and its architect Celebrating its centennial anniversary, the Denver Art Museum decided to feature an exhibition to educate visitors about the museum's unique qualities and to see it in a new way. Working together with Craig Miller, curator of the museum's Design and Architecture Department, designers developed a concept and approach consisting of the marriage of two major elements: the integration of the work of Gio Ponti, the museum's architect, and the decision to let architecture and graphics (i.e., typography, photography and drawing) have equal voices.

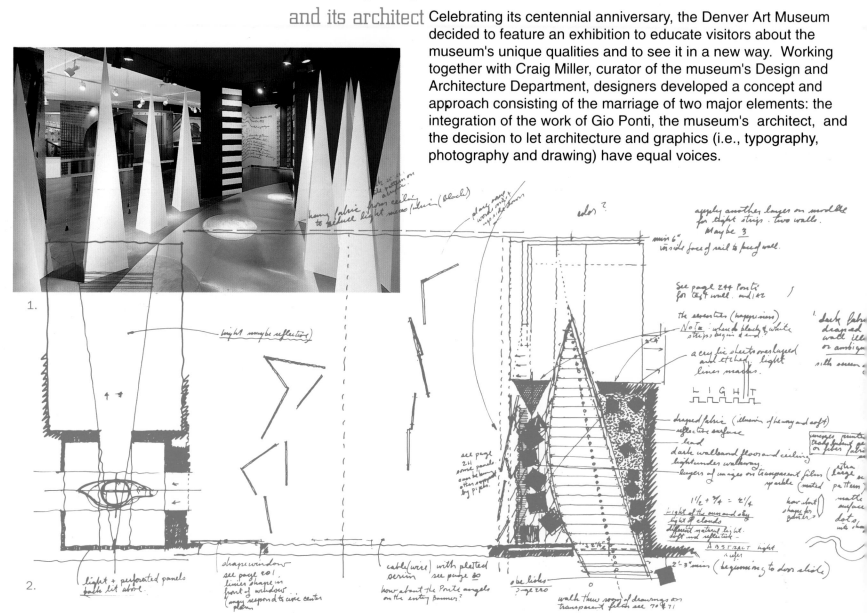

1.

2.

5.

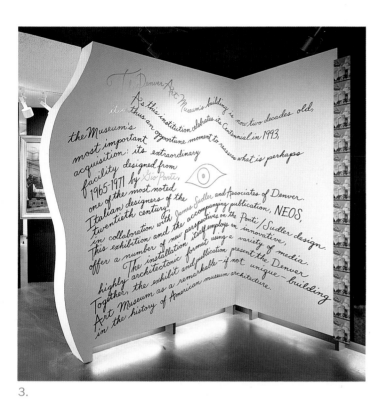

3.

1. Entrance to exhibit conveys a sense of the wonder and magic of architecture.
2. Design study of entrance plan.
3. Amorphous introductory text panel with playful script treatment contrasts with entrance.
4. Giant portrait of architect Gio Ponti peers from behind his work.
5. Details of dimensional display walls.
6. Frames in display are designed to mimic the architecture.
7. Past , Present and Future wall demonstrates traditional display technique.

6.

4.

7.

2.

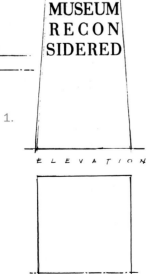

MAIN ENTRY LOBBY

THE A
RT OF
ARCHI
TECTU
RE - TH
E DENV
ER ART
MUSEUM
RECON
SIDERED

PONTI EXHIBITION
OB·1   22 OCT
3/4" = 1'-0"

1.

ELEVATION

PLAN

4.

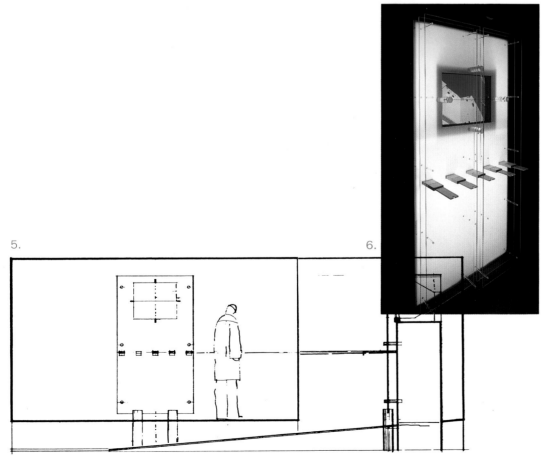

5.   6.

Project Facts

A team of two designers and two assistants worked "too many hours to count" on the one year seven month assignment. Overall project budget was $100,000, of which implementation was $62,500 and design was $37,500. Of the design budget, $7,000 was for photography. The project scope included conceptual design, schematic design, design development, construction documents and supervision of installation. Since no artwork existed beforehand, the architectural design itself became the exhibition; for one section, designers art directed all photography and redrew the museum's floor plans.

Technical Information

Aluminum, gypsum board, medium-density fiberboard, Plexiglas, and large-format photographic transparencies were specified. Patterns were applied to the aluminum used for flooring. Transparencies were wrapped around three dimensional objects. Several unusual elements posed challenges for fabricators and installers, including 20 foot photo-murals, images hanging from the ceiling as well as wrapping them around objects, and fabrication of obelisks and Plexiglas altar.

Design Details

Encouraged by a client open to new ideas as long as they fit the budget, designers sought to challenge people to participate. In the first, transitional space, designers wanted people to leave the everyday world behind and enter the world of the museum; the walls are mirrored, the floor is metal, and visitors walk through a forest of obelisks leading to the intro room. These elements relate to Ponti's work or to components of the building. In the exhibition, designers deliberately reversed the scale of objects: Gio Ponti's portrait is large (ten x ten feet) and the museum's overview is small (six x nine inches). Typography becomes walls and photographs are three dimensional.

Credits

Design: Wesselman Design, Inc. and Anthony Pellechia Architects, Seattle, WA
Design Team: Anthony Pellecchia and Kathy Wesselman, Design Directors; Petra Schwartze, Joel Bakken
Architect: Anthony Pellecchia
Fabrication: Newcastle Construction, Denver, CO (contractor); Communication Industries, Denver, CO (signage, graphic fabrication); Reed Photo Art, Denver, CO (photographic reproductions)
Photography: Thomas Arledge, Denver, CO

Wiehle-Carr
"FRANK LLOYD WRIGHT
CALIFORNIA PROJECTS"

Creating a context for an architect's legacy

An extension of the traveling exhibition "Frank Lloyd Wright: Decorative Designs Today," featuring furniture and accessories now in production, relates these elements to eight of the architect's Los Angeles projects. For the 1,200 square foot exhibit, on display for a six-week period at the Pacific Design Center's Murray Feldman Gallery in West Hollywood, California, designers carefully selected a limited number of projects to demonstrate the breadth of Wright's California work without exceeding a modest budget.

1.

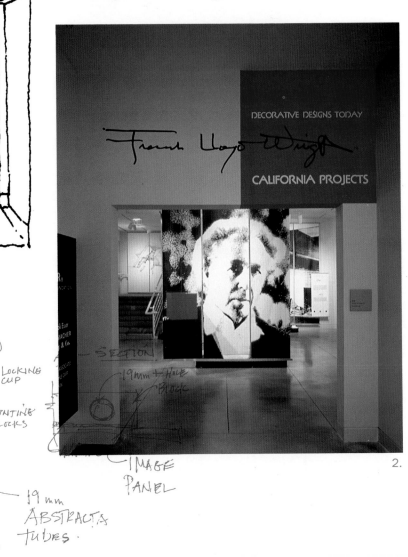

2.

3.
SIDE VIEW & BACK VIEW
IMAGE
LOCKING CLIP
MOUNTING BLOCKS
CONCRETE BASE
SLEEVE INSET IN CONCRETE BASE
19 mm ABSTRACTA TUBES.
SECTION
19 mm + HOLE BLOCK
IMAGE PANEL

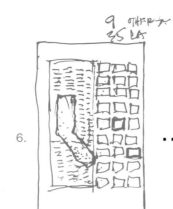

6.

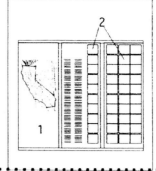

Wall - 2
Topic Intro—Cal/S.C. Projects
text & images on existing wall

7.

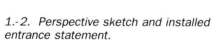

4.

5.

1.-2. Perspective sketch and installed
entrance statement.
3. Study for typical panel and base
construction.
4. Enlarged strips of architectural elevations
are backgrounds for actual artifacts.
5. Photograph of original installation is foil
for Wright desk.
6. Early study and installation drawing of
photo wall.
7. Concept sketch and finished vignette
showing integration of architect's design
and actual Wright chairs.

Project Facts
Two designers spent about 300 hours on
the F. Schumacher & Company project. Curatorial work,
design and fabrication lasted nine weeks.

Technical Information
Xerographic enlargements on paper,
laminate covered platforms for furniture, Plexiglas
cases for some decorative objects; wood moulding
details and trim were specified. The exhibit makes
generous use of large images (one being 20 feet high)
suspended in front of walls or used as space dividers.
The three foot width limitation of these materials
necessitated a panel-like mounting with up to four
strips hung side by side from wooden battens.
Typical elements are eight feet high.

Design Details
This extension of a larger show had to work
aesthetically with existing show elements. The
previously designed portion of the show related
foreground three-dimensional pieces to full sized
black and white backdrops of room settings where the
pieces originated. Designers enhanced dimensionality
by suspending all graphic and caption elements on
wires away from walls by a few inches, or by using
them as space dividers. Typestyles, colors and
details were derived from or sympathetic to Wright's
own use of these elements.

Credits
Design Firm: Florian-Wierzbowski Architecture, Chicago
Design Director: Paul Florian
Curatorial and Design Consultants: Louis Wiehle,
Christopher Carr/Wiehle-Carr, Los Angeles, CA
Installer: Curatorial Assistance, Los Angeles, CA

1.

B.J. Krivanek Art + Design
COMMEMORATIVE WALL-
JEFFERSON HIGH SCHOOL, LOS ANGELES

Bringing role models to an inner city community

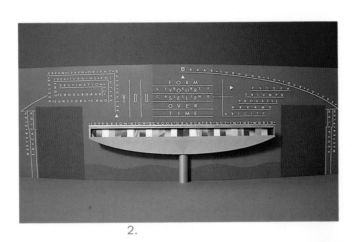

2.

Jefferson High School in South Central Los Angeles has had several prominent graduates, including Dexter Gordon, Alvin Ailey, and Nobel laureate Ralph Bunche. In the school's most public space, the lobby of its auditorium, B.J. Krivanek designed an installation that draws attention to its history of success and invites students to imagine the possibility of similar achievement in a very human, non-intimidating manner: Interspersed at random in a display of photographs, they encounter their own reflections in mirrors. Says the designer, "While complementing the original Streamline Moderne architecture of the campus, this public art program restores a sense of dignity and purpose to an embattled educational environment."

1. Exterior view of "moderne" high school, which influenced project design.
2. - 4. Dimensional presentation board, elevation diagram and project installation.
5. Concept sketch showing detail in elevation and section.
6. Detail of installation showing formal arrangement of typography and photographs.
7. Mirrors, which punctuate photos of successful graduates, provide inter-action with passing students.

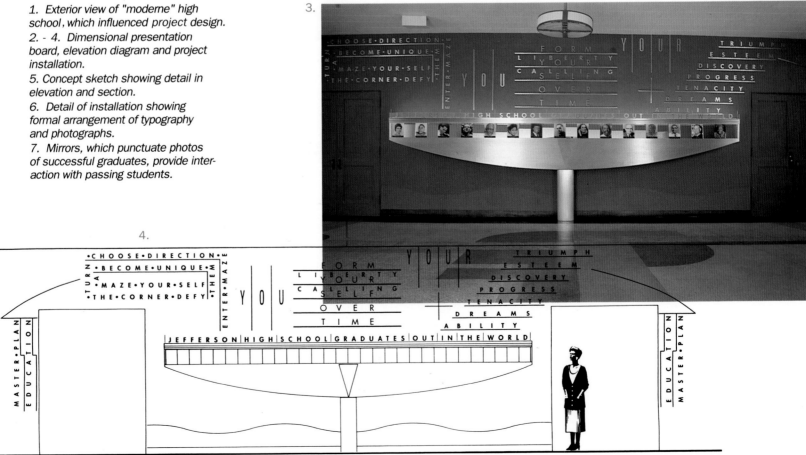

3.

4.

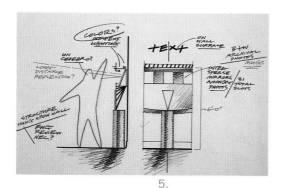

5.

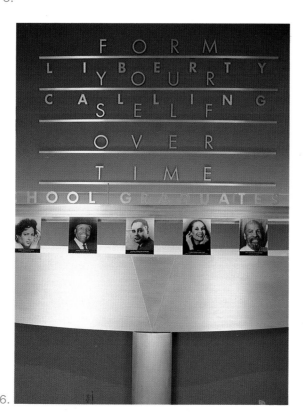

6.

7.

Project Facts

Funding from the Los Angeles Endowment for the Arts and The Jefferson High School Alumni Association comprised the $15,000 overall project budget, of which only 10 percent was allocated for design services; designing and researching the project involved considerable pro bono time.

Technical Information

Aluminum is used extensively for all structural forms, selected for its natural color and for the futurism it represented in the 1930's (the date of the original building). Thick acrylic shields the image; it is heavily defaced by tagging and periodically replaced. Neon was selected for indirect illumination — green to wash the wall behind the continuum, pale orange to wash the images within. The gray-green wall color was selected to relate to the lobby's existing terrazzo floor, with a deep blue waiving motif below to suggest a precarious balance. Inscriptions, mainly in Futura, are precision cut from brushed aluminum. While a schematic model was constructed early on, all design details were established via working drawings only. Illumination effects were extrapolated from the experience of the neon fabricator.

Design Details

Facing an imminent grant deadline, the designer seized upon the basic concept: to present images of role models within a horizontal continuum, so that students would randomly encounter reflections of themselves. From there, design development proceeded quickly; the designer's energy was focused primarily on writing the selection of materials, lighting and typography.

Credits

Design Firm: B.J. Krivanek Art+Design, Los Angeles, CA
Design Team: B.J. Krivanek, Design Director; David Rieger
Archival Research: Robert Perry
Photo Credit: Edmund Barr
Fabricators: AHR Ampersand, Glendale, CA;
Neonics, Marina del Rey, CA

Albert Woods Design Associates
"IN THE LINE OF DUTY"

Raising the public's awareness of an
ongoing commitment to veterans disabled
in the line of duty A 2,000 square foot traveling exhibition commissioned by Disabled American Veterans (D.A.V.) personalizes disabled veterans for the visitor. Designed for use in a variety of unknown spaces, the exhibit has a flexible layout and integrated lighting. Shippable units can be combined to form large-scale unbroken forms. Most challenging to designers were compiling the necessary statistical and visual information for a program on worldwide distribution of armed forces, and selecting individual veterans for video interviews.

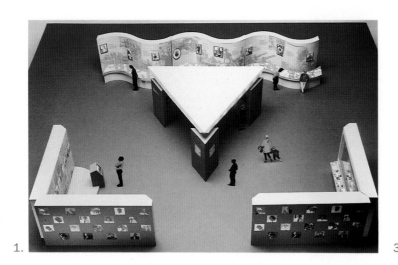

1.

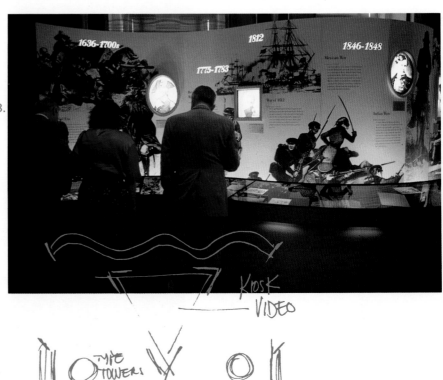

3.

1. - 2. Concept study and model of ideal exhibit plan.
3. Cases are internally lit to avoid dependence on existing lighting.
4. One of several interactive stations that allow visitors to use devices designed to aid the disabled.
5. Installation overview.
6. Collage style photos and caption wall.

2.

4.

5.

6.

Project Facts

Design and production of the year and a half project for Disabled American Veterans involved a team of five designers. The project scope included total responsibility for all research, design, specifications and supervision of production. Designers also produced printed graphics and all audiovisual programs.

Technical Information

Fabrication involved a variety of techniques. Opaque surfaces were hard wearing laminates edged with wood trim. To avoid dependence on existing lighting, all illumination is internal except for footlights for vertical walls.

Design Details

The exhibit needed to make disabled veterans real people, not statistics. This resulted in a central presentation of video interviews with a variety of veterans. A special touch controlled interactive program enabled visitors to explore the United States' ongoing worldwide commitment of Armed Forces.

Credits

Design Firm: Albert Woods Design Associates, New York
Design Team: Albert H. Woods, Design Director; Krister Olmon, Ileana Truneanu, Scott Briggs, Elizabeth Blades, Kay Gudmestad, Leslie Nowinski, Brian Unger, Carol Wilson, Robert Kurilla, Daniel Gross, Lora Myers, Nola Schiff, Sharon Edwards
Fabricator: Robert Schultz and Associates, Inc., Temple City, CA
Photographer: Sylvia Plachy

Pentagram
"THE POWER OF MAPS"

Showing the significance of maps as instruments
of communication, persuasion and control

A display of more than 400 historic maps at the Cooper-Hewitt
Museum in New York is accompanied by a questioning narrative
that reveals the subjective nature of these ostensibly objective
documents. Collaborating with museum staff and curators,
Pentagram partners Peter Harrison and James Biber worked to
shape and animate the installation, and to engage visitors as they
were guided through the galleries. The elements they developed
echo the folding forms of paper maps. By using these common,
tactile forms in an unusual way, they reinforced the theme of the
show and encouraged visitors to examine familiar objects from a
different point of view.

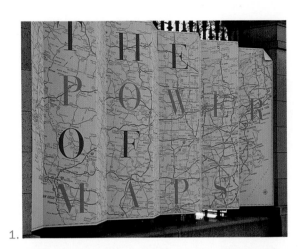
1.

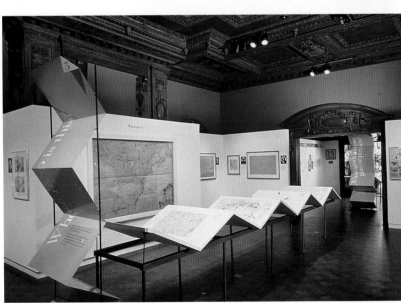
2.

3.

4.

5.

1. Exterior sign of folded aluminum.
2. Installation overview.
3. Folded steel tower signs act as area markers.
4. Exhibit entrance viewed through "torn" map.
5. Signature mapfolded table displays contrast with flat walls of exhibit.
6. Thin steel rods support tower signs.

6.

Project Facts

A team of two designers and two architects designed large directional signs, theme statement panels and display tables as well as the exhibition program for the five month exhibit.

Technical Information

The exhibit's main identity is a continuous folded piece of steel, with type and images silkscreened directly onto its powder coated surface. Clips on flanking support rods hold the folded element in place. The exterior fence is made from a series of seven panels of folded sheet aluminum, with graphics silkscreened directly onto the metal surface.

Design Details

The form and content of the exhibition was intended to surprise and involve visitors from beginning to end. It educated the viewer in stages to illustrate the theme that every map is subjective. Each room made the visitor aware how different political situations, historic events, and individual motivations have shaped the making of maps. The exterior sign for the exhibition ran along the fence around the Carnegie Mansion, which houses the Cooper-Hewitt collections. Designers created a folding form that was both symbolic and functional: Creased and dog-eared like a road map, it was easy to read from a vehicle traveling down Fifth Avenue. Its background image was Route 66 from New York to San Francisco.

Credits

Design Firm: Pentagram Design, New York, NY
Design Team: Peter Harrison, Partner/Designer; James Biber, Michael Zweck-Bronner, Architect; Christina Freyss, Designer
Fabricator: Rathe Productions, New York, NY
Photo Credits: Bill Jacobson (interiors); Peter Mauss Esto (interiors); Reven T.C. Wurman (exterior signs)

Albert Woods Design Associates
"MADE IN AMERICA"

Taking advantage of a museum's
in-house capability

A 50,000 square foot multimedia exhibition on the industrial history of the United States fills one thematic area within the immense Henry Ford Museum in Dearborn, Michigan. The circulation plan allows visitors to enter, exit and move through the exhibit by means of a variety of pathways. Because of a limited budget, the team had to design to maximize use of the museum's in-house shop capability and to take advantage of donations of technical help and hardware.

1.

2.

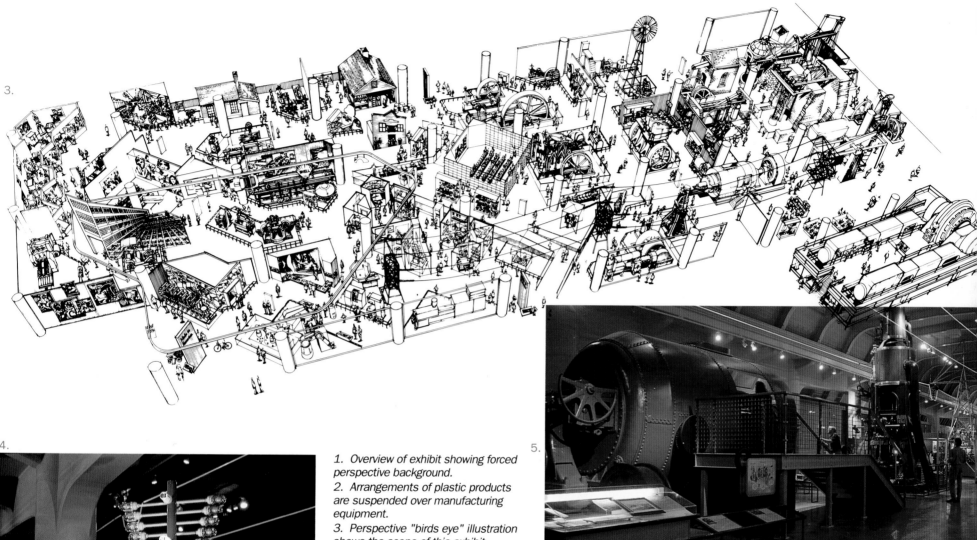

3.

4.

1. Overview of exhibit showing forced perspective background.
2. Arrangements of plastic products are suspended over manufacturing equipment.
3. Perspective "birds eye" illustration shows the scope of this exhibit.
4. Interactive electrical display.
5. Stairs lead to cutaway view of dynamo interior.

5.

1.

1. Detail of products on moving track.
2. Exploded views are usually drawn, This exploded Model T shows the simplicitiy of the auto.
3. The scale of some objects are large and seem to be embedded in the floor.
4. View from entrance.
5. Photographs "float" on corrugated steel wall.
6. View of corridor from raised display platform.

2.

3.

4.

5.

6.

Project Facts

Nine designers worked on the two year assignment for The Henry Ford Museum. Overall project budget was $6 million, of which $3 million was implementation. The exhibition is permanent.

Technical Information

An extruded aluminum railing system and perforated and corrugated steel were specified. Fiber-optic transmission lines transmitting light were also used to express energy. The exhibition uses basic metal stud construction with sheet metal cladding. Basic wall height is 13 feet; however, some elements extend to the 40 foot ceiling, including transmission towers and the Highland Park Plant. A flexible over-head track system provides lighting.

Design Details

Within the huge, open museum space, the exhibition is given its own color and finish palette for variety. Designers took advantage of the need to make full use of the high bay industrial space to provide dramatic vistas and dynamic features, including actual transmission towers spaced 100 feet apart with glowing fiber-optic transmission lines, an over-head conveyor system, and a photomural factory set with motion picture images of workers within projected onto its windows. Color, type, and materials express the industrial theme.

Credits

Design Firm: Albert Woods Design Associates, New York
Design Team: Albert H. Woods, Design Director; Krister Olmon, Ileana Truneanu, Scott Briggs, Elizabeth Blades, Katherine Oudens, Paul Pickard, Diane Dufault, Nola Schiff, Lora Myers
Film Production: New Deal Films, Albuquerque, NM; Slide Factor, Boston, MA
Interactive Program: Albert Woods Design Associates
Audiovisual: Boyce Nemec Design, Norfolk, CT
Lighting: Donald L. Bliss, Maywood, NJ

The Burdick Group
THE PHILIPS COMPETENCE CENTER

Illustrating a corporation's technical
capabilities and accomplishments

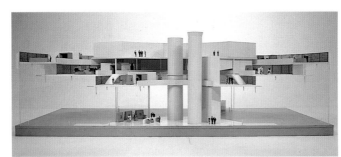

1.

Philips, a diversified global corporation, had offices located throughout the city of Eindhoven as well as internationally, but lacked a central corporate facility until The Burdick Group proposed a new use for an existing dome-shaped building built in the 1960's. Named the Philips Competence Centre, the building now serves as an international meeting place open to visitors, business partners, clients, employees, future employees, and, by invitation, public groups. The exhibit concept developed from the fact that product innovations by diverse divisions had grown from a group of shared technical core competencies. Taking examples of innovations from each division, designers illustrated how these competencies were involved in their development. Interactive exhibits explain innovations as diverse as the compact disc (CD), high-definition television (HDTV), compact lighting, and medical products such as ultrasound and MRI. Interactive computer stations give visitors the opportunity to explore these innovations.

2.

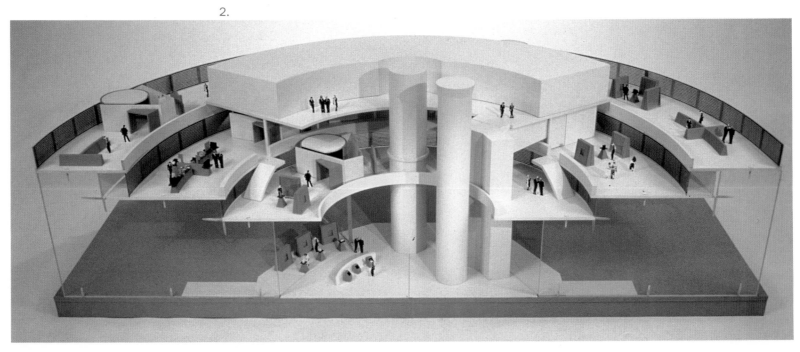

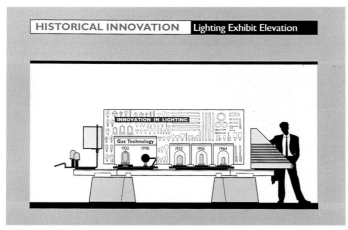

HISTORICAL INNOVATION | Lighting Exhibit Elevation

3.

1. - 2. Scale model section.
3. Lighting exhibit elevation sketch.
4. Scale model of theater and exhibit case.
5. Full size graphic panel mockup.

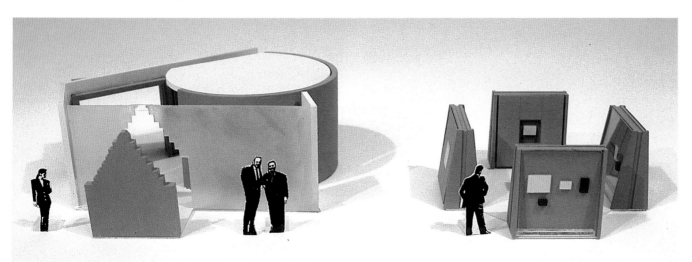

4.

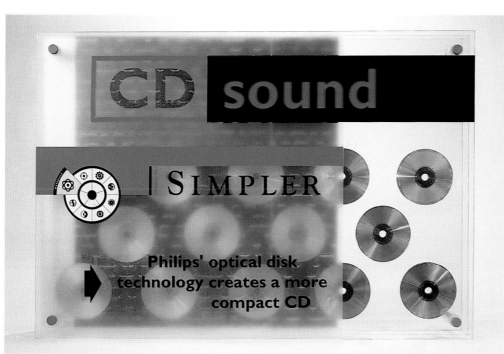

5.

1.

2.

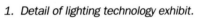

1. Detail of lighting technology exhibit.
2. Exhibit panel detail showing multiple surface design approach.
3. System of video panels.
4. Exhibit panel detail.
5. Communications technology exhibit features touchscreen monitor.
6. Detail of touchscreen interface, an emerging design discipline.

3.

4.

5.

6.

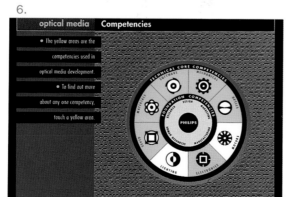

Project Facts

The two year project for Philips involved 15 designers. The scope of work extended to the corporate visitor's center's planning and design, concept development and master plan as well as design of interiors and exhibits.

Technical Information

The design palette was simplified to a few materials with a neutral but technical base: steel and bead-blasted aluminum, etched and clear glass. Structural materials are used for armatures that can house a large amount of electromechanical devices. Color comes from the graphics and a continuous, glowing light wall that extends around the perimeter of each of three "rings." Illumination comes from a 12 volt suspended lighting system developed by the designers.

Design Details

Designers took a layered approach to information, beginning with a 10 minute film supplied by computer programs, headline and copy, and diagrammatic graphics. Graphic colors are coordinated with a colored light wall that expands the windowless space visually and provides the subliminal message that lighting is at the core of Philips' identity — the company began at the turn of the century as a light bulb manufacturer. Central to the exhibit vocabulary is the structural "armature" used throughout the Centre. These support the computer stations, interactive exhibits and graphics illustrating each product innovation. In addition to the armatures, "monoliths" and other large cases were also developed, as were theater enclosures for the orientation film and for films located throughout the upper rings.

Credits

Design Firm: The Burdick Group, San Francisco, CA
Design Team: Bruce and Susan K. Burdick, Design Directors; Bruce Lightbody, Associate, Project Director; Jon Betthauser, Senior Designer, Technology Integration; Aaron Caplan, Johnson Chow, Jerome Goh, Cameron Imani, Mark Jones, Carolyn Morton, Christoph Oppermann, William Smock, Cindy Steinberg, Pino Trogu, Jeff Walker, Steve Wiersema
Fabricators: Carlton Benbow Contracts Ltd., Devon, England; Gielissen BV, Eindhoven, The Netherlands

Bowman Design
EMF EDUCATION CENTER

An interactive facility for exploring
complex public health issues

In response to public concern about the possible effects of electromagnetic fields, or EMF, Southern California Edison dedicated a 1,200 square foot seminar and classroom facility to the issue. Working with input from a wide variety of science and health consultants, designers developed exhibits to present basic information and stimulate discussion. Despite a committee approval process and strict local Title 24 fire and electrical codes, designers nonetheless met a fixed opening date.

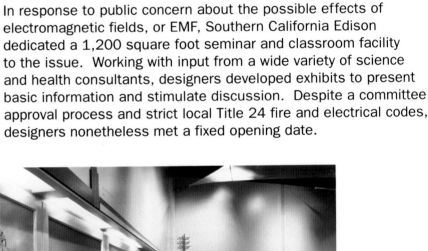

1.

2.

1. Dramatic lighting highlights built in display case.
2. + 4. Display surrounds classroom setup.
3. Pushbuttons allow visitors to interact with display.
5. - 6. Understated written narrative supports hands on exhibitry.

3.

4.

5.

6.

Project Facts

Two designers worked an estimated 2,000 hours on the nine month project for Southern California Edison Company. Their involvement was part of an extensive team effort to identify content and integrate the facility. In addition to these responsibilities, the assignment included mechanical engineering, text writing, and project management.

Technical Information

Class A birch ply construction, painted finishes, color core laminates, aluminum components and a nylon mesh interior ceiling were specified. Walls were built as oversized units to minimize panel seams. All interactive mechanisms were custom designed. Coherent, overall graphics are permanent. Lighting scenes are computer-controlled.

Design Details

Design had to promote a non-hierarchical discussion and exploration of complex issues with a potentially apprehensive audience, and to impart credibility and integrity. Exhibits needed to provide fundamental information to stimulate discussion and debate. All demonstrated phenomena are real, not simulated. Nylon ceiling "wings" suggest a blending of science and aesthetics.

Credits

Design Firm: Bowman Design, Los Angeles, CA
Design Team: Tom Bowman, Principal; Alison Goodman (graphic design), Dexter Powell and Herb Bentley (drafting)
Architect: Criterion Associates, Costa Mesa, CA
Fabricator: Grondorf-Field-Black & Company, Irvine, CA; The New Curiosity Shop, Mountain View, CA (electronic components)
Special Consultants: American Video (audiovisual and lighting system); Los Angeles and San Diego County Offices of Education (content and curriculum)

Jack Biesek is president of Biesek Design, a California-based environmental graphic design firm that has pioneered the use of computers for all aspects of EGD work including planning, designing, and project management. Mr. Biesek is a member of the board of directors of the Society for Environmental Graphic Design and served as president of the organization in 1990-91.

JACK BIESEK

The New Environmental
Graphic Design Document

Environmental graphic design consists of many layers of simple ideas that combine to create a complex fabric of information. Consider the hundreds of signs of differing sizes, shapes and configurations that comprise many projects and you begin to understand why this type of work requires careful organization and attention to detail.

Like most other designers, I now use computers to simplify and manage tasks. The benefits are so obvious that debating their merits is by now a non-issue. Computers enable us to deal with many different kinds of data — words, drawings, and mathematical representations — simultaneously. We can now manipulate images in hitherto unimaginable ways, customize type-faces in a few hours' time, and complete production work with unprecedented speed. Computerization has another important though often overlooked impli-cation: The work of many individuals can now be combined into one unified, seamless presentation (i.e., the process doesn't show who contributed what, or where specific efforts started and stopped). The finished document makes a pow-erful statement about professional design skills and the synergy of collaboration.

MOVING BEYOND ESTABLISHED CONVENTIONS

For all their importance in communicating ideas, design drawings generally have not been the focus of much critical review or creative insight, nor have the enhanced production capabilities of new hardware and software been fully applied to them. By and large, environmental graphic designers have been content to inherit from architects the conventional format of blue-prints. Given the affinities between the two professions, this is understandable. But as environmental graphic design continues to develop along somewhat independent lines, designers are turning to new formats. Are blueprints always the best way to use two-dimensional means to communicate three-dimensional concepts? I, for one, have always felt intimidated by them, and I know that my sentiments are shared by many clients. Additionally, the large-format sheets are cumbersome to format, store and retrieve. As a result, I now use advanced graphic design production tools to develop customized documents. Not only do clients find these more compelling and easy to read, but they can be used to help suggest an assignment's overall visual direction, and they can further the consistent image of my own communications.

During computerization's "transitional period" in the mid-1980's, I used a hybrid approach combining an Apple Macintosh Plus computer with conventional cut-and-paste techniques to generate my first 8 1/2-by-11 inch design documents. Since that time, the 8 1/2-by-11 inch booklet (as well as 8 1/2-by-14 inch and 11-by-17 inchs formats) has remained the standard of our office. It is concise and convenient (whether for faxes or overnight mes-senger), easy to lay out, easy to use for presentations, and significantly easier to produce (in-house versus at a service bureau). In effect, design and presentation began to merge into one inseparable process.

Corporate identity manuals provided additional inspiration. For clari-ty and proficiency, they served as excellent models. Documents influenced by their look and feel proved accessible to client, project architect, contractor and fabricator alike. Moreover, they pointed a way to making a statement about the level of a project's integrity vis-á-vis the supporting documentation.

THE NEED FOR SOUND DATA MANAGEMENT

Organizing information for environmental graphic design naturally lends itself to computerization: The process is highly detailed, and design criteria usually require periodic modification. In early stages especially, the many elements of an environmental graphics program remain in flux. Designing, tracking and managing several hundred or several thousand signs in a large sign program is not uncommon. Detailing what signs will say (via a graphics schedule) and where signs will be installed (via sign location maps) as well as call-outs for colors, materials and fabrication techniques (via construction detail drawings) is a part of every project.

With respect to design documents, computers offer significant man-agement as well as visual advantages. Data can be much more readily built into design criteria. It becomes the designer's responsibility, however, to learn to organize projects and manage data accordingly. The Society for Environmental Graphic Design (Cambridge, MA) offers a "process guide" that outlines a project planning framework. It is a good place to start for ideas that can be applied to managing the several file cabinets' worth of information stored in your computer.

EQUIPMENT AND SKILLS: THE RIGHT STUFF.

At the risk of sounding dated all too soon in an environment where technology changes quickly, I'd like to outline the computer tools a graphic designer currently needs to complete a typical assignment in today's competi-tive environment. Certain activities require specialized tools, but generally an adequate setup currently means a computer with 16 megabytes of RAM and 200 megabytes of memory augmented by a large color monitor. Unless you have a penchant for pioneering (and significant financial resources,) it is wise to stay away from experimental technology. Wait for equipment to enter the mainstream to discern between what's leading edge and what's *bleeding edge*.

Design and drawing skills remain imperative, though with a computer the distinction between these tasks can begin to become blurred. Adobe Illustrator, Aldus Freehand and other drawing programs are good for developing concepts and refining ideas. They have good typographic controls and export files to Adobe Photoshop (a good program for creating a

48 pt ABCDEFGH
PQRSTUVW
efghijklm
xyz0123456

48 pt type for non-ADA copy
on doors signs (types A, A.1).

5/8"
65 pt ABCD

5/8 inch caps as required by ADA
for tactile copy on door signs (types A, A.1, A.2).

1"
103 pt ABC

1 inch caps as required by Title 19
for stairwell code signs (type H).

PCC Optima Medium is a customized version of the Adobe Optima
typeface. The weight has been increased to optimize the effectiveness
of the typeface for signing purposes. This font has been altered
electronically and is available in Macintosh format from the designer.

simulation of a sign drawing combined with a photograph). For technically-oriented designers, StrataVision 3D and other 3D modeling programs allow the creation of three-dimensional shapes that can be viewed from any perspective. These programs include tools for lighting as well as surface finish, mapping and reflectance. Another frontier for designers includes working in architectural CAD (computer-aided design) programs and data file exchanges that allow designers to import files such as floor plans and elevations from clients and architects.

WHERE IS THE DIGITAL HIGHWAY TAKING US?

It's entirely possible that multimedia will influence the look of presentation and design documents radically; the widespread use of multimedia by environmental graphic designers, to say nothing of the business community in general, remains at least a few years away. How their potential for interactivity will affect the design process remains to be seen.

Multimedia notwithstanding, computers have currently reached something of a technological plateau. Innovations have slowed considerably. No budding technologies are in the works of a scale comparable to that of bringing mainframe computing power to the PC format. Still, we can expect our computer systems to become much quicker (more horsepower) and more specialized (design workstations). The digital highway (i.e., information via your telephone line) is being built right now, and computers will be able to access information from around the world with increasing speed. Sophisticated computer systems offering ten to fifty times the power of the most powerful Macintosh Quadra are also on the horizon, and with them an entire new group of programs — few of them compatible with existing systems — to master. With high-powered equipment, design may become highly compartmentalized.

Design of information is changing rapidly and environmental graphic design will tie in more and more with other forms of marketing and information services. Designers can help this process evolve by encouraging a spirit of collaboration with other design professionals (architects, industrial designers, marketing specialists, etc.) and educating friends and clients about how good design helps everyone. With the design process extended to the presentation document, the medium becomes the message: Not only does our documentation clearly communicate our design intent, but it becomes a tangible representation of good design in itself: easy to read, produce and manipulate, an unambiguous and attractive tool for communication.

Dining Environments

Orchestrated spaces shape the enjoyment of meals.

The Graphics Studio
THE BURGER THAT ATE L.A.

Upholding a quirky architectural tradition

The Brown Derby is gone. The Big Red Piano is gone. The Mile-High Cone is gone. Even as the fantasy architecture of Los Angeles was mostly memory, the Burger That Ate L.A. arrived to uphold an old tradition and capture the wacky, innocent spirit of an earlier time. Exterior graphics literally enact the restaurant's name: A giant hamburger appears to have taken a bite out of a stylized city hall.

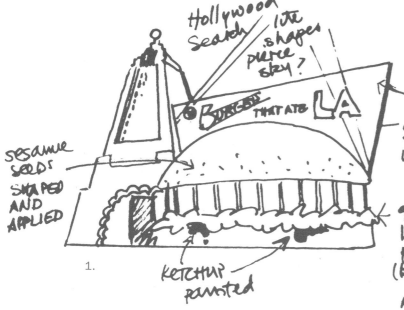

Hollywood Search lite shapes pierce sky?

BURGER THAT ATE LA

sesame seeds shaped and applied

ketchup painted

GOOGIE STYLE WALL

green leafy plant (birds nest fern) or lettuce

1.

1. Concept sketch.
2. Restaurant exterior.
3. Interior with 30 foot tomato slice ceiling.
4. Signature illustration.
5. Detail of entrance showing "Burger's Bite".

2.

3.

counter
seats
pickle
green
vinyl

4.

7624 MELROSE AVENUE
LOS ANGELES

5.

Project Facts

The designer spent 20 to 30 hours over a six week period on the assignment for restaurateur David Alderman. Design budget was $7,500; implementation budget, $18,000. The scope of work included exterior and interior graphics, interiors consulting, and a complete printed graphics program for the restaurant's launch.

Technical Information

Large scale interior and exterior graphics are paint and plaster. Signs are silkscreened aluminum. The exterior sign is floodlit from above and illuminated from below by uplights concealed in the shrubbery. Entry sign is 12 x 18 inches. The giant tomato slice above the counter is 30 feet in diameter.

Design Details

The client wanted the restaurant to exemplify the city's rich tradition of programmatic architecture. Beyond that, the designer found inspiration for the primary colors and bold typography of the hand lettered identity signs in an old bullfight poster.

Credits

Design Firm: The Graphics Studio, Los Angeles, CA
Designer: Gerry Rosentswieg
Architect: Solberg and Lowe, AIA, Santa Monica, CA
Fabricator: Merit Sign Company, Sun Valley, CA
Other Collaborators: Charles White III, Los Angeles, CA (signature illustration)
Photo Credit: Ferguson Kirchner, Newport Beach, CA

Debra Nichols Design
BAYSIDE CUISINES AT ONE MARKET

A food court expands on an architect's themes

The facade of a classical European arcade inspired the new design for a 10,000 square foot food court in San Francisco, CA, the first phase in a 1.5 million square foot renovation. Architect Cesar Pelli added grilles and lattice structures to a building with almost no architectural inspiration to expand upon; Nichols extended his theme of linear bars and grilles. All elements, from the logo through the signage for office towers and retail, are based on transparency and the patterns achieved in the layering of perforated metals, glass and metal leaf. For the food court, designers developed food sculptures as a counterpoint to the vocabulary of linear bars used in the logo. Averaging five feet across, the abstract sculptures are fabricated of rolled metals. Designed entirely in model form in paper, they were fabricated directly from the models. To create interesting clusters of food imagery, the sculptures were subsequently arranged by hand. The team worked with tenants to incorporate food elements and perforated metal forms in their signage.

PAINTED ALUM. SUPPORT TUBES COLOR C-1 CAPPED ENDS

PAINTED PERFORATED METAL PANEL COLOR C-4 BOTH SIDES & ALL EDGES

PAINTED ALUM. HORIZONTAL SUPPORTS COLOR C-2

PAINTED STEEL BRACKET COLOR C-2

2" OVERLAP OF "CUISINE" BEYOND HERE.

SEE DETAIL FOR TYPOGRAPHIC DIMENSIONS

"CUISINE" FABRICATED HOLLOW METAL LETTERS PAINTED FACE, SIDES & INTERIOR. COLOR C-5

"BAYSIDE" FABRICATED HOLLOW METAL LETTERS PAINTED FACE, SIDES & INTERIOR. COLOR C-6

· ARTWORK FOR TYPOGRAPHIC LAYOUT TO BE SUPPLIED BY OWNER
· FIELD VERIFY DIMENSIONS FOR ALIGNMENT W/JOINTS SUPPORTS COLOR C-3

ALIGN W/JOINT

① ELEVATION - SIGN TYPE "A"
1/2" = 1'-0"

1.

2.

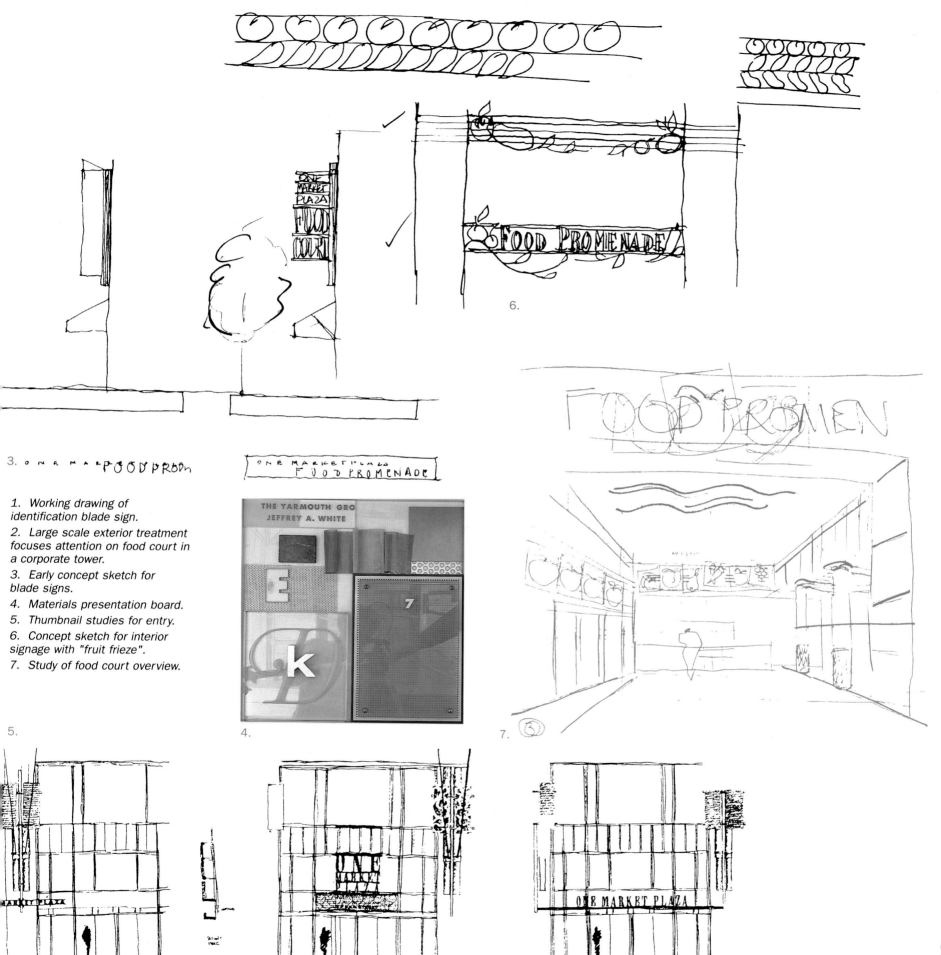

3. ONE MAI FOOD PROM

1. Working drawing of identification blade sign.

2. Large scale exterior treatment focuses attention on food court in a corporate tower.

3. Early concept sketch for blade signs.

4. Materials presentation board.

5. Thumbnail studies for entry.

6. Concept sketch for interior signage with "fruit frieze".

7. Study of food court overview.

5.

4.

7.

3.

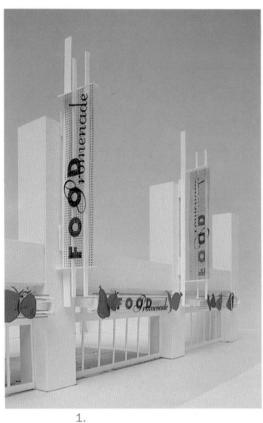

1.

4.

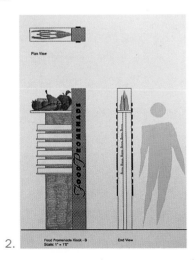

5.

1. Presentation model of
exterior signs.

2. Presentation board of directory.

3. Exterior sign.

4. Interior food court identity
incorporates rolled and overscaled
metal food sculptures.

5. Detail of sculpture.

6. Model showing decorative
food treatment.

7. Actual wall sculpture.

8. Early study model for sculpture
tomato forms.

2.

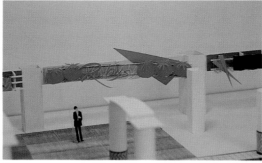

6.

7.

8.

Project Facts

The project for owners One Market Building Ownership, The Yarmouth Group, and CB Commercial Real Estate Group involved three designers over a nine month period. Implementation budget was $150,000. Scope of work included logo design, all signage elements related to entries such as canopy design, street-scaled vertical signs, tenant directory, retail tenant guidelines and retail tenant signs.

Technical Information

Metallic paints, perforated aluminum, steel tubes, and laminated glass were specified; signs were sandblasted, rolled, and constructed. The fabricator made the rolled food sculptures by studying the designers' models; there were no working drawings that could convey dimensionality. Vertical 30 foot exterior blade signs were also structurally challenging. Food sculptures measure five feet in diameter on 30 foot wide canopy signs. They are illuminated by ambient light.

Design Details

The graphics program extends the spirit of the architecture while also offering a counterpoint to it: Graphics extend the architect's concept of additive grilles and sculpture against which designers have placed volumetric, sculptural forms on some signs — treating sculpture as logos against linear architectural elements. Layering and transparency were also a part of the design approach. To emulate certain combinations of architectural features, designers used an elongated serif typeface juxtaposed against or layered under bold, chunky type.

Credits

Design Firm: Debra Nichols Design, San Francisco, CA
Design Team: Debra Nichols, Design Director; Roxanne Malek, Lori Powell, Designers
Architect: Cesar Pelli & Associates, New Haven, CT
Fabricators: Arrow Sign Company, Oakland, CA; Martinelli Environmental Graphics, San Francisco, CA

THARP DID IT
BLACKHAWK GRILL

Celebrating the classic automobile

The Blackhawk Grill features a different classic automobile in the bar each month. In developing a visual identity for this singular Danville, CA restaurant, designers worked as an integral part of the interior and architectural team. Their challenge was to develop an identity that would be distinctive yet at the same time compatible with other, differently themed restaurants owned by the same group. The "BG" logo, reminiscent of the Rolls Royce ligature, is actually a stylized interpretation of a hawk.

1.

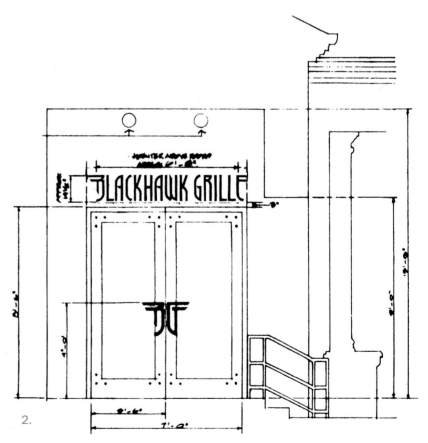

2.

1. Restaurant entrance.
2. Working drawing of entry doors and detail of logo handles.
3. Host station.
4. Flexible wine menu can be altered as needed.
5. Vintage hubcaps serve as mood lighting sconces.

Project Facts

A team consisting of three interior designers, two architects and four graphic designers spent three months on the California Cafe Restaurant Corporation (San Francisco, CA) project. Scope of work included identity, signage, and architectural detailing. Graphic design budget was $8,500.

Technical Information

Door handles are powder coated aluminum; the wine by the glass board is constructed of galvanized aluminum with magnetic strips that can be cleaned and reused. Interior designers created wall sconces from old hubcaps. The ligature was to have been sandblasted on the hubcap, but Tharp opted to have it cut from a piece of vinyl that looks like brushed aluminum. The host station, co-designed by Tharp Did It and the interior design firm, is constructed of wood and a back lit curved aluminum plate that was pegged from the surface, allowing internal lighting to create a halo effect.

Design Details

The interior design firm selected materials that subtly referred to the automotive technology of a bygone era. Graphic designers followed this precedent, combining eclectic design elements with deco styled graphics and hand drawn logotype and ligature. Printed graphics such as menus, wine labels and stationery employ a photographic texture of the restaurant's exterior walls.

Credits

Design Firm: THARP DID IT, San Francisco, CA and Portland, OR
Design Team: Rick Tharp, Design Director; Jana Heer, Jean Mogannam, Kim Tomlinson, Designers
Interiors: Engstrom & Hofling, San Rafael, CA
Fabricator: Eclipse, Point Richmond, CA

3.

4.

5.

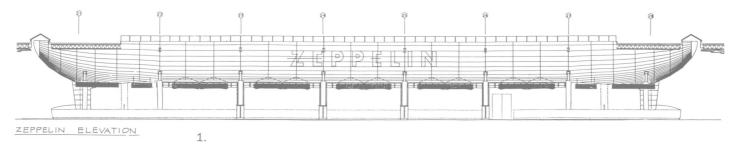

ZEPPELIN ELEVATION

1.

Sussman/Prejza & Co.
THE ZEPPELIN

An unusual metaphor helps a food court lift off

The site of a former airship field is also the location of Roosevelt Field, New York's first shopping center. Appropriately, Sussman/Prejza's architectural design and identity for the renovated center's new 29,000 square foot food court refers to the location's past. The food court is organized around the metaphor of a zeppelin airship. An oval measuring 200 x 60 feet, it doesn't fit traditionally into the surrounding retail space. Instead, it fights the edges of the space as if it has landed at a loading dock.

While getting past overused "food market" or "market-place" metaphors typical of food courts, the design also offers a practical solution to the food court's challenging racetrack (as opposed to u-shaped) layout. In effect, the zeppelin enables the food court to serve as the mall's central focal point.

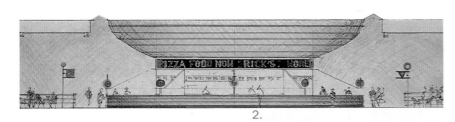

2.

1. Architects elevation of food court structure.

2. Presentation board shows relationship of canopy to food court tenants.

3. Logotype study.

4. Canopy is structural steel with an aluminum skin.

5. Food court acts as reference point in shopping mall.

6. Presentation board detailing zeppelins nose.

7. Food court overview shows unique race track shape.

8. Color and structural detail.

3.

4.

5.

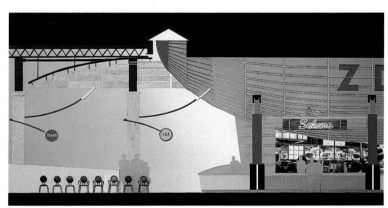

6.

7.

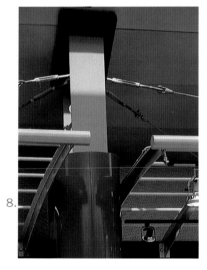

8.

Project Facts

A team of five designers worked some 1,500 hours over an 18 month period on the assignment for Corporate Property Investors (New York, NY). Implementation budget for the zeppelin skin and tenant canopies was $950,000. Design budget was $130,000. Overall scope of work for Roosevelt Field included interior color, food court architectural design, and project signage.

Technical Information

Designers specified structural steel, stainless steel cables, architectural perforated and anodized aluminum, and a ceramic tile floor. All components were prefabricated and assembled on site. Their dimensions were determined by computer model. The fabricator is based in California; installation took place in New York. Every panel at the ends of the zeppelin is different, for a total of 400 different shapes and sizes. Continuous metal panels are 8 x 2 feet. The structure is illuminated by daylight from within and outside, and at night by neon and halogen lighting.

Design Details

The food court's unusual, racetrack shaped layout as well as limited control of tenant storefront design guided the project. An aesthetic of "minimalist gigantism" juxtaposed against typical repetitive elements of mall architecture creates an unexpected change of scale and level of reference.

Credits

Design Firm: Sussman/Prejza & Co., Inc., Culver City, CA
Design Team: Fernando Vazquez, Associate in Charge, Design Director; John Johnston, Roseline Seng, Traer Price, Chuck Milhaupt, Ena Dubnoff
Architect: Sussman/Prejza, Design Architect (Zeppelin); Marty Dorf & Associates, Los Angeles, CA, Architect of Record (Zeppelin); RTKL & Associates, Baltimore, MD (Roosevelt Field Renovation)
Fabricator: Peter Carlson Enterprises, Studio City, CA
Other Collaborators: Theo Kondos & Associates, New York, NY (lighting design) ; Charles Pankow Builders Ltd., Garden City, NY (general contractor)

Communication Arts
WIZARDZ

A magical experience that you can see, drink, eat and buy

Wizardz is a 200 seat dinner theater themed around magic. Challenged to develop a "never seen before" experience in Los Angeles for a budget of $150 per square foot, designers decided to take the Wizardz name into "the greatest unknown" — the universe and the galaxies. Neon in the ceiling shows the orbits of the planets. A spiraling wizard's cap with stars and moons towers above the bar. Crackling neon that seems to hold up the canopy of the bar creates a lightning effect. Starlight patterns enhance the walls and ceilings. Magic wands, mirrors, and visual illusions create an unexpected and thrilling recreational environment. The bar/lounge becomes a focal point, crowning the street at CityWalk, Universal Studios' newest attraction.

1.

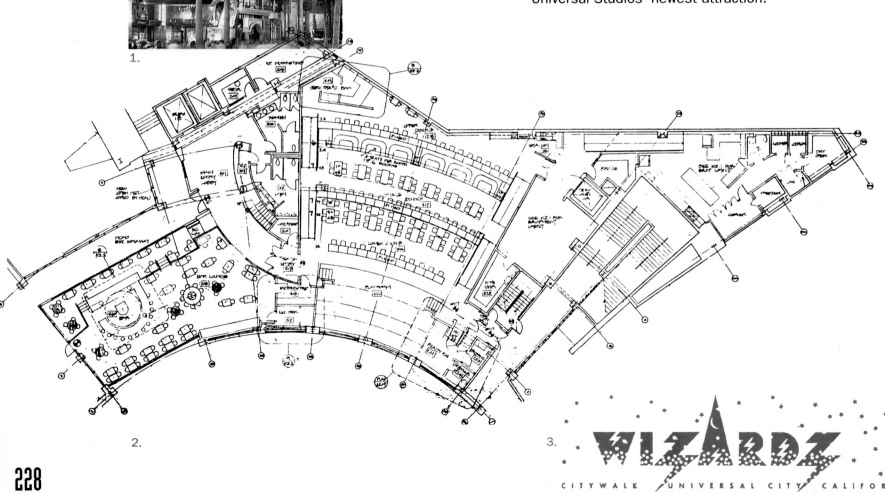

2.

3.

WIZARDZ
CITYWALK / UNIVERSAL CITY / CALIFORNIA

4.

Project Facts

A five person team worked approximately 4,500 hours over a 16 month period for Giles Enterprises. Overall project budget was $3.3 million, of which $2.2. million was implementation and $600,000 was design. (Additional funds went to special effects.) Scope of work for the theater, restaurant, bar, lounge and gift shop included all interior space allocation, circulation, finishes, fixtures and furnishings, graphics, logos and signage.

Technical Information

Materials included glass, metal, wood, plaster, carpet, neon, plastics, vinyl, resin, mylar, day glow paint and fabrics. Bent metal and glass elements have multi color faces and cut out celestial shapes. Plastics and glass are edge lit. Fabrication techniques included metal shaping, glass blowing and large scale air blasting. Fabricators in several locations throughout the U.S. worked with very tight budgets and tight schedules. Many items were built directly from conceptual three dimensional sketches. Elements range in size from 1/8 inch square to 20 feet. Varied lighting includes neon, fluorescent, internal, external low voltage theater, sequential, choreographed and more.

Design Details

To attract visitors up 20 feet off the street, designers sought to provide a mysterious, magical experience within the context of the hard to impress Los Angeles marketplace. The Wizardz cone cap, crackling neon and proscenium lightning bolts are unusual highlights of the experience.

Credits

Design Firm: Communication Arts Inc., Boulder, CO
Design Team: Richard Foy, Design Director; Mike Doyle, Lydia Young, Todd Cail, John Ward, Paul Mack
Architect: Ray Hirata Architects, Venice, CA
Fabricators: BTS Construction, San Diego, CA; Sheet Metal Fabrications, Salt Lake City, UT; Wesnic, Jacksonville, FL; Rainbow Sign, Boulder, CO; Benjamin Brothers, Boulder, CO; Alger Lighting, Los Angeles, CA; Pacific Westline, Los Angeles, CA
Other Collaborators: Patti Giles, Robert Hanover
Photo Credit: Grey Crawford, South Pasadena, CA

5.

6.

1. High impact restaurant exterior competes favorably with other attractions.
2. Second level plan showing 200 seat dinner theatre.
3. Project logo.
4. Elaborate flashing neon ceiling enlivens lounge area.
5. Proscenium lightning bolts are a dramatic part of the lighting scheme.
6. Magic motif extends to mosaic tile treatment in restrooms.

David Carter Design Associates
ANZU

Fusing East and West, old and new

Anzu represents the first real attempt at introducing "Pacific Rim" cuisine to the Dallas area. For the 3,011 square foot Japanese restaurant, owners wanted "a very sophisticated image on a shoestring budget." In addition, designers needed to create a look and feel that would attract a broad range of diners.

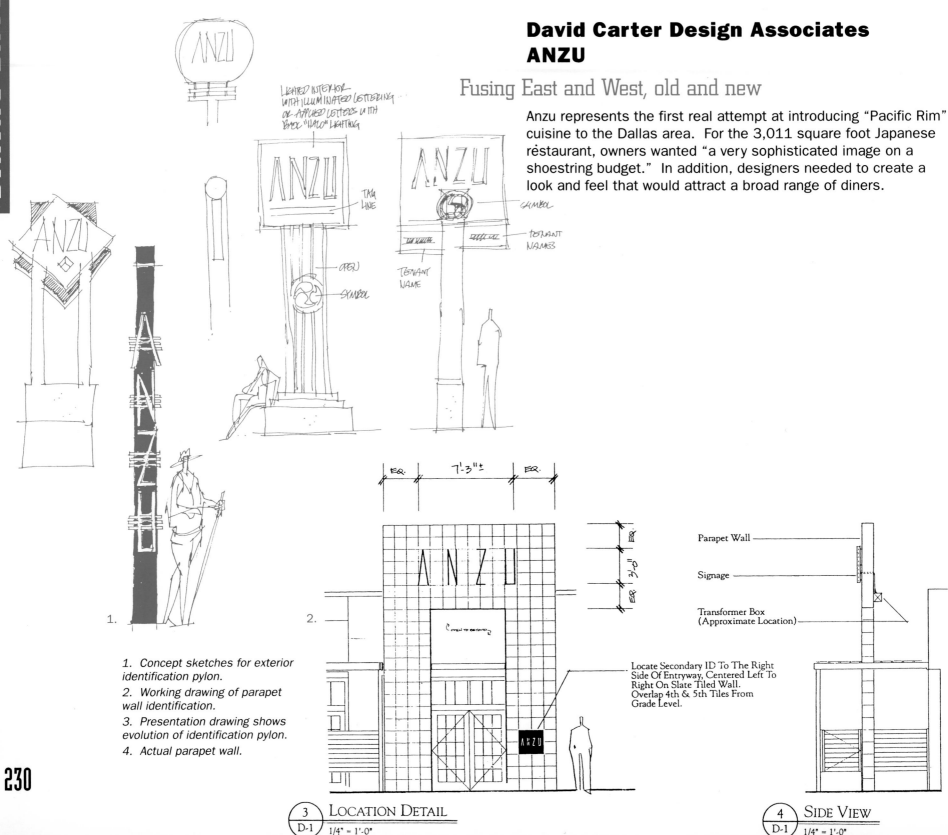

1. Concept sketches for exterior identification pylon.

2. Working drawing of parapet wall identification.

3. Presentation drawing shows evolution of identification pylon.

4. Actual parapet wall.

Locate Secondary ID To The Right Side Of Entryway, Centered Left To Right On Slate Tiled Wall. Overlap 4th & 5th Tiles From Grade Level.

Parapet Wall

Signage

Transformer Box (Approximate Location)

3 LOCATION DETAIL
D-1 1/4" = 1'-0"

4 SIDE VIEW
D-1 1/4" = 1'-0"

3.

4.

Project Facts

The Nakamoto Restaurants, Inc. assignment involved four designers working on and off over a three month period. Scope of work included identity, logo, exterior signage (pylon and two building identities), menu and related print and collateral.

Technical Information

Aluminum reverse channel letters with gold leaf faces and returns are mounted to the projecting monolithic wall. Each three foot letter is individually halo illuminated with white neon tubing. Eye level, two foot square entry plaque consists of a smooth, natural wood panel with raised metal letters incised into it.

Design Details

Simplicity and budget were guiding factors; signage needed to convey a harmonious environment. Special typography was used in designing the logo. Colors and materials were chosen to communicate a warm, old yet new, sophisticated image. As the vertical wall added to the entrance was not technically attached to the building, it violated the city's sign ordinance. In a subsequent meeting with a city inspector, representatives of the client and project team successfully argued its case.

Credits

Design Firm: David Carter Design, Dallas, TX
Design Team: Lori Wilson, Design Director; Stephen Papathopoulos, Sharon LeJeune, Lynn Pendergrass, Jim Rucker.
Architect: Paul Draper & Associates, Dallas, TX
Fabricators: Industrial Design, Inc., Dallas, TX

1.

Susan Roberts: Art, Color, Design
THE SALAD BOWL

Oversized bowls and murals brighten an eating area

The Salad Bowl is a 4,000 square foot fast food restaurant in New York City whose name and identity are reflected in oversized bowls and fruit shapes reminiscent of French pottery and Matisse cutouts. The painted bowls transform a long, narrow, windowless eating area into an indoor courtyard, giving the maximum impact for a low budget, drywall and paint project.   The designer needed to visualize and paint on curved surfaces, and, in response to budget restrictions and opening deadlines, to design murals that she could paint in less than two weeks with the help of one assistant.

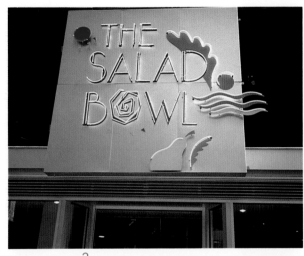

2.

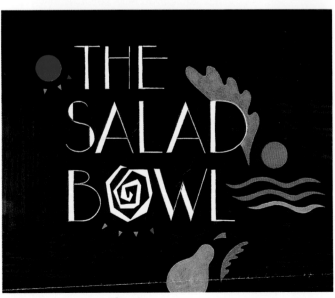

3.

4.

1. Overview of restaurant.
2. Neon identification.
3. Early study for street signage.
4. Detail showing super-scaled salad bowl.
5. Salad bowl size makes small scale space seem larger.
6. Surreal sculptures play mind trips with scale.
7. Matisse inspired patterns brighten a windowless interior.

5.

6.

7.

Project Facts

The designer's client was the architect, with whom she collaborated on the six month project for owner Orhan Ayhan. The assignment consisted of designing an identity for the restaurant and applying it to a neon sign, menu and murals; and selecting the restaurant color palette.

Technical Information

Fiberglass was originally specified for the bowls, but the fabricator could not deliver on time, so the order was cancelled. The architect and construction crew built the bowls with metal ribs like a boat. Thin strips of drywall were bolted to the ribs to form the curving shapes and then spackled to cover joints. This solution allowed the construction crew to continue on schedule. The exterior sign is 10 feet square. Bowls measure approximately 10 feet high and 24 feet around. Concealed halogen light sources accentuate the sculpture and define the courtyard walls.

Design Details

Architectural color selections for walls, ceiling, floor, ceramic tile, banquette upholstery and other elements required coordination and constant refinement as the availability of materials and other aspects of the project changed — "a complicated and time consuming part of this job." The bowls are fanciful and dramatize scale. A false perspective was created by making the blue bowl at the rear of the eating area smaller and less brightly colored than the yellow bowl up front; the rear bowl recedes to make the space seem longer than it really is. The restaurant opening coincided with a Matisse exhibition at the Museum of Modern Art, as customers admiring the Matisse like murals would have been pleased to note.

Credits

Design Firm: Susan Roberts: Art, Color, Design, Athens, GA
Design Team: Hugh Boyd, Boyd Associates, Montclair, NJ, Design Director; Susan Roberts, Graphic Designers/Muralist/Colorist
Architect: Hugh Boyd, Boyd Associates, Montclair, NJ
Fabricators: Hamilton Woodworking, Blairstown, NJ; Commercial Stainless, Bloomsburg, PA; The Lighting Practice, Philadelphia, PA
Other Collaborator: Alfred De La Houssaye, New York, NY (pear sculpture)
Photo Credit: Dub Rogers

Lance Wyman is the principal of
Lance Wyman Ltd. in New York.
He has taught at the Parsons
School of Design in New York
for the past 20 years and was
founding President of the SEGD
Education Foundation

LANCE WYMAN

Multicultural Environmental Graphic Design

We commonly think of culture as the cumulative activities and achievements of any given period or group of people, including their tools, crafts, agriculture, economics, arts, religious beliefs, traditions, language and history.

A *multicultural* environment is one that mixes two or more cultures. It can be an event such as the Olympics, an international airport, or a city where residents, workers and visitors come from different ethnic backgrounds. For a graphic designer, devising ways to communicate effectively in a multicultural environment is always a challenge. Different traditions, languages and histories can get in the way. They can also show the way. One characteristic common to all multicultural systems is that "icons" can be used to cross over language barriers and, in many cases, to enforce a sense of place or culture.

USER-FRIENDLY ICONS

I use the term *icon* rather than *pictograph*, *pictogram* or *symbol* because it was icons, a term made popular by the Apple Macintosh, that contributed so much to making the computer "user friendly." Icons are not new — you find them in cave paintings no less than on computer screens — and we are still learning how to design and use them. Whatever they're called, however, the principal remains the same: We live in a world of familiar objects and activities that can be pictorially referenced (icon) as well as more abstractly referenced (word), and when a situation warrants, icons can help make communication simple, direct and multilingual (user-friendly.)

AN EARLY INSTANCE OF MULTICULTURAL DESIGN

For the 1962 International Trade Exposition in Zagreb, Yugoslavia (now Croatia), the United States Department of Commerce sponsored an exhibition of American products for leisure time ranging from cosmetics to camping gear. What was needed was an effective communicator where different languages were spoken -- in other words, a symbol that was not tied to any particular alphabet or language, universal enough to be understood by an international audience.

As the project designer, I developed an icon of an hourglass (representing time), containing a sun and moon (suggesting day and nighttime activities) in a way to make *time* an important focus of the exhibition.

The icon was applied not only as a flat image; it became the basis for a number of site structures including a 50 foot entrance gateway and a modular fence around the exhibit, and pointed to an important direction in my own future work integrating visual communication as an integral part of the three dimensional environment.

The hourglass icon wasn't formally tested to determine how well it communicated; I relied more on a process of combining what seemed obvious images and relying on feedback from the client as to their appropiateness.

Testing visual icons, especially those intended for multicultural environments, is very complicated. Feelings and emotions are involved as well as rationality, and these make objective evaluation extremely difficult. A good icon evaluation would have to establish criteria to determine appropriateness of visual content (familiarity vs. time required to learn and retain), comprehension (legibility based on content and style), taste (a respectable image). To date, I suspect we rely on an informal selection process and common sense.

MEXICO '68

I first went to Mexico in 1966 when invited to compete in an international competition to design the graphics for the upcoming summer Olympic games. Not speaking Spanish or knowing much about Mexico, I was in for a cultural shock. A crash course in Mexican culture was necessary. It consisted of visits to the Museum of Anthropology and the markets and streets of Mexico City as well as talking to the writers and architects who had started work on the project, and going through the photo archives of the Olympic publications department. The result was winning the Mexico '68 logotype and the graphics for the games. The logotype was Sixties Op Art kinetic typography generated from the five-ring Olympic symbol, which suggested imagery found in Mexican pre-Hispanic art and Mexican folk art. By expressing a sense of place and culture, it visually exclaimed the games were in Mexico and set the tone for the graphics program. Applications ranged from postage stamps to a two-ton sculptural sign.

The program also included a system of icons designed to identify the 19 sports events. The sport icons designed under the direction of Katzumie Masaru for the 1960 Tokyo Olympics were a guiding light. The Tokyo sport icons were bold stick figure images, designed with system-unifying consistency. For the Mexico icons, we chose to focus on an expressive detail, a part of the athlete's body or a piece of equipment, to develop icons similar to the glyphs found in Mexican pre-Hispanic cultures. The icons supported a sense of place and functioned as an international language on directional signs, on tickets, and in the media. They effectively eliminated the need for sport names in different translations.

Prior to Tokyo, sport events for the 1948 Olympics held in London were represented by line illustrations within shields. Sport icons, designed specifically for each Olympics, have become a tradition. The icons for the recent Barcelona games created a sense of place (Catalonia) through imagery based on the work of Joan Miró. Icons for the 1994 Winter Olympic Games in Lillehammer echoed ancient stone petroglyphs.

THE ROLE OF ICONS IN MULTICULTURAL TRANSIT SYSTEMS

Following the Olympics, I stayed in Mexico to design the graphics for the Metro, Mexico City's new rapid rail transportation system. The program includes an "M" logo to identify the Metro, color coding to identify lines, and icons to identify the Metro services and stations.

In addition to names, we identified each station with an icon that makes reference to an important nearby landmark or associated activity. Most research was accomplished by talking to the large team of engineers and architects who were designing and building the Metro. They represented the various communities throughout the city that the Metro would eventually service; their knowledge often helped in determining an appropriate image.

A grasshopper identifies Chapultepec Park Station. (Chapultepec means "Grasshopper Hill" in the ancient Nahuatl language of the Aztecs.) A remnant of the aqueduct that carried water through the city during Colonial times stands near the entrance to the Sevilla Station and is the icon for the station. A stack of apples represents Merced Market, a central marketplace of the city. A round Aztec Pyramid to the Wind, uncovered during the excavation of the Pino Suarez Station, is restored as part of the station and is used as the icon.

The icons play two important roles: First, they assist local residents, some of whom can't read, and tourists who have difficulty pronouncing and remembering station names such as Juanacatlan, Chapultepec, and Cuauhtemoc. When applied to signs and maps, the icons also become a visual reference to the history and activities that Mexico City embraces.

Here it's important to mention a key design criterion: Each icon is intended to be a familiar image, an image that can be described in any spoken language (pyramid, butterfly, grasshopper, bell, headdress, etc.) Directions such as "take this line to the *grasshopper* station" can be spoken in Spanish, English, Japánese, and so on.

After returning to New York in 1971, my first project was in Washington, D.C. in partnership with Bill Cannan (Wyman & Cannan), designing maps for the Washington Metro and complete identity/wayfinding systems for the Washington Mall and National Zoo. As a tourist capital and the seat of our Federal government, Washington is a quintessentially multicultural city, and we included icons in each of the systems. Those designed for the Washington Mall reflect some of the nation's multicultural roots and influences. The Lincoln Memorial is a structure of Greek columns, the Washington Monument is an Egyptian Obelisk, the Capitol Dome is based on the architecture of Ancient Rome, and the Smithsonian Castle echoes medieval England .

Currently, I am collaborating with Paul Arthur to design a wayfinding system for the Toronto Transit Commission (TTC.) Paul is a multicultural wayfinding pioneer, and more recently the co-author of *Wayfinding – People, Signs, and Architecture* . (McGraw-Hill Ryserson Limited, 1992)

Part of the planning is to identify TTC rapid transit stations with pictorial icons. As in Mexico City, icons are designed to be familiar images that can be said in different languages; at the same time, they reflect differences in style and cultural significance. In Toronto, for example, an Indian headdress based on the Native American cultures indigenous to Canada is used as the icon to represent the Spadina Station; in Mexico City, a Native American heáddress is used for the Moctezuma Station, but it is an Aztec configuration. The helmet used as the icon for Toronto's Museum Station is that of an English knight; a Spanish colonial helmet identifies the Cortez Station in Mexico. Just as the Mexico City Metro icons contribute to creating a sense of place and culture that is Mexico City, the TTC icons are intended to evoke Toronto.

RESPONSIBILITIES OF THE ENVIRONMENTAL GRAPHIC DESIGNER

As environmental graphic designers, it is important to keep in mind that what we contribute to streets, buildings, and public spaces has a direct effect on people's lives. I don't suggest that icons alone can accomplish everything —word messages, photo images and color-coding are some of the other forms commonly used in a visual communications system — but they *can* play a very important role, especially for a multicultural environment. They can cross communication barriers and contribute to making public spaces and events easier to understand and safer to use. They can be designed to instill an environment with the vitality of its inherent uniqueness, creating a sense of place, a sense of culture, and a sense of pride.

Tradeshow Spaces

Commercial exhibits are high-impact marketing environments.

Copeland Hirthler
Design+Communications
BASF SHOWROOM

Making a showroom part of a bigger marketing graphics picture Using neon columns, lighting and photo murals, designers found the means to rework an existing showroom on a limited budget. Existing beams, walls, and built-in shelving units remain the same, but the Neocon display now builds on the company's product introduction graphics for a consistent marketing image.

1.

1. Showroom entrance.

2. Overview of showroom color, textures and patterns refer to the product line.

3. Eccentric shaped buttresses separate product environment.

4. Corrugated plastic models are incorporated into display.

5. Marketing graphics echo showroom design vocabulary.

2.

3.

4.

5.

Project Facts

To complete the four month assignment for BASF Fibers Inc., a team of two designers worked approximately 150 staff hours.

Technical Information

Together with photo murals, neon and custom graphics, the exhibit's three dimensional models, made of corrugated plastic, were fabricated in Atlanta and installed in Chicago. Lighting conforms to building restrictions.

Design Details

Copeland Hirthler had previously established the client's current marketing and corporate image, which the showroom was also to reflect. The display concept reinforces and complements the product line, drawing attention to features, color, and performance.

Credits

Design Firm: Copeland Hirthler, Atlanta, GA
Design Team: Brad Copeland, Design Director;
Kevin Irby, Designer
Fabricator: Ideas, Atlanta, GA
Photo Mural: Meteor Photo, Atlanta, GA

Earl Gee Design
CHRONICLE BOOKS
TRADESHOW EXHIBIT

A radically different environment for the display of books

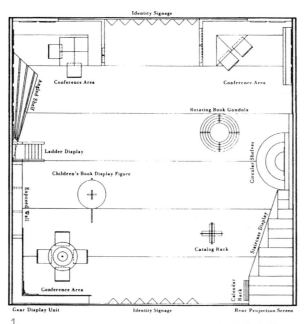

1.

A gear, ladder, staircase and standing figure serve as metaphors for work, progress, attainment and humanity in an environment unlike anything ever seen before at the annual American Booksellers Association event. Beyond conveying the publisher's vision of innovation, uniqueness, and quality, the exhibit also displays a large quantity of books in a variety of ways: self standing displays for new releases, racks for finished proofs, shelves for prototype dummies, and a spine out for backlist titles. Semi private conference areas in the 30 x 30 ft. cross aisle environment seat from two to six people.

2.

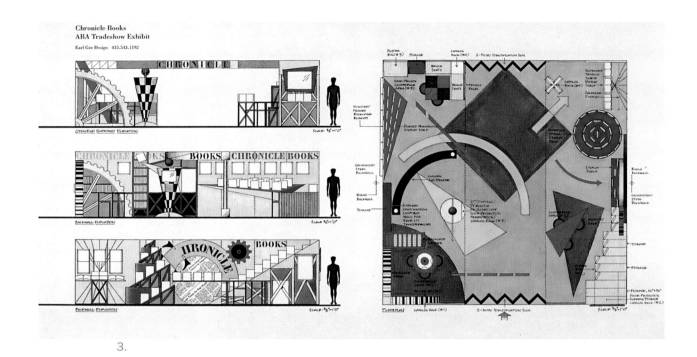

3.

1. Floorplan showing
cross-aisle plan.
2. Overview showing central
aisle entry.
3. - 4. Presentation boards
showing graphic plans of
floor, elevations and wall
graphics.
5. Presentation model.

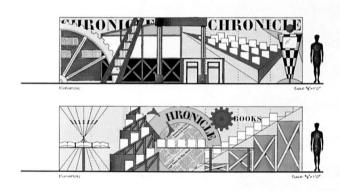

4.

5.

1.

3.

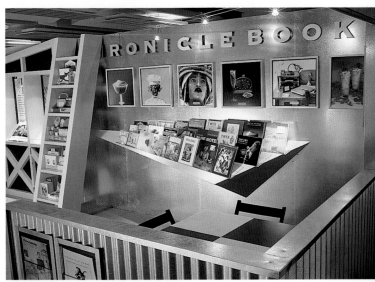

4.

2.

5.

1. Dynamic and varied display forms create an interesting approach to selling books.

2. Privacy panels create a private office space.

3. Display draws upon Russian constructivist stage designs.

4. Detail showing compound-angle wedge shelf with angled book slots.

5. Detail of display tower.

6. Detail of ladder display fixture.

7. Overview showing new corporate identity and symbol.

6.

7.

Project Facts

San Francisco based Chronicle Books is a publisher of high quality illustrated books on diverse topics. One designer completed the assignment in four months. Overall budget was $75,000: $15,000 for design and $60,000 for implementation.

Technical Information

The design specified light maple wood and galvanized steel backwall panels. Cantilevered zig-zag aluminum header signage with a 20 ft.span uses perforated steel support sections. Protruding from the back wall, a compound-angle wedge shelf has angled book slots. Display elements did not exceed 8 ft. show regulation height. Moveable high intensity halogen spotlights highlight the books and create a theatrical lighting effect.

Design Details

Working from the idea that Chronicle "sees things differently," as embodied in the company's new "reading glasses" corporate identity, the designer turned to a "Russian Constructivist stage design" aesthetic as inspiration for a highly functional environment, the ultimate "machine" for the display of books.

Credits

Design Firm: Earl Gee Design, San Francisco, CA
Designer: Earl Gee
Fabricator: Watermark/Barr Exhibits, San Rafael, CA
Collaborator: Chronicle Books, San Francisco, CA: Jack Jensen, Publisher; Drew Montgomery, Marketing Director; Michael Carabetta, Design Director

Looking
PANEL CONCEPTS SHOWROOM

Using a showroom to reposition a company's product

For a 4,000 sq. ft. showroom in Los Angeles's Pacific Design Center, designers developed a comprehensive display that is sufficiently structured to allow a visitor to experience a clear product presentation unassisted by showroom staff. Building on an existing architectural configuration, the team updated the graphics and re-used some of the existing product. At the front of the showroom, designers substituted detail prints suspended on wires for actual products, which would have been too large to display effectively. Besides contributing to a gallery effect, the prints allow important details to be highlighted.

1.

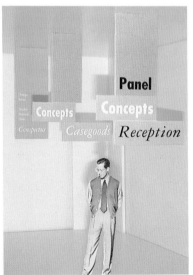

3.

4.

1. Showroom overview showing furniture with photographic details.
2. Sign installation.
3. Presentation model.
4. Seating display uses repetition as its theme.
5. Early entry identification working drawing.
6. Floor plan.
7. Tensioned cables support floating product photos.
8. Showroom design reveals a modernist aesthetic.

2.

Actual Ceiling

Bottom Edge of Occassional Beams

18.42"   25"

Panel Concepts 10.4"

2.8"

11.8"

Reception 14.2"

11.3"

7'0"   Overall Length 61.89"

5.

6.

7.

Concepts

Systems

Three.0

8.

Project Facts

A team of four designers spent 150 hours over a three month period to complete the assignment for Panel Concepts, Inc.

Technical Information

The display incorporates lightweight plastic sign panels and toned black and white photo prints on plastic laminated foamcore. Materials were silk-screened, painted, and cut. Sign installation required access to the ceiling; an unusual ceiling system of tight, maze-like compartments made installing signs difficult. Track lighting illuminates the 36 x 48 in. photo panels and 16 x 60 in. sign panels.

Design Details

The showroom coordinates with product presentation, typestyle and colors in print and advertising programs. Designers applied a modernist goal of high clarity in the presentation of product groups and individual products, each shown in prototypical context. Otherwise, they strove for aesthetic neutrality. Product names on the two-sided sign panels are visible from a distance; explanations are visible at close proximity. Sign panels are hung in easily accessible but invisible brackets.

Credits

Design Firm: Looking, Los Angeles, CA
Design Team: John Clark, Design Director; Paul Langland, Marianne Thompson, Designers
Fabricators: Jon Richards Company, Guasti, CA; Olson Color Expansions, Los Angeles, CA; Stat House, Los Angeles, CA
Other Collaborators: John Musch, Panel Concepts, Los Angeles, CA; Carla Simi, Simi Studios, Studio City

Tim Girvin Design
MICROSOFT CD ROM CONFERENCE

Illustrating the wonder of a new digital world

When Microsoft convened an international conference at the Hilton Convention Center in Anaheim, California to unveil its CD ROM technology, the company wanted to convey the fascination people experience when exposed to the possibilities of this new digital world. With event graphics as well as an extensive print collateral system, designers placed highly technical information in a playful and whimsical context.

1.

ENTRY GRAPHICS
4.

2.

3.

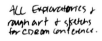

ALL Explorations & rough art & sketches for CDROM conference.

5.

MICROSOFT

1. + 3. Studies for oversized neon and plastic show icons.

2. Icons and banners enliven large auditorium.

4. Study for entry graphic.

5. Banner with show logo.

6. - 7. Design explorations and finished display kiosks.

8. Simple design themes unify disparate conference locations.

9. Larger than life plastic cutouts carry directional information.

6.

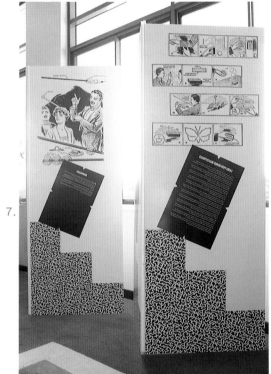

7.

8.

9.

Project Facts

Three designers and one production artist spent approximately 400 hours on the three month project for Microsoft Corporation. Scope of work included developing the identity and all print and promotional pieces for the conference as well as signage, interior and exterior banner treatments, and exhibit design.

Technical Information

Sintra compressed laminate material, ripstop nylon, neon, mylar and PVC pipe were specified. Designs were screen printed. Large PVC pipe was painted to look like an oversized magician's wand. Banners measure 10 x 18 feet; kiosks 4 x 8 feet; neon elements, 12 feet. Neon was placed on staging and spot lights were used to illuminate banners.

Design Details

In keeping with the "magic of CD ROM technology" conference theme, designers turned to "magic" as inspiration for imagery that was fun and exciting yet also elegant. Impact was enhanced by larger than life figures that were used as signage panels and the large application of neon on staging fronts. Bright colors were selected to contrast against the facility's neutral interior.

Credits

Design Firm: Tim Girvin Design, Inc., Seattle, WA
Design Team: Stephen Pannone and Tim Girvin, Design Directors; Kevin Henderson
Illustration: Anton Kimball and Tim Girvin
Fabricators: Color & Design, Seattle, WA; Turner Exhibit, Edmond, WA

Pentagram
MOHAWK TRADE SHOW DESK

A traveling trade exhibit uses simplicity to amplify an
advertising theme How does a design assignment express a theme of *not*
designing — or overdesigning — as an approach to creating form?
Architect James Biber's traveling display for Mohawk, a major
paper company, provides a succinct answer. His low budget,
short turnaround solution builds on an advertising campaign
created by Pentagram partner Michael Bierut. The campaign,
"When is Good Design No Design?" urged designers not to waste
paper on frivolous or unnecessary pieces. Amplifying this, the
exhibit designer's solution was to create a generic set of forms
required for the display — a table, chair, and lamps — to say, in
effect, "All we need is a table, a chair, and some light." The
items were then papered in the mill wrap designed by Pentagram
for the reams and rolls that Mohawk sells. The result is a
furniture ensemble that clearly says "Mohawk."

1.

2.

3.

*1. - 3. Travelling display uses
packing crate to complete exhibit.*
*4. All display elements are
papered in signature mill-wrap.*
5. Detail of "wrapped" lamp.

4.

5.

Project Facts

A team of two designers spent two months on design and fabrication of the Mohawk Paper Company project. The project will have a two-year life-span. Overall budget was $40,000, of which $15,000 was design and $25,000 was implementation.

Technical Information

Inexpensive, readily available materials were specified, in keeping with the theme of simplicity: Kraft paper, medium-density fiberboard (MDF), standard packaging crate, banner cloth, scaffolding pipe and connectors. The table measures 2 ft. 6 in. by 6 ft. A backlighted banner erected on the display's packing crate illuminates the tableau — lamps are installed inside the crate.

Design Details

The exhibit needed to be set up and broken down by one person, and to fit through all doors. In keeping with the ad campaign, the exhibit emphasized restraint, efficiency and economy of means, "undesign" - a message further dramatized by the crate, which remains at the trade show site, collecting labels and stickers as it travels from one show to the next. As with other elements, it communicates that nothing is wasted; everything becomes a part of the display. For large events, any number of the setups can be displayed together to create a large scale version of the individual display.

Credits

Design Firm: Pentagram, New York, NY
Design Team: Michael Bierut and James Biber,
Design Directors; James Biber, Project Architect;
Michael Zweck-Bronner, Assistant;
Mill Wrap Design: Lisa Cerveny, Pentagram
Illustrator: Michael Bull, Pentagram
Coordinator: Karla Coe, Pentagram
Fabricator: Rathe Productions, New York, NY
Photo Credit: Kevin T.C. Wurman

Dennis S. Juett & Associates
WILLIAM M. THOMPSON
'THE VITAMIN COMPANY' EXHIBIT

The packaging is the exhibit.

A unique, modular display featuring the line of vitamin and mineral food supplements makes use of empty product bottles to showcase every product the company produces. The 40 foot display (comprising ten 4 x 8 ft. panels) is totally self-contained, with all product bottles glued in place. Easy to set up and dismantle, panels lock together and electrical elements plug together.

1.

1. Model of trade show display.
2. Color study using actual product labels.
3. Installation shot of completed exhibit with labels creating a rainbow effect.

2.

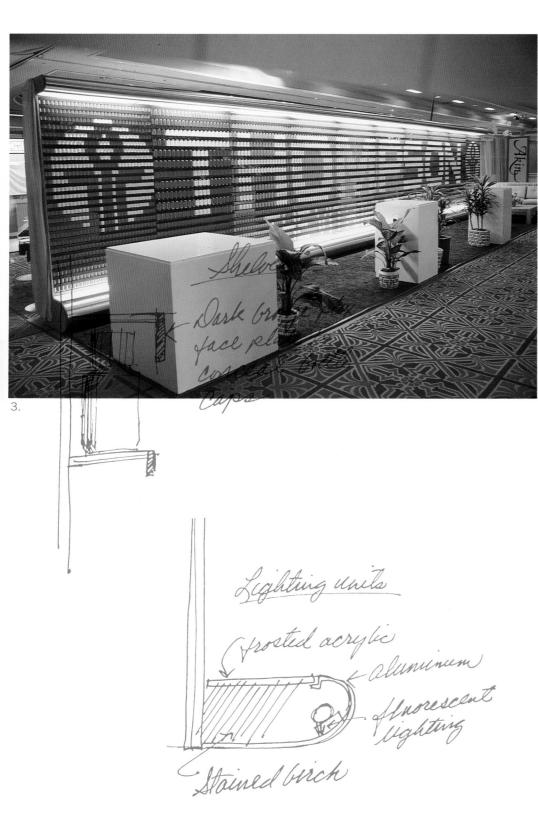

3.

Shelves

Dark orange
face plate
conceal bottle
caps

Lighting units

frosted acrylic

aluminum

fluorescent
lighting

Stained birch

Project Facts

To develop the concept, design and supervise implementation of the assignment for the Carson, CA based William M. Thompson Co., a team of two designers worked approximately 100 hours over a five-month period.

Technical Information

The exhibit makes use of basic techniques and simple materials: 3/4 in. plywood, 3/4 in. birch, aluminum, acrylic panels, electrical components, empty product bottles, and product labels. Display shelves are approximately 3 in. high, with dark orange plexiglas face plates to conceal bottle caps. Stained birch and aluminum cases with frosted acrylic panels contain fluorescent lighting fixtures.

Design Details

The display was created with approximately 5,000 product bottles ranging in size from 50 to 350 cc and representing the full range of a line of more than 420 products. The arrangement of bottles established the typestyle; product packaging created the colors.

Credits

Design Firm: Dennis S. Juett & Associates, Pasadena
Design Team: Dennis S. Juett, Design Director;
Jeffrey Lawson, Designer
Fabricator: William M. Thompson Co., Carson, CA

Mauk Design
EXPERVISION EXHIBIT

Creating an oasis amid clutter to communicate a product's advantage A strong use of typography to drive home a product's primary advantage makes perfect sense for a company whose innovative software scans any typeset document and recognizes individual letterforms. Designers covered the walls of Expervision's 30 x 30 foot peninsula exhibit with problem typeforms that competitors' products can't recognize. A series of cones displays five particularly difficult documents and, on their opposite side, showcases the company's packaging. Ultimately, designers succeeded in giving a newcomer the look of a leader in its category.

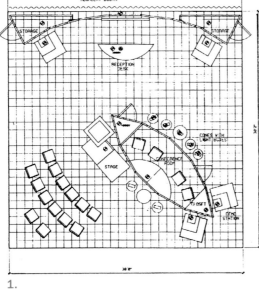

1.

2.

3.

1. Floorplan.
2. Axonometric drawing shows how the space functions.
3. Exhibit overview.
4. Color concept sketch explores materials and fabrication options.
5. Display fixtures present product information.
6. Detail of display wall showing "problem" letterforms and actual letters which competitors scanners cannot read.

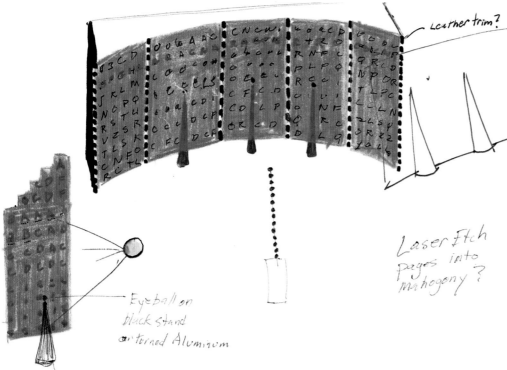

Leather trim?

Laser Etch pages into mahogany?

Eyeball on black stand unturned Aluminum

4.

5.

UNIVERSAL CHARACTER RECOGNITION

6.

Project Facts

Two designers spent approximately 150 staff hours over three months on the project for Santa Clara, CA based Expervision. Overall project budget was $105,000, of which $20,000 was for design and $85,000 for implementation.

Technical Information

Fabrication is conventional but uses a reconstituted mahogany veneer for all wall surfaces. Except for stock resin dimensional lettering, type is silkscreened. Flooring is a snap together antifatigue mat. Cones were originally to be gold painted, but California EPA restrictions on metallic gold paints yielded a dull, mustard-colored paint. In desperation, designers opted to leaf them in Dutch metal, an amalgam of tin and brass, and then clear coat them. Since the fabrication budget made no provision for gold leaf, the design firm's entire staff did the leafing themselves. The exhibit is illuminated by MR 16 size downlights on rods.

Design Details

Working with an 18-ft. height limitation, designers coordinated the exhibit concept with existing product packaging, which is inspired by the look of leather-bound books. Designers used this Old World feeling, which communicates product quality, to emphasize the client's *new* technology, displaying images their competition cannot recognize. Cones serve as "visual arrows," pointing to type samples as well as product.

Credits

Design Firm: Mauk Design, San Francisco, CA
Design Team: Mitchell Mauk, Design Director; Francis Packer, Designer
Fabricator: Admore, San Francisco, CA and Boston,
Typography: Design & Type, San Francisco, CA;
Adobe Software, Mountain View, CA

1.

Bowman Design
VISIONS OF REALITY

Introducing a virtual reality company

At an all important annual convention of amusement park and attraction companies, newcomer Visions of Reality introduced itself and its product with a 20 x 60 foot environment. Designers created a stylized exhibit that communicated a sophisticated corporate look as well as the high tech space theme of the company's virtual reality game. Besides a tight budget and short production cycle, designers needed to adapt to changing product criteria — the product was being developed as they designed. Their solution features visitor interaction with the product, and works like a real store.

2.

3.

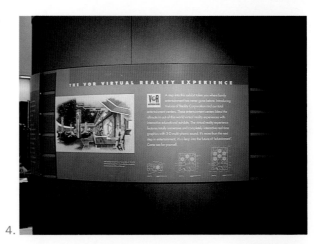

4.

5.

6.

1. *Dimensional logo identifies exhibit entry.*
2. *Shaped overhead panel uses space images to reinforce high-tech theme.*
3. *Display encourages interaction with product.*
4. *Information panel decorates conference area.*
5. *Graphic "wings" call attention to exhibit game pods.*
6. *Curved panel detail.*
7. *Working drawing.*
8. *Video stack.*

Project Facts

Three designers logged some 250 hours on the 90-day Visions of Reality Assignment. Overall project budget was $100,000, of which $25,000 was design and $75,000 was implementation. The scope of work included design concept, theme, details, graphic design and project management.

Technical Information

Truss, birch ply exhibit construction and Zolatone paint were specified, with duotone photographs applied to the exhibit's curved "wings." Commonly used construction methods were employed. Panels measure 4 by 8 feet. The circular conference room is twelve feet high. Graphic wings measure six and a half by six and a half feet. The exhibit is illuminated by show lights from the wall as well as clip-on MR 16's on the truss.

Design Details

Imagery supported the vision of a high tech space game; designers focused attention on the exhibit's game pods. Suspended above them, curved graphic "wings" carry duotone astronomical photos as well as crosshairs and computer like numbers to designate each pod. Dark, neutral colors highlight graphics and game pods, and text appears in a clean, simple Futura typeface.

Credits

Design Firm: Bowman Design, Los Angeles, CA
Design Team: Tom Bowman, Design Director; Christina Chang, Robert Condon
Fabricators: Grondorf Field Black & Company (exhibits and graphics), Irvine, CA; Colorhouse, Burbank, CA (photographs and duotones)

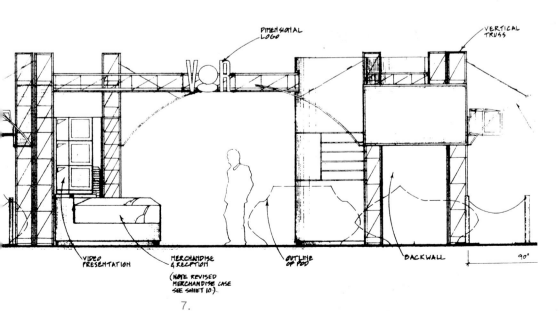

7.

8.

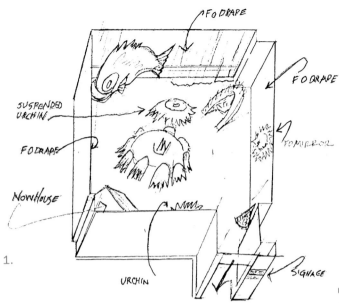

1.

GoldmanArts
DESIGNER'S SATURDAY

Transformation of an annual interior design market

Held in New York City, Designer's Saturday is the largest East Coast contract furnishings/design market event. Designers brought intense color to a relatively neutral site with a series of large, bright and unusual forms that interpret underwater creatures beginning with a 35 foot "Neon Nudibranch" that scales the outside of the building, its 140 appliquéed tentacles waving as they would with the underwater currents. The program continues inside, providing continuity through a 37 floor plan. The solution overcomes budget constraints, time restrictions on exterior installation, and a limited time for execution.

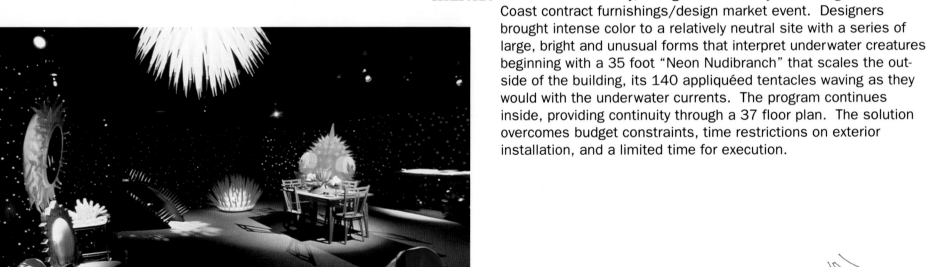

2.

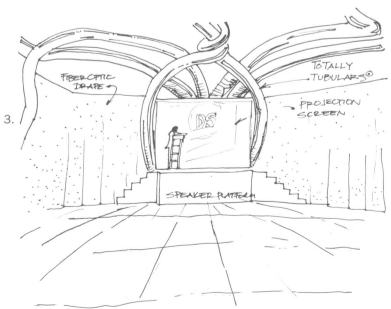

3.

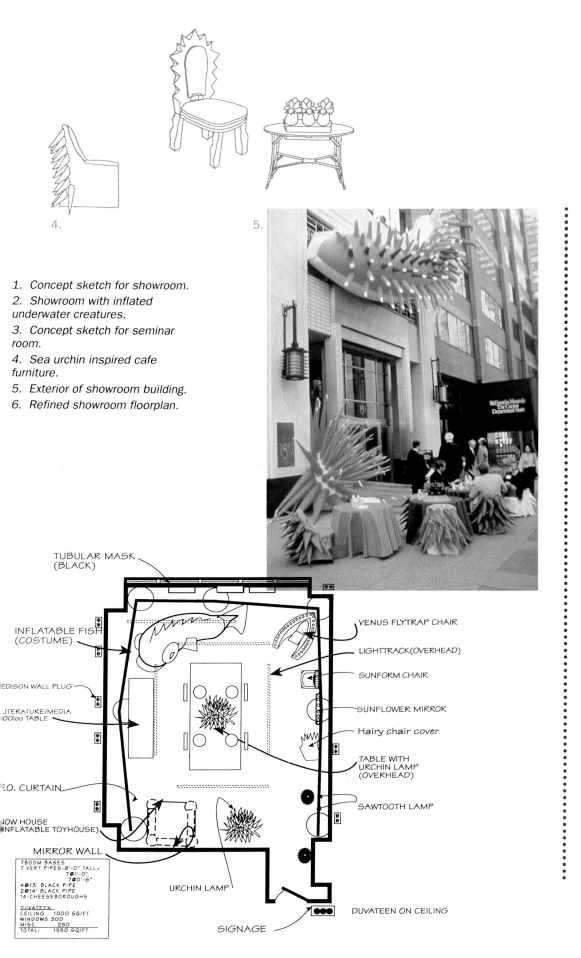

1. Concept sketch for showroom.
2. Showroom with inflated underwater creatures.
3. Concept sketch for seminar room.
4. Sea urchin inspired cafe furniture.
5. Exterior of showroom building.
6. Refined showroom floorplan.

TUBULAR MASK (BLACK)

INFLATABLE FISH (COSTUME)

EDISON WALL PLUG

LITERATURE/MEDIA OOloo TABLE

O. CURTAIN

OW HOUSE NFLATABLE TOYHOUSE)

MIRROR WALL

7800M BASES
7 VERT PIPES-8'-0" TALL+
7@1'-0"
7@0'-6"
4@13' BLACK PIPE
2@14' BLACK PIPE
14-CHEESEBOROUGHS

DUVATEEN
CEILING   1000 SQ/FT
WINDOWS 300
MISC.   250
TOTAL: 1550 SQ/FT

URCHIN LAMP

SIGNAGE

VENUS FLYTRAP CHAIR

LIGHTTRACK (OVERHEAD)

SUNFORM CHAIR

SUNFLOWER MIRROR

Hairy chair cover

TABLE WITH URCHIN LAMP (OVERHEAD)

SAWTOOTH LAMP

DUVATEEN ON CEILING

Project Facts

A two person team spent approximately 35 hours designing the display for the Architects and Designers Building's 25th Annual Designer's Saturday, Overall budget was $33,000, of which $11,100 was design, $6,000 was production, and $15,900 was installation and rental. Scope of work included exterior design for the facade, interior directional decor, event decor and showroom design.

Technical Information

Large scale cold air inflatables, a fiber optic drape, inflatable props, furniture and lighting were specified. Industrial fabrics were put to decorative use. Fiber optic drape involved patented construction techniques. Besides the drape, pin spots provided additional illumination. Largest display elements measure 35 feet across; smallest, one foot.

Design Details

Underwater creatures provided inspiration for transforming the space, building and event into a new experience. In coordination with the exterior installation, the outdoor cafe was adorned with "Hairy Chair Covers" for the tables and urchin like centerpieces. A 20 foot diameter Neon Urchin is displayed directly outside the cafe. Inside, fiber optic curtains carry the "beyond this world" theme to the seventh floor seminar and function room. The designers' own showroom was an underwater restaurant setting using urchin lamps, centerpieces, chair covers and additional elements in displaying their line of furniture and accessories.

Credits

Design Firm: GoldmanArts, Boston, MA
Design Team: Jon Goldman, Design Director;
Steven Rosen, Designer
Fabricator: Mainlight, Inc., Wilmington, DE (fiberoptic)
Other Collaborator: Production Arts, New York, NY

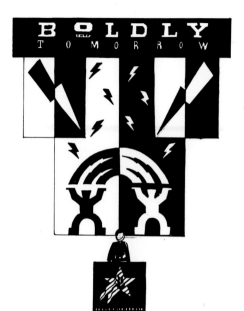

1.

3.

Hornall Anderson Design Works
FOOD SERVICES OF AMERICA:
BOLDLY INTO TOMORROW CAMPAIGN

Using high-energy graphics to
strengthen the team

Each year, Food Services of America holds a partnership building conference with its vendors. Conference campaign graphics need to express the energy and excitement of that partnership. For the 1992 conference, designers developed a figure known as the "Incaman" to convey boldness and evoke the event's Scottsdale location, and a "rainbolt" to symbolize the transformation of energy. All components were shipped in crates, and required a single person to set up.

2.

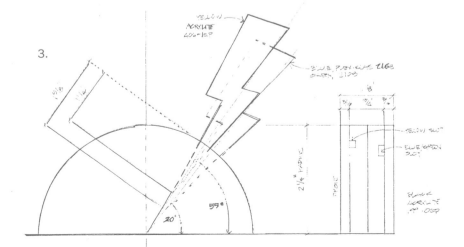

5.

6.

1. Concept study for podium.
2. Actual podium.
3. "Rainbolt" working drawing showing large scaled application of "rainbolt", an event icon.
4. Presentation sketch of monumental event identity.
5. Actual monument sign.
6. Tabletop display.
7. Exploration of "Incaman", an event icon.

7.

Project Facts

Four designers worked approximately 400 hours on the six month project for Food Services of America. The scope of work included designing an identity, graphic kit of parts, and background set to reinforce the "Boldly into Tomorrow" theme.

Technical Information

Half inch white and black gatorfoam and eight inch EPS foam with plastic laminate faces were specified. Two by eight foot patterns were silkscreened onto the gatorfoam. Installers needed to set up the environment in similar conference rooms on different floors every other day, for a total of three setups. Elements were illuminated by existing incandescent and fluorescent spotlights.

Design Details

Designers sought ease of installation and a strong visual impact in a predominantly burgundy colored room with hot colored panels and icons, and with the massive, focal "Incaman" element. Their design communicated boldness, energy, power in partnerships, making connections, and synergy — ideas that reinforce the conference theme.

Credits

Design Firm: Hornall Anderson Design Works, Seattle
Design Team: Jack Anderson, Design Director; Cliff Chung, Jani Drewfs, Leo Raymundo
Fabricators: HOW-Mac, Seattle, WA (Incamen, dimensional lightning bolts); Popich Sign Company, Seattle, WA (graphic panels and vendor signs; Avita Textiles, Seattle, WA (banners).

Mauk Design
PARITY "VOS" EXHIBIT

Finding a strong metaphor to introduce a product

1.

A stopwatch serves as the organizing idea behind a dramatic, impactful design introducing a new phone mail software product. The theme stresses the speed of using "VOS" software for writing applications. Reflecting a deep understanding of the tradeshow environment, the design team looked to conventional fabrication methods to meet the 10 x 20 foot environment's limited budget.

2.

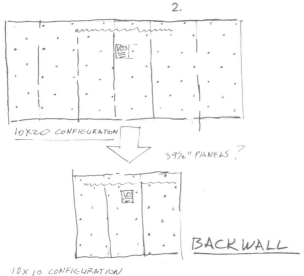

10X20 CONFIGURATION

39½" PANELS ?

BACKWALL

10X10 CONFIGURATION

3.

4.

1. Concept model showing alternate design direction.
2. Concept sketch explores display wall flexibility.
3. - 4. Finished display wall.
5. Concept drawing of literature stand.
6. Completed installation.
7. Concept sketch.

260

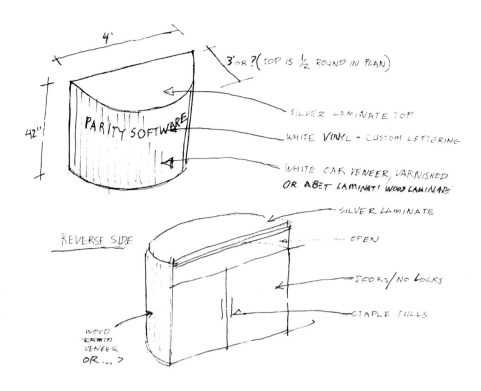

4'

3' OR ?(TOP IS ½ ROUND IN PLAN)

42"

PARITY SOFTWARE

SILVER LAMINATE TOP

WHITE VINYL - CUSTOM LETTERING

WHITE OAK VENEER, VARNISHED
OR ABET LAMINATI WOOD LAMINATE

SILVER LAMINATE

REVERSE SIDE

OPEN

DOORS/NO LOCKS

STAPLE PULLS

WOOD VENEER
OR ...?

LITERATURE STAND - QUAN 1

5.

6.

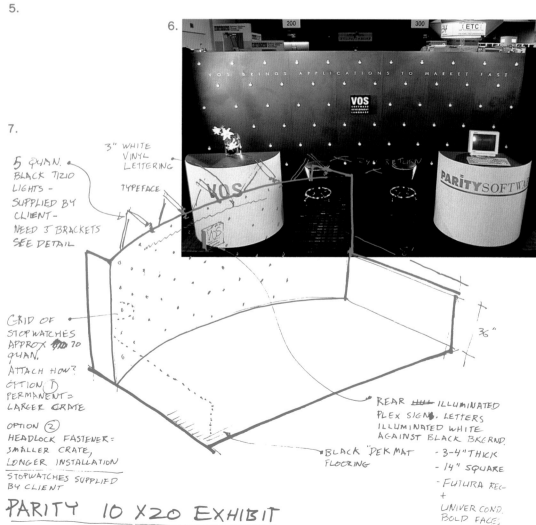

7.

5 QUAN.
BLACK TIZIO
LIGHTS -
SUPPLIED BY
CLIENT -
NEED 3 BRACKETS
SEE DETAIL

3" WHITE
VINYL
LETTERING

TYPEFACE

GRID OF
STOPWATCHES
APPROX 970 70
QUAN.
ATTACH HOW?
OPTION ①
PERMANENT =
LARGER CRATE

OPTION ②
HEADLOCK FASTENER =
SMALLER CRATE,
LONGER INSTALLATION
STOPWATCHES SUPPLIED
BY CLIENT

36"

REAR ILLUMINATED
PLEX SIGNS. LETTERS
ILLUMINATED WHITE
AGAINST BLACK BKGRND.

BLACK "PEK MAT"
FLOORING
- 3-4"THICK
- 14" SQUARE
- FUTURA REG-
+
UNIVER COND.
BOLD FACE.

PARITY 10 X 20 EXHIBIT

Project Facts

A three-designer team completed the assignment for Parity Software Development Corporation (San Francisco, CA) over a three month period. Overall budget was $23,000, of which $8,000 was for design and $15,000 for implementation.

Technical Information

Designers specified laminate covered wood, choosing an Italian laminate for pedestals for its realistic wood grain pattern. Facing the challenge of how to mount stopwatches to the wall without ruining their mechanisms, designers tapped the backs of the watch cases, but not deep enough to penetrate them entirely, then threaded in a 1/8 in. screw

Design Details

Opting for a classic versus a high tech aesthetic, designers used simple, restrained typography to communicate the primary product advantage — speed of programming. An array of 56 operating stopwatches mounted to the back wall drives the message home. Designers worked with existing space limitations: an 8 ft. height limit at the exhibit's back wall and a 4 ft. height limit on its front half.

Credits

Design Firm: Mauk Design, San Francisco, CA
Design Team: Mitchell Mauk, Design Director;
Tim Mautz, Designer
Fabricator: Watermark Exhibits, San Rafael, CA
Photo Credit: Andy Caulfield, Los Angeles, CA

Environmental Signage and Graphics
PROJECT CHECK LIST

While each project may vary in scope, sequence and services, this check list provides general breakdown of the steps of a typical signage and graphics project.

The Proposal

- ☐ Identify or hear about project
- ☐ Obtain RFP (request for proposal) or general information
- ☐ Request budget information
- ☐ Review architect's drawings
- ☐ Visit project site
- ☐ Identify competing design firms
- ☐ Draft proposal of services, fees, expenses and schedule
- ☐ If selected for interview (short list), prepare presentation
- ☐ Rehearse interview, including answers to likely questions

The Agreement (Contract)

- ☐ Resolve contract type (flat fee, time-and-materials, etc.)
- ☐ Resolve expense reimbursement
- ☐ Resolve terms and conditions (payment schedule, termination, arbitration, etc.)
- ☐ Review with attorney
- ☐ Execute agreement

Programming and Analysis

- ☐ Meet to clarify goals
- ☐ Review architect's drawings
- ☐ Interview user groups, operations staff, etc.
- ☐ Review codes and regulations (fire, building and safety, federal, ADA, etc.)
- ☐ Analyze flow of pedestrians and vehicles
- ☐ Identify decision points and information needs
- ☐ Create wording for typical signs and identify sign types
- ☐ Locate typical signs on plan drawings
- ☐ Create list of sign types and quantities
- ☐ Review with owner and architect

Schematic Design

- ☐ Develop "thumbnail" concepts for all sign types
- ☐ Organize into "family" of signage elements
- ☐ Review with owner and architect
- ☐ Develop preliminary budget for fabrication and installation

Design Development

- ☐ Refine schematic concepts into final designs
- ☐ Select materials and fabrication techniques
- ☐ Resolve relationship to architecture, landscape, hardscape, etc.
- ☐ Review with owner and architect

Construction Documents

- ☐ Develop instructional "design intent" working drawings for signs
- ☐ Write specifications for fabrication and installation
- ☐ Finalize location plans showing each sign element
- ☐ Review with owner and architect

Bidding and Award of Contract

- ☐ Issue construction documents to qualified vendors for bidding
- ☐ Review bids with owner and architect
- ☐ Assist in selection of vendor(s) for contract award

Supervision

- ☐ Review and approve submittals form vendor(s) (shop drawings, color matches, patterns, etc.)
- ☐ Review work in vendor(s) shop(s)
- ☐ Review installation of typical sign elements at site
- ☐ Prepare punch-list for vendor completion

Trade Show and Interpretive Design
PROJECT CHECK LIST

While each project may vary in scope, sequence and services, this check list provides general breakdown of the steps of trade show and exhibit design project.

The Proposal
- ☐ Identify or learn about project
- ☐ Request RFP (request for proposal) or general information
- ☐ Request budget information
- ☐ Review proposed site or architect's drawings
- ☐ Identify competing design firms
- ☐ Draft proposal of services, fees, and expenses
- ☐ If selected for interview (short list), prepare presentation
- ☐ Rehearse interview, including answers to likely questions

The Agreement (Contract)
- ☐ Resolve contract type
  (flat fee, time-and-materials, percentage, etc.)
- ☐ Resolve expense reimbursement and mark-up
- ☐ Resolve terms and conditions
  (payment schedule, termination, arbitration, etc.)
- ☐ Review with attorney
- ☐ Execute agreement

Programming and Analysis
- ☐ Meet to clarify goals
- ☐ Define preliminary content
  (information, artifacts, products, etc.)
- ☐ Establish theme, story or narrative concept
- ☐ Develop detailed content outline
- ☐ Develop tentative space plan block out
- ☐ Develop "script"

Schematic Design
- ☐ Develop "thumbnail" concepts for spaces, walls, displays, etc.
- ☐ Identify location for all items from content outline
- ☐ Select display techniques and materials
- ☐ Develop preliminary budget
- ☐ Review with Client

Final Design
- ☐ Refine schematic concepts into final designs
- ☐ Develop final display text and captions
- ☐ Select final photographs and visuals
- ☐ Select final materials and fabrication techniques
- ☐ Develop final budget
- ☐ Review with owner

Fabrication/Installation Documents
- ☐ Prepare detailed working drawings and specifications
- ☐ Prepare artwork for photo-processed
- ☐ Review with client

Bidding and Award of Contract
- ☐ Issue documents to qualified vendors for bidding
- ☐ Review bids with client
- ☐ Assist in selection of vendor(s) for contract award

Supervision
- ☐ Review
- ☐ Review work in vendor(s) shop(s)
- ☐ Review installation at site
- ☐ Prepare punch-list for vendor completion

DESIGNING & PLANNING ENVIRONMENTAL GRAPHICS

A book like this doesn't spring into existence without a great deal of time and effort by many people, starting with the firms who submitted material to be reviewed for *Designing and Planning Environmental Graphics,* to the staff members who unfailingly responded when we asked for more material, even when it was in deep storage, or who recreated material to explain more fully a project. We would like especially to thank Sandy Whitman at Wayne Hunt Design and Lisa Woodard and Joan Borgman at The Graphics Studio for their invaluable support and continuing good nature.

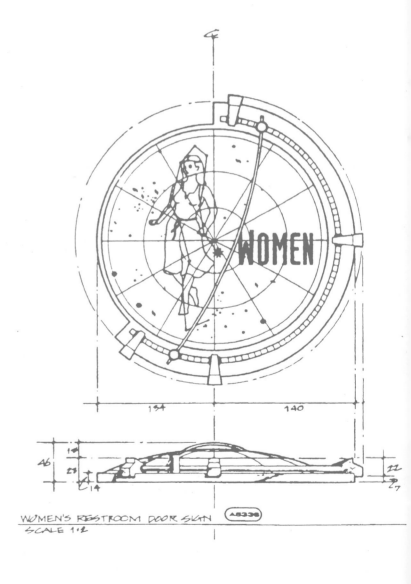

WOMEN'S RESTROOM DOOR SIGN
SCALE 1:2